CAMBRIDGE TEXTS IN THE
HISTORY OF PHILOSOPHY

══

MEDIEVAL JEWISH
PHILOSOPHICAL WRITINGS

CAMBRIDGE TEXTS IN THE HISTORY OF PHILOSOPHY

Series editors
KARL AMERIKS
Professor of Philosophy, University of Notre Dame

DESMOND M. CLARKE
Professor of Philosophy, University College Cork

The main objective of Cambridge Texts in the History of Philosophy is to expand the range, variety and quality of texts in the history of philosophy which are available in English. The series includes texts by familiar names (such as Descartes and Kant) and also by less well-known authors. Wherever possible, texts are published in complete and unabridged form, and translations are specially commissioned for the series. Each volume contains a critical introduction together with a guide to further reading and any necessary glossaries and textual apparatus. The volumes are designed for student use at undergraduate and postgraduate level and will be of interest not only to students of philosophy, but also to a wider audience of readers in the history of science, the history of theology and the history of ideas.

For a list of titles published in the series, please see end of book.

MEDIEVAL JEWISH PHILOSOPHICAL WRITINGS

EDITED BY

CHARLES MANEKIN

University of Maryland

CAMBRIDGE
UNIVERSITY PRESS

CAMBRIDGE UNIVERSITY PRESS
Cambridge, New York, Melbourne, Madrid, Cape Town, Singapore, São Paulo, Delhi

Cambridge University Press
The Edinburgh Building, Cambridge CB2 8RU, UK

Published in the United States of America by Cambridge University Press, New York

www.cambridge.org
Information on this title: www.cambridge.org/9780521549516

First published 2007

Printed in the United Kingdom at the University Press, Cambridge

A catalogue record for this publication is available from the British Library

Library of Congress Cataloguing in Publication data

Medieval Jewish philosophical writings / edited by Charles Manekin.
p.   cm. – (Cambridge texts in the history of philosophy)
Includes index.
ISBN 978-0-521-84023-1 (hardback) – ISBN 978-0-521-54951-6 (pbk.)
1. Philosophy, Jewish.   2. Philosophy, Medieval.   I. Manekin, Charles Harry, 1953–
II. Title   III. Series.
B755.M42   2007
181′.06 – dc22   2007032990

ISBN 978-0-521-84023-1 hardback
ISBN 978-0-521-54951-6 paperback

Contents

Introduction

Jewish thinkers have been engaged with the fundamental questions of human existence from time immemorial, but, with the significant exception of Philo Judaeus, they began to compose philosophical[1] treatises only in the ninth century of the common era. Philosophical speculation can be found in post-Biblical and rabbinic literature, albeit in rudimentary form, but philosophical writing in the manner of the Greeks achieves preeminent status among the Jews only in the Middle Ages. Why did the Jews compose so many works of philosophy between the tenth and fifteenth centuries, when they had produced virtually nothing beforehand? The phenomenon of medieval Jewish philosophy is all the more remarkable when one takes into account the often precarious nature of Jewish existence during this period, the need for institutions and financial resources to support a leisure class of scholars, the focus of rabbinic Jewish culture around traditional texts, and a Talmudic antipathy towards "Greek wisdom."

Part of the answer is that medieval Jewish intellectuals combined a culturally ingrained sense of spiritual and intellectual superiority with an awareness of their deficiencies in the area of philosophy. On the one hand, they saw themselves as the sole heirs of a divine revelation that constituted not only a history of the world, but also a repository of all wisdom, theoretical as well as practical. On the other, they knew that only a small number of scholars of their faith had engaged in studying philosophical works, compared with the canonical books of Judaism, and that

---

[1] The terms "philosophical" and "philosophy" used here include matters pertaining to natural science and medicine as well as philosophy, proper.

philosophical knowledge was to be found among the gentiles. Accordingly, some conceived of their project as recovering an authentic Jewish scientific-philosophical tradition that had been lost. It did not bother these intellectuals that they were relatively few in number, compared to the Talmudists. That was to be expected, given the esoteric nature of the enterprise. Only students who were properly prepared – that is, who had first studied philosophy – were entitled to unlock the "secrets of the Torah," which they interpreted as philosophical in nature. This required that students be trained in philosophy, which necessitated the production of primers, manuals, encyclopedias, and philosophical commentaries.

Historians have often neglected this production, focusing their attention instead on medieval Jewish philosophy's preoccupation with the conflict between the Jewish and Greek traditions, between religion and science. This may be because of the enormous influence of Maimonides, who wrote his *Guide for the Perplexed* for Jews who had difficulty reconciling the truth of Jewish teachings with those of the philosophers. The most famous works of medieval Jewish philosophy follow this pattern; although they may contain political philosophy, philosophical theology, and even science, their focus is on understanding Judaism and reconciling its truth claims with those of philosophy, whenever possible.

Yet while this aspect of medieval Jewish philosophy is important, it is mistaken to claim that Jewish intellectuals in the Middle Ages were interested only in religious philosophy. Such a claim reflects the interests of some modern scholars[2] more than of the medieval Jewish philosophers themselves, who saw their aim as the pursuit of wisdom *tout court*, interpreting that in terms of the love, knowledge, and awe of God. It is likewise mistaken to claim that only two Jews in the Middle Ages, Isaac Israeli and Solomon ibn Gabirol, produced works of "pure" philosophy, rather than philosophical interpretations of Judaism. A considerable number of works in Hebrew logic, philosophy, and medicine are extant in manuscripts that await critical editions and study. These commentaries and compendia bear witness to Jewish interest in topics that did not have direct bearing on questions of religious philosophy. There are only slightly fewer

---

[2] For the traditional historiography of Jewish philosophy, see Steven M. Wasserstrom, "The Islamic social and cultural context," in: *History of Jewish Philosophy*, eds. Daniel H. Frank and Oliver Leaman (London/New York: Routledge, 1997), pp. 93–114. Cf. Dimitri Gutas, "The Study of Arabic Philosophy in the Twentieth Century: An Essay on the Historiography of Arabic Philosophy," *British Journal of Middle Eastern Studies* (2002) 29: 5–25, esp. 12–15.

manuscripts extant of the Hebrew translations of the *Treatise on Logic* attributed to Maimonides – a work with no Jewish content – than those of his famous *Guide of the Perplexed*, and it is by no means certain that more people read the latter than the former.

Interestingly, the production of "pure" philosophy flourished more among Jewish intellectuals who lived in the Christian world – especially in Spain, Provence, and Italy – than those who lived in Muslim Spain, Northern Africa, and the Near East. The reason is not hard to surmise: the acculturated Jews in Islamic lands were able to read philosophy with commentaries in Arabic; there was no need for them to transmit these works into Hebrew and to comment upon them. By contrast, Jewish intellectuals in Christian Europe generally did not read Arabic or Latin, and so had to appropriate the philosophical material through translation and commentary in Hebrew. Once this appropriation was completed, there was a corpus of "pure" philosophy in Hebrew that laid the foundations for a Hebraic philosophical tradition which lasted well into the modern period. In renaissance Italy there were Jewish teachers and translators of Averroes' commentaries; around the same time, prominent Jewish savants in Spain were debating issues of scholastic philosophy in Hebrew, such as the ontological status of universals. No doubt this was considered as a "marginal" intellectual activity by their traditionalist opponents, as it was by modern Jewish historians who were interested in philosophy of religion. Even though Jewish intellectuals lacked the institutional resources of the Christian university, and a philosophical tradition akin to that of the Church Fathers, they did not neglect purely philosophical matters.

Whether the philosophy studied and taught by medieval Jewish philosophers was "pure" or "applied," it was characterized by two overarching principles: the unity of truth, and its accessibility to human reason. The first principle was implicitly adopted by all the philosophers appearing in this anthology, even those who are highly critical of the truth-claims of the Aristotelians. There may be truths that are difficult to obtain by unaided reason, but they are in principle reconcilable with it. Thus, the Aristotelian philosophers viewed the idea of creation *ex nihilo* as absurd, but to Maimonides it was not only not absurd, but true, whereas according to Gersonides, its truth can be demonstrated. Medieval Jewish philosophers disagreed more over the epistemic status of beliefs backed by traditional authority than about those grounded in reason. Do the latter beliefs provide certainty? Maimonides says no; Albo disagrees; Saadia holds the middle position that rational speculation *increases* the certainty of one who believes on the basis of traditional authority. None of the philosophers holds that reason is an unreliable instrument when used properly.

The medieval Jewish belief in the supremacy and authority of reason derives in part from the belief that God is described by the Aristotelians as reason or intellect (Hebrew: *sekhel*). If God is intellect, and we humans are created in His image, then it is intellect that binds us to God. Even Crescas, whose theology is more voluntaristic than that of the Aristotelians, does not exempt God from being subject to the laws of logic. And it is noteworthy that the major medieval Jewish philosophers, unlike their Christian counterparts, did not develop a voluntaristic divine command theory of ethics. God's justice may often be unfathomable to the medieval Jewish philosophers, but it is never irrational or the product of an arbitrary will.

As we shall see in the introductions to specific texts, medieval Jewish philosophers were very much creatures of their time and their intellectual milieu. I have employed the common practice of categorizing them according to the dominant perceived influence: Kalamic, neoplatonist, Aristotelian, Averroist, etc. This is a convenient way of arranging the material, but it fails to do justice to the individual authors, who, we should never forget, are more than just the sum total, or pale image, of their authorities, even in the Middle Ages. Terms like "minor figure," "unoriginal," and "derivative" have no currency in the medieval mindset.

Saadia Gaon: *The Book of the Beliefs and Convictions*

Saadia ben Joseph al-Fayyūmī (882–942), the leading rabbi of his day and the dean ("gaon", pl. "geonim") of the academy in Sura (present-day Iraq), is generally recognized as the first medieval Jewish philosopher of note. That reputation is based primarily on his *summa* of religious philosophy, *The Book of the Beliefs and Convictions* (or *The Books of the Choicest Beliefs and Opinions*), which was one of the first philosophical works translated from Arabic into Hebrew. It is not an exaggeration to say that Saadia helped shape much of the rabbinic thought that is characteristic of traditional Judaism. His moderately rationalist presentation of rabbinic

Jewish doctrine managed to survive not only because it was theologically more palatable to the traditionalists than Jewish Aristotelianism and neoplatonism (not to mention kabbalah), but also because it was not associated by his traditional readers with any foreign philosophical school.

Yet scholars since Maimonides (1138–1204) have recognized that Saadia's philosophy was deeply influenced by "Kalām" (literally, "speech" or "discourse"), the term used to designate the rationalist theology that began to develop in the beginning of the eighth century. As a result of the Islamic conquests that extended from Spain to Persia, including the prominent centers of culture in the Middle East, and because of the enlightened policies of the Abbasid rulers, classical philosophy, science, and belles lettres were transmitted to the Islamic world in the form of translations, commentaries, and manuals. The absorption of peoples of different faiths and ideologies, coupled with the exposure to philosophy, led some Muslims to imitate the example of Christian theologians and to develop subtle theological defenses of their dogmas; indeed, the very attempt to formulate Muslim dogma dates from this period. The Kalām theologians positioned themselves between the orthodox, who felt no need to mount a sophisticated defense of the faith, and the philosophers, who viewed Greek philosophy, with its commentarial tradition, as paramount. The most famous early school of Kalām was the Mu'tazila, which became the semi-official theology of the Abbasid emperors during the early ninth century. The Mu'tazilites viewed reason as a reliable instrument for acquiring knowledge and deciding the correctness of moral judgments. If the demands of reason ran counter to the simple meaning of the text of the Qur'ān, then the latter had to be interpreted accordingly.

Saadia's *Beliefs and Convictions* follows the pattern of a Mu'tazilite theological work. Its ten treatises fall unevenly into the two chief areas of Mu'tazilite inquiry, divine unity and divine justice. Its introduction addresses epistemological topics, including a defense of the ability of humans to achieve knowledge through reason. According to Saadia, human error results from an incomplete knowledge of the object and method of inquiry, as well as a careless approach to one's research. He complains that his generation in particular is beset by perplexity: "I have seen men sunk, as it were, in a sea of doubts and covered by the waters of obscurity, and there was no diver to bring them up from the depths and no swimmer to grasp their hands and bring them to shore" (Introduction). Whether this was merely a rhetorical flourish, or whether there was a real crisis of religious belief among Saadia's coreligionists, is not clear. In any event, Saadia's purpose in the book is to remove their doubts and to render their beliefs not merely true but also certain. He does not hesitate to proclaim the superiority of belief "on the basis of speculation and education" to belief "on the basis of tradition alone."

Saadia differs from later Jewish philosophers in his understanding of what brings about certainty, and what methods one should employ in order to remove doubts. He initially lists three "principles" that provide us with certain knowledge: observation, intellect, and necessary inference. Observation provides us with reliable sense-knowledge so long as our senses are healthy and we guard ourselves against illusions. As for intellectual knowledge, Saadia states that "whatever is conceived in our intellect free of all defects is to be regarded as true and indubitable knowledge." This includes not only theoretical but moral knowledge as well. Indeed, one of the underlying assumptions of the *Beliefs and Convictions* is that humans can discover ethical principles and imperatives, provided that they think clearly and rationally. The third operation is necessary inference, which is not so much logical consequence but rather the inference to the necessary conditions of an existent state of affairs. The inference can be direct, as when we observe smoke and infer the existence of fire. It can also involve several steps, as when we observe the ingestion and excretion of food, and infer the existence of an unobserved digestive process. Saadia realizes that people may be mistaken in their inferences, and so he provides a list of maxims that will ensure their validity – guidelines that can also be employed in scriptural exegesis.

In addition to these three principles, Jews are said to possess a fourth, namely, authentic tradition. Saadia appears to offer conflicting statements about this principle's status. On the one hand, it is said to be based on the first two; on the other hand, it is said to confirm the first three. For Saadia, reason and revelation are mutually reinforcing, since any contradiction between the two is only apparent.

This belief in the essential harmony between faith and reason supports Saadia's defense of rational investigation against the objections of the traditionalists. The defense appears to have been purely theoretical, since the geonim, unlike the Kalām theologians, constituted the orthodox within rabbanite Judaism. Saadia not only reinterprets the Biblical and rabbinic dicta that apparently forbid or limit rational investigation; he underscores the importance of that study for understanding Biblical prophecy, and for answering ideological opponents. As for the objection that such investigation is dangerous because it may lead to heresy, Saadia, ever the philosophical optimist, claims that this will not occur if the investigation is carried out rigorously and carefully.

Saadia asks why divine revelation is needed at all, given that unaided reason can attain truth in both theoretical and moral spheres. His answer is that while reason can eventually derive the moral truths taught in scripture with certainty, this is a process that takes time, is fraught with difficulty, and is not for everybody. Since God did not wish the Jews to remain without religion in the meantime, or that the investigators be pressured into finding their answers in a hasty and careless manner, He revealed to them the truths amidst wonders and miracles.

Solomon ibn Gabirol and Shem Tov Falaquera: *Excerpts from "The Source of Life"*

When Saadia was espousing a kind of Jewish Kalām in Babylonia, the physician Isaac Israeli was writing works of neoplatonist philosophy in Northern Africa. Neoplatonist ideas entered the Arabic world chiefly through adaptations of Plotinus and Proclus in books known as the *Theology of Aristotle* (in two versions), and the *Book of the Pure Good* (in the Latin West, the *Liber de Causis*). Among those ideas one finds the notion of a hierarchy of being; the eternal emanation of being from the One that is beyond being; the crystallization of being in a series of "hypostases" that mediate between the One and the world; the descent of the soul from the One, and its subsequent journey back to it. Neoplatonic concepts also reached the Arabs via neoplatonically inclined commentators on Aristotle, such as the Muslim philosophers al-Fārābī and Ibn Sīnā; even a more orthodox Aristotelian like Ibn Rushd was not immune to neoplatonic influences.

However, a purer form of neoplatonism can be found in *The Source of Life*, a remarkably original work by the eleventh-century Spanish Jewish poet and philosopher, Solomon ben Joseph ibn Gabirol (c. 1020–c. 57). One is hard pressed to find anything like it in medieval philosophical literature. Presented as a dialogue between master and pupil, the work was intended as the first volume of a projected trilogy; unfortunately, the second and third volumes were never written, due to the author's untimely death. Athough the original Arabic text has been lost, some citations are found in *The Garden*, a philosophical work by the twelfth-century Spanish-Jewish poet, Moses ibn Ezra. Gabirol's work was translated into Latin in the twelfth century as *Fons Vitae* by the Spanish archdeacon Domingo Gundisalvi, with the aid of John of Spain, and was influential in late twelfth- and thirteenth-century scholastic philosophy. In the thirteenth century Shem Tov ben Joseph Falaquera abridged and translated the work into Hebrew in numbered paragraphs. Although neither the *Source of Life* nor Falaquera's abridgement appears to have had much influence on subsequent Jewish philosophy, Gabirol's system is interesting in its own right, and represents the crowning achievement of medieval Jewish neoplatonism. His emphasis on the primacy of divine will reappears in Jewish philosophers such as Maimonides and Crescas, albeit in different forms.

According to Gabirol, the soul begins its journey to God through the knowledge of matter and form among the lowest form of being, i.e., sensible things and corporeal substance. From there it moves on to the knowledge of the simple substances that are intermediate between First Substance and corporeal substance, until it achieves the knowledge of universal matter and universal form. Once the soul has achieved this knowledge and the knowledge of God's action/will, it has achieved all that can be known about the First Substance, which is the purpose of human existence. Gabirol thus begins the *Source of Life* with a treatise on the existence of matter and form in sensible things.

In Treatise Two we move from the level of sensible substance (body) to a higher level of corporeal substance. Whereas the first sort of substance possesses a corporeal matter that supports the visible forms of the qualities (figure, color, etc.), the second sort of substance possesses a spiritual matter that supports the form of quantity, or corporeity.

Gabirol provides in Treatise Three a battery of demonstrations for the existence of substances that are intermediate between the First Agent (God) and the substance that supports the categories. Some of these demonstrations are based simply on the idea that, if there is any relation between God and corporeal substance, which are utterly different from each other, then there must be some intermediate entity or entities that bridge the ontological gap, just as the sensible forms of the soul are intermediary between the intellectual forms of the intellect and the corporeal forms of corporeal substance.

The constant refrain that the lower is the image of the higher because the lower emanates from the higher, is the nub of the argument for two of Gabirol's best-known claims: first, that all of created existence, including simple substances, possesses matter and form, and, second, that the varieties of matter and form are united within universal matter and universal form. The first thesis (the theme of Treatise Four) sounds odd at first: how can simple substances be *composed* of anything? Gabirol's answer is that substances are called "simple" in relation to what is inferior to them in the hierarchy of being, and "composite" in relation to what is superior to them. This assumes that the relation of form to matter does not render a substance *in itself* composite; on the contrary, form gives a particular kind of existence to an entity; matter sustains its existence. In another formulation, Gabirol claims that each substance is form for its superior substance and matter for its inferior substance in the hierarchy of being. We see then that matter and form are relative terms and that substances are both matter *and* form.

Universal matter and universal form, as conceived in themselves, are the subject of Treatise Five. Here Gabirol offers a new description of universal matter and form via their properties. Universal matter and universal form are found in all created existents but, as prime matter and prime form, they are ontologically prior to all other created existents; combined, they constitute the universal intellect. Much of Falaquera's abridgement of this treatise, the longest of the book, is devoted to the universal intellect, which, lacking its own proper form, is the totality of all forms. The identification of universal form with the form of universal intellect ensures that the real and the knowable are coextensive.

In addition to the properties of universal matter and form described above, Gabirol notes that form is active in the process of emanation (a favorite image is that of the sunlight permeating and penetrating where it can), and that matter moves to receive the form out of love and desire for the source of the form, namely divine will. This is very different from the Aristotelian notion of matter as a passive and inert receptacle. He argues that because universal matter is created together with universal form, and hence close to the "source of life," universal matter is infused from the outset of creation with the light of unity (from universal form) which awakens within it the desire to receive more light. All actually existing matter is already informed in some manner.

Moses Maimonides: *The Guide of the Perplexed*

Andalusian Jewish philosophy reaches its peak in the writings of Rabbi Moses ben Maimon (whence the popular acronym "Rambam"), known to the Arabs as Abū 'Imran Mūsā ibn Maymūn ibn 'Abd Allāh, and to the scholastics as Maimonides or Rabi Moyses. Maimonides was born in Cordoba, Spain, in 1138, to a distinguished family of jurists and communal leaders. After the Almohad conquest of Southern Spain, and the subsequent persecutions of Jews and Christians, Maimonides' family left Cordoba and spent the next eighteen years or so traveling through Spain, Northern Africa, and Palestine, before settling in Egypt in 1166. Shortly after he arrived there, Maimonides completed his first major work, a commentary on the basic law code of rabbinic Judaism, the Mishnah (c. 1168). Over the next ten or so years, he labored on a comprehensive code that was to include "all the Laws of the Torah and its regulations, with nothing omitted." After the dissemination of the *Mishneh Torah* (*Code of Law*, 1178–80), his only major work written in Hebrew, Maimonides became famous throughout the Jewish world.

Maimonides discusses in these early legal writings "the fundamentals of the Torah," i.e. the fundamental beliefs and opinions underlying the divinely revealed Law. These include belief in the existence, unity, incorporeality, and absolute priority of God, who alone is to be worshiped; prophetic revelation, and the supremacy and immutability of Mosaic revelation; divine omniscience, reward and punishment, the coming of the Messiah, and the resurrection of the dead. Maimonides implies that in order to accept these beliefs, especially the theological ones, one needs at least a rudimentary understanding of them. This suggests that there is a religious obligation to study the fundamentals of the Law, especially the theological ones; otherwise, one is left with a misleading and false conception of God and His relationship to the world.

In the *Mishneh Torah* Maimonides expands upon the philosophical theology that underlies Jewish belief in God's existence, unity, and incorporeality. Moreover, the commandments to love and fear God, we are told, presuppose an examination of nature, which, in turn, presupposes a rudimentary knowledge of physics and metaphysics. So Maimonides provides in his law code a précis of Aristotelian cosmology and physics, which he appears to accept without reservation. At this point in his literary career, there is little in his philosophical writing that distinguishes him from the Muslim Aristotelians, especially al-Fārābī and Ibn Sīnā. But ten years later he declares his independence from the philosophers and attempts to stake out a middle path between them and the dogmatic theologians of the Kalām.

The context of the new development is his defense of the world's createdness in the *Guide of the Perplexed* (c. 1190). For the first time in his writings, Maimonides declares belief in creation out of nothing to be a fundamental of the Torah, second only to the affirmation of divine unity. This declaration put him squarely in the camp of the theologians. Some harmonizing philosophers, notably Ibn Sīnā, and arguably Gabirol, had tried to give a philosophical intepretation of creation as eternal or continual, which would make it compatible with the Aristotelian thesis of the world's eternity. Maimonides may have accepted a similar interpretation of the world's creation in his legal writings. But he explicitly rejects it in the *Guide,* because he there accept that our view about the world's origins has direct implications for our concept of God. If the world is eternal or proceeds eternally from God, he argues, then divine causality is natural and not voluntary. This means that God did not choose to create the world in the way that he did, but rather that it proceeded (and proceeds) from him of necessity. In that case, Maimonides reasons, God cannot change the wing of a mosquito or the leg of a fly. Such a limit to divine power implies the destruction of the Law.

But Maimonides makes it clear that he does not wish to be associated with the Kalām theologians, whose philosophical principles and methods he severely criticizes. He feels that their religious and ideological commitments overly influence their science, and that they buttress their views with discredited theories. Since the science that Maimonides accepts is mainly Aristotelian, which implies the eternity of the world, he is in a dilemma. His way out is first to argue that the eternity of the world has not been demonstrated, and hence that the creation of the world is possible. He then offers proofs that he concedes are not conclusive but merely probable on behalf of the creation of the world.

It is a tribute to Maimonides' acuteness that he realized the implications for his (Aristotelian) philosophy of including creation *ex nihilo* as a fundamental principle, although he may not have realized how far reaching the damage would be. Yet he was compelled to do so in order to remain faithful to what he considered to be the "fundamentals of the law."

Isaac Albalag: *The Emendation of the "Opinions"*

After a century of translation activity from Arabic into Hebrew, beginning in the twelfth century, Aristotelianism emerged as the philosophical school *par excellence* among the philosophically minded Jews of Southern France and Northern Spain. Students now studied Ibn Rushd's paraphrases, compendia, and commentaries of Aristotle, many of which had been purged, at least to some extent, of the neoplatonic elements that had shaped the Aristotelianism of al-Fārābī and Ibn Sīnā. At the same time, Maimonides' *Guide of the Perplexed* was widely read and commented upon, and here too the impact of Aristotelianism was felt. Some readers implied that Maimonides secretly adhered to Aristotelian naturalism, and that his statements to the contrary were intended for non-philosophers. These readers were doubtlessly influenced by Ibn Rushd's view that philosophical truths and theories should be concealed from non-philosophers, who would only mistake them as heretical. By reading the *Guide* through an Averroist prism, they were able to harmonize the two main philosophical authorities of the period, Maimonides and Ibn Rushd.

As for Ibn Sīnā, although few of his philosophical writings were actually translated into Hebrew, it would be mistaken to say that his doctrines were neglected. Several of Ibn Sīnā's writings were available in Spain as late as the fourteenth century, and some Arabic-reading Jewish philosophers made use of them. Besides, the Jewish intellectuals who read only Hebrew were familiar with Ibn Sīnā's main doctrines in logic, physics, and metaphysics from Ibn Rushd's restatement and criticisms in his commentaries, and from al-Ghazālī's exposition of Ibn Sīnā's philosophy in the widely read *Opinions of the Philosophers*. Ironically, two of the most Averroistic philosophers of this period, Isaac Albalag and Moses of Narbonne, were responsible for disseminating the views of Ibn Sīnā through their commentaries on the *Opinions*. Both viewed al-Ghazālī's work as a well-written summary of philosophy for beginning students, so long as it was supplemented by their own critical notes and comments from an Averroist perspective.

Albalag was active at the end of the thirteenth century, probably in Catalonia. In 1292, he composed his only surviving work, *The Emendation of the "Opinions."* Albalag saw the *Opinions* as a "middle way common to philosophy and popular beliefs." He took it upon himself not only to translate the text but also to transform its method from the popular mode of philosophizing to the demonstrative. Where al-Ghazālī deviated from the truth, Albalag would be there to provide the correct (Averroist) doctrine.

One such deviation concerns the question of metaphysical indeterminism and its implications for divine foreknowledge. Ibn Sīnā's metaphysics is strictly determinist. Although only God necessarily exists in Himself, and all other things have merely possible existence, they are all causally determined to exist when they exist. At one point in the *Opinions* al-Ghazālī argues that if future events were only possible with respect to their causes, and not necessitated, then they would be undetermined. In that case God could not have foreknowledge of their existence, since knowledge is always through necessitating causes. Al-Ghazālī explains further that if future events are always necessitated by their causes then we can infer not only that they are knowable by God, but we can also understand *how* they are so knowable: God's complete knowledge of the causes enables Him to foresee whether and when future events will come to pass. According to al-Ghazālī, God's knowledge is like that of an omniscient astrologer who knows all future possible events because he knows the hierarchy of the causes that determine them. However, God, unlike the astrologer, has complete knowledge of the causes.

With respect to metaphysical determinism, Albalag, like Ibn Rushd, rejects the distinction between things that are possible in themselves, yet necessary with respect to their causes. It is true that effects necessarily follow from their causes when those causes are *essential*. But this is not true of *accidental* causes, which do not necessitate their effects. Some effects are possible because their nature does not dictate the final outcome. In such cases the outcome is essentially possible, and it is not necessary (as Ibn Sīnā claims).

Consider, he writes, the case where Reuben inadvertently damages his eye with his finger when he raises his hand. It is impossible to foreknow this event, or the time of its occurrence, because the causal sequence does not conform to any order; nor does the existence of the effects follow necessarily from the existence of the causes. The damaging of the eye does not follow necessarily from the raising of the finger, nor is the meeting of the finger with the eye a necessary event when the finger is raised, even though the damaging of the eye follows necessarily from the finger meeting it, and the finger meeting it follows necessarily from its being led in a straight line to the eye. For the finger's being led on that line to the eye has no cause except for Reuben's inadvertent action. For Albalag, a cause necessitates its effect when and only when there is something in the nature of the cause that necessitates a particular effect, and something in the nature of the particular effect that renders it necessitated.

Yet if some future events are undetermined, especially those that occur as a result of human choice, does this imply that God does not know them? Albalag says no. It implies only that God does not know them in the way that al-Ghazālī suggests, which is the way of an omniscient predicter. Albalag does not elaborate on his view of divine knowledge. He may adopt the position offered by Ibn Rushd elsewhere, that God knows things insofar as they exist within His essence in the noblest way possible. Still, Albalag recommends teaching al-Ghazālī's theory as appropriate for the multitude, since it will be easy for them to grasp.

Albalag's critical gloss on al-Ghazālī's position on divine knowledge was the first time a Jewish Aristotelian responded to the challenge of Avicennan determinism, but it was by no means the last. The Jewish scientist/philosopher Abner of Burgos (c. 1270–c. 1346) composed several treatises in which he advocated strict causal determinism based on Avicennan metaphysics. According to Abner, God's eternal knowledge causally necessitates, via the instrumentality of the heavenly bodies, the temporal existence of individual substances and accidents. Since human volitions are accidents, they too are necessitated, but this does not make them any less voluntary. Agents are said to will something, insofar as they accord, desire, and choose it, even if this results from compulsion, *a fortiori* if the compulsion is not felt. Abner's deterministic views achieved notoriety only after he converted to Christianity, adopted the name Alfonso de Vallodolid, and began to write polemical treatises against the Jews and Judaism. Yet despite his apostasy, Abner was admired by Jewish savants for his philosophical prowess. His former student and chief adversary Isaac Polgar called him "quick-witted and knowledgeable in the ways of religion and philosophy," and Narboni considered him to be "one of the most distinguished of his generation." Narboni was so impressed by Abner's philosophical acumen that he doubted the sincerity of the apostate's commitment to determinism, and even to Christianity.

An examination of Abner's writings and arguments shows that he had already been committed to Avicennan determinism as a young man, and that he had worked out its philosophical and religious implications in early writings. Moreover, even after his much-publicized conversion, his causal determinism (which he also called the "divine decree" and "predestination") remained a live option for Jewish philosophy. It re-emerges, as we shall see below, in the philosophical theology of the leader of Spanish Jewry in the late fourteenth and early fifteenth centuries, Ḥasdai Crescas. Both the apostate Abner and the orthodox Crescas had a common enemy in Jewish Averroists like Albalag, Polgar, and Narboni who, in their eyes, denied God's omniscience and individual providence, and over-intellectualized Judaism.

Moses of Narbonne (Narboni): *The Treatise on Choice*

Moses of Narbonne's *Treatise on Choice* (1361), his response to Abner's *Epistle on the Divine Decree*, was one of the last things this prolific author wrote. Born in Perpignan at the end of the thirteenth century, he spent most of his life in Spain, where he composed commentaries on works by Ibn Rushd, al-Ghazālī, and Ibn Ṭufayl. He is best known for his commentary on the *Guide of the Perplexed*, which he completed around the same time as the *Treatise on Choice*.

Narboni begins his short work by citing the deterministic theses of Abner and then claiming that Aristotle had already showed their absurdity. He attempts to show that Abner's brand of determinism implies fatalism, notwithstanding Abner's protests to the contrary. For if God has decreed that Reuben will be rich, then he will be rich no matter what he does, and he need not do anything. Narboni's arguments indicate that he does not appreciate the distinction between Abner's causal determinism, which masquerades under the name of the "divine decree," and a more simplistic view of fatalism. More importantly, he attacks Abner's causal determinism by repeating at length the main points from Aristotle's *Metaphysics* that had occupied Albalag.

With respect to God's knowledge, a subject that had occupied him considerably in his commentary to the *Guide*, Narboni appeals to Ibn Rushd's claim that "God knows Himself which, in a certain respect, is all existing things. Therefore, when he thinks himself, he thinks all existing things in a more excellent manner." God does not know things as particulars – because these are apprehended by the senses – or as universals – because these are abstracted from the sensible particulars. Rather, in thinking Himself, he is able to understand all that will occur as a result of this divine productive knowledge.

Gersonides: *The Wars of the Lord*

Rabbi Levi ben Gershom ("Ralbag," "Gersonides", 1288–1344) was medieval Jewry's most intellectually diverse philosopher, making contributions to logic, mathematics, astronomy, astrology, physics, biology, psychology, philosophy, rabbinics, and Biblical exegesis. He left behind philosophical commentaries on Ibn Rushd's summaries and paraphrases of Aristotle that are extant in many manuscripts, some of which were translated into Latin. He also wrote extended commentaries on the Torah, the books of the early prophets, and some of the later biblical writings, including a commentary on the book of Job, which was one of the first Hebrew books to be printed.

Relatively little is known about Gersonides' life. He lived in various towns of the Languedoc area of Provence, which did not then belong to the Kingdom of France. That was lucky for him, since he avoided the persecutions and expulsions that his coreligionists endured during those years. Gersonides spent several years in Avignon, and he may have been acquainted with Pope Clement VI. He speaks of contacts with Christian clerics who shared his interests in astronomy. There is evidence that he earned his livelihood as a professional physician, astronomer, and moneylender.

It has been said of Gersonides that he strived to be original in all that he undertook. His earliest literary work was an attempt "to correct the errors" in Aristotle's theory of the modal syllogism. His commentary on Euclid's *Elements* attempted to construct a geometry without axioms. His voluminous treatise on astronomy, in which he criticized his predecessors, included astronomical tables based largely on his own observations. In his commentary on the Torah he claimed to have discovered the legal rules of inference by which established rabbinic law was derived from the Torah, a claim that led him to be accused (two centuries later) of intending to compose a new Talmud! Because of his philosophical worldview Gersonides has been called an "Averroist," but that is an error; there is hardly a significant doctrine of Ibn Rushd that he does not criticize and reject.

Gersonides' major work, *The Book of the Wars of the Lord*, was composed over a twelve-year period. Originally intended to discuss the creation of the world, its scope expanded to include six controversial sets of problems that had stymied previous philosophers: (i) Is the rational soul immortal, and are there degrees of immortality? (ii) Do humans predict the future (e.g., in dreams or prophecy) by chance or essentially? (iii) Does God know existing things, and if so, in what way? (iv) Is there divine providence, and if so, does it extend to individuals? (v) How do the movers of the heavenly bodies move them? How are they related to each other and to God? (vi) Is the universe eternal or created, and if created, then how?

The fifth treatise, a consideration of cosmology, may seem out of place in a book of philosophical problems. Yet cosmology for Gersonides is the ultimate science, since the heavenly bodies and their movers are the most noble creatures in the universe. At the top of the hierarchy of being is God, the First Cause, from whom emanates directly the incorporeal intellects, the movers of the spheres. Each intellect governs a celestial sphere whose soul possesses a partial representation of the univeral order within the mind of God, each of which is called the "nomos" (law) or the "intelligible plan of the existents." The different partial representations account for their different celestial influences upon sublunar entities. The goal of these influences is to preserve and maintain the sublunar world.

Because the apprehension of each celestial sphere is a partial one, Gersonides posits the existence of an intellect that coordinates the different influences. This is the Agent Intellect, the "giver of forms," which possesses in its soul the intelligible plan of sublunar existence. This is not the same as the more comprehensive intelligible plan of all existence that is within God's soul, although Gersonides is fond of saying that the plans are "in a certain manner" the same. To use an Aristotelian analogy, if God is like the commander of an entire army, then the Agent Intellect is like the captain of a unit, who arranges his soldiers according to his understanding of the commander-in-chief's plan.

This brief description of Gersonides' picture of the world provides the context for the problem considered in the third treatise: "Whether or not God knows particular sublunar things, and if He does, in what manner does He know them?" If we give the problem a Gersonidean interpretation, its answer is related to the answer to another question:

Are particular sublunar things *scientifically understandable*? Gersonides' answer is a qualified "yes"; they are understandable insofar as such things are determined according to the plan within the soul of the Agent Intellect (which is "in a certain sense" the same plan that is within the soul of God). Gersonides makes a similar point earlier in the *Wars* where he argues that future events can be known before they occur because such things are determined according to the plan within the soul of the Agent Intellect. The sort of knowledge to which he refers here is not sense-knowledge. It involves understanding why a thing is what it is, and why it cannot be otherwise. All knowledge of sublunar things is via knowledge of the plan that orders them. When we say that God knows sublunar things, we mean that He knows and determines the plan from which these things follow.

In chapter 3, Gersonides subjects Maimonides' theory of divine knowledge (as he understands it) to a devastating critique. He correctly points out that, if there is no shared meaning between the term "knower" when applied to God and to other knowers, which he takes to be Maimonides' position, then there is no philosophical justification to apply the term "knower" to God. Whether this argument is a *reductio ad absurdum* of Maimonides' theory, or of Gersonides' own understanding of it, is a subject for another place; here one should note the two main assumptions that both philosophers hold in common. First, there are problems predicating terms that denote essential attributes of God. Maimonides thinks that these problems are insurmountable; Gersonides does not. Second, there is no proportion between God and His creatures – Maimonides thinks that this rules out the possibility of essential predication; Gersonides does not. Gersonides accepts a type of predication of attribute-terms – predication by "priority and by posteriority" – which Maimonides does not discuss. Would Maimonides have rejected this sort of positive predication, or, what is similar to it, predication by analogy? That question needs to be examined further.

Ḥasdai Crescas: *The Light of the Lord*

The flourishing of Arab Aristotelianism among Jewish savants in Provence and Spain, in the early to mid-fourteenth century, was followed by a conservative reaction in Spain and Italy in the late fourteenth and early fifteenth centuries. The Aristotelian worldview was rarely challenged, but the "enlightened" interpretation of the Jewish religion, i.e., the synthesis of Aristotelian naturalism and intellectualism with rabbinic Judaism, was soundly rejected by most thinkers. Spanish Jewish philosophers denied that human happiness consists in intellectual perfection, that the Biblical stories and rabbinic legends are to be interpreted as philosophical allegories, and that divine activity should somehow be naturalized. They emphasized the uniqueness of the Jewish people, the spiritual value of faith, and the efficacy of divine will and grace. Some have called the Spanish Jewish philosophers "theologians," but that is primarily because the texts that entered the Jewish literary canon from this period were dogmatic and theological in nature. Apart from the fact that there was never a clear distinction between theology and philosophy in Jewish philosophy – on the contrary, philosophical theology was subsumed under metaphysics in the Arab and Jewish Aristotelian tradition – this is historically inaccurate. Some of the Spanish Jewish philosophers who were most averse to Jewish Aristotelianism wrote commentaries on Aristotle, or "pure" philosophical treatises. They were simply less willing than their predecessors to fashion Judaism from Aristotelian cloth.

This conservative reaction has at times been presented as a natural reaction to the overly philosophical interpretation of Judaism that was typical of fourteenth-century Provence. Others point to a Spanish Jewish conservative tradition extending back to Judah Halevy in the twelfth century, Moses ben Naḥman and Meir ben Todros Abulafia in the thirteenth century, and Isaac Bar Sheshet and Nissim of Gerona in the fourteenth century. Still others see it in light of the difficulties of Spanish Jewry in the fifteenth century, which culminated in their mass expulsion in 1492. But recently scholars have noted the impact of the contemporary Christian religious and intellectual environment on fifteenth century Spanish Jewish intellectuals. Christian scholasticism had rejected the intellectualism and naturalism of Arab Aristotelianism already in the thirteenth century. The elevation of the will over intellect, the superiority of faith to reason, the emphasis on piety and the observance of religious precepts over the study of science and philosophy, the voluntarist reading of divine omnipotence – these and many other doctrines had parallels within Spanish Jewish philosophy, although rarely were they openly acknowledged.

The most vehement critic of Jewish Aristotelianism was Ḥasdai Crescas (c. 1340–1412), a prominent rabbi and leader of the Spanish Jewish community. Born in Barcelona, he studied under the noted Talmudist Nissim of Gerona, and acquired a reputation as a rabbinic scholar. In 1387 he moved to the capital of Aragon, Saragossa, where he was awarded the title "member of the royal household," and where he taught rabbinics and philosophy. His proximity to the court afforded him protection in the anti-Jewish riots that swept Spain in 1391, but a royal order of protection arrived too late to save his son in Barcelona.

Aside from a polemical anti-Christian tract and a philosophical sermon, Crescas left only one work, the *Light of the Lord*. The *Light* is an exposition of the fundamental principles of Judaism. It was intended to be the first part of a comprehensive work whose second part would be devoted to Jewish law. Crescas wanted the work to replace the twin pillars of Jewish law and philosophy: Maimonides' *Mishneh Torah* and the *Guide of the Perplexed*. But the second part was never composed, and so Crescas' impact on subsequent Jewish culture was limited.

The selection from the *Light of the Lord* takes up the themes of divine knowledge, determinism, and human choice. Crescas believes that God's knowledge determines things to be as they are, but he appears to waver between two types of determinism. The first is metaphysical determinism, the view that things are causally determined to exist in the way they exist by an external determinant. In this case the external determinant is God's "knowledge and conception of His will." However, Crescas often adheres to a weaker version of determinism that claims that, although divine foreknowledge entails the occurrence of future possibles, it does not causally necessitate them. The claim is found in Crescas' discussions of divine knowledge, Mosaic prophecy, and human choice. Here Crescas implies that future possibles are genuinely possible. How does one deal with these two very different ways of looking at divine knowledge? One possible interpretation is that Crescas' "theological determinism" belongs to a later stratum of the *Light of the Lord* and reflects scholastic influence. Perhaps Crescas' initial acceptance of Ibn Sīnā's and Abner's metaphysical determinism was tempered in later years as a result of his new acquaintance with scholastic treatments of divine foreknowledge. Rather than replace the old with the new, he presents them as alternatives.

As for the appropriateness of divine reward and punishment, given the truth of metaphysical determinism, Crescas offers two methods of reconciliation which, although they share elements in common, are independent of each other. His first method is to distinguish sharply between divine equity or justice (*yosher elohi*) and other forms of justice. God legislates, rewards, and punishes out of love for his creatures, in order that they achieve their ultimate real happiness. The commandments that He promulgates and their recompense motivate humans to act in such ways as to lead them necessarily to this goal. Since God is not Himself benefited or wronged by anything, a retributive model of divine justice, which repays good with good and bad with bad, is inappropriate. Retributive justice is appropriate, however, for political justice (*yosher medini*), the aim of which is, presumably, to guarantee social well-being. Crescas holds that political justice requires people to be able to choose without any compulsion or coercion at all. He probably means by this to exclude inadvertent actions rather than not causally necessitated actions. If this interpretation is correct, then Crescas holds that it is unjust politically to punish someone for an inadvertent crime, but not according to divine justice, where the punishment is intended to benefit the agent.

Crescas feels that divine sanctions are appropriate only when the agent feels no coercion or compulsion, i.e., when they are voluntary, for only then are they acts of the agent's soul. Here Crescas parts company with his predecessor Abner of Burgos, who held that, since divine recompense follows from actions necessarily, there is no difference between the recompense of one who acts under compulsion and one who does not; somebody who is forced to drink poison will die just as quickly as one who drinks it willingly. It may seem initially that Crescas' insistence upon voluntariness as a prerequisite for the appropriateness of reward and punishment, and his distinction between felt and unfelt compulsion, puts him squarely in a long compatibilist tradition, which views determinism as compatible with the moral appropriateness of praise and blame. Compatibilist determinists believe that agents are to be praised or blamed for what they do voluntarily, even though they bear no ultimate responsibility for their character, desires, genetic dispositions, etc., which determine their volitions. As long as they can do what they want to do, without being compelled to do it, or (according to some) as long as their actions arise from their character, then praise and blame are appropriate.

But Crescas offers no justification of this sort. Rather, he begins his second method of reconciliation by saying that the goal of acts of worship and good deeds is for the soul to achieve states of desire and joy, through which the soul attains conjunction with God, who is absolute pleasure and love. This joy is nothing other than the pleasure of the will in doing good. So it is fitting for reward and punishment, i.e., the soul's conjunction with

God and its separation, to follow from voluntary actions, for only these activate the soul through desire. Here "fitting" simply means something like "reasonable," not "morally appropriate." Crescas seems to be saying that it makes sense that reward and punishment are linked to the states of the soul, not that reward and punishment are morally appropriate because they are so linked. If this is correct, then Crescas has simply taken the rationalist solution offered by the Jewish Aristotelians – that spiritual reward follows upon the perfection of the intellect – and has substituted will for intellect. Through desire and love one conjoins with God, who is desire and love. This is not the move of a soft determinist, who wishes to justify ascriptions of praise and blame.

Because Crescas requires voluntariness in order for reward and punishment to be "fitting," he needs to explain how God can reward and punish beliefs, which he holds are involuntary. To do this he posits the existence of "something conjoined, attached, and concomitant to beliefs, and this is the pleasure and joy that we experience when God grants us His belief and the diligence to apprehend its truth, which is without a doubt a matter of volition and choice." Crescas does not believe that pleasure and joy are freely chosen by us; they are as metaphysically determined as anything else. But they are acquired without any *felt* compulsion, as when, for example, we delight in our knowledge that God exists. Crescas concludes by saying that volition is significant for determining the reward and punishment for actions as well as for beliefs, although he allows that inadvertent actions also are subject to punishment.

Crescas' second method, which is not found in Abner, accords well with his emphasis upon the will rather than the intellect. But it does not represent a softening of Crescas' determinism; indeed, from various parts of the *Light of the Lord*, it appears that Crescas, like Abner, is a determinist of the astral sort. In the section on human choice, he repeats Abner's claim that the will, understood as the accordance of the appetitive and imaginative faculties, is determined by the heavens. In another passage, he goes farther than Gersonides by making the *intellect* subject to astral determinism.

Yet when Crescas confronts the question of astral determinism at the end of the *Light*, as well as in his discussion of individual providence, he allows that at least certain choices are not subject to stellar influence. It may be that, in the discussion of choice, he simply appealed to astral determinism in order to present a stronger case for determinism. More likely, this is one of the many inconsistencies in the book. But whether human choice is subject to astral determinism or not, Crescas implies that it is subject to metaphysical determinism – except in those passages that demur from determinism and were probably added later.

Joseph Albo: *The Book of Principles*

Crescas had several students who became prominent philosophers in their own right. One was the Spanish rabbi Joseph Albo (c. 1380–1444), whose *Book of Principles* (c. 1425) is arguably the last major treatise of medieval Jewish philosophy to make any significant impact on Jewish intellectual life. The book is part religious polemic, part systematization of religion, and part *summa* of Jewish religious philosophy.

As religious polemic, the *Book of Principles* attempts to show that the Christian and Muslim religions do not have the status of divine law, and that the only two laws in effect that are genuinely divine are the Mosaic Law (for Jews) and the Noahide Law (for gentiles). To show this, Albo proposes and defends what he considers to be the necessary principles and branches of *any* divine law, and then examines various religions to see whether they include these principles or not; if they do, and if they provide complete proof of the veracity of their messenger, then they are divine. Christianity is disqualified, mainly because it substitutes belief in the Trinity and the Incarnation for the principle of divine unity and incorporeality, and because it substitutes belief in the arrival of the messiah and his resurrection for divine reward and punishment. Islam is disqualified because it substitutes belief in predestination for divine providence, which vitiates belief in reward and punishment for actions undertaken voluntarily. Albo also holds that neither religion provides complete proof of the veracity of its messenger.

Before Albo elaborates on the principles of divine law he considers what he calls natural law and conventional or nomic law. Natural law comprises those laws which are universal and necessary for man insofar as he is political by nature; "all those measures which are calculated to maintain the political group and to enable the people to live in a suitable manner." These include the bare minimum of laws that maintain justice and suppress wrong, and that apply to all societies. Albo may have appropriated the terms "natural law" and "conventional law" from the Christian tradition, but he uses them differently. "Natural law" is closer to the notion of "governmental law" that one finds in the *Kuzari* of Judah Halevy (twelfth century), i.e., laws that are necessary for the survival of humans as political creatures. More important, however, are conventional or "nomic" laws, i.e. laws promulgated by a lawgiver or ruler in order to promote human welfare. If the purpose of natural law is to ensure survival, the purpose of nomic law is to promote human flourishing and, more accurately, to perfect the welfare of a given society. Nomic law can include laws requiring the worship of gods or God and the performance of good actions. divine law includes the law of the first two categories but in a much more perfect state, because the lawgiver is an omniscient and benevolent God. So not only does the divine law teach the correct beliefs essential for human happiness that are not found in nomic law; it provides for justice and morality in a much better way.

Albo stipulates three principles (i.e., necessary presuppositions) of any divine law: God's existence, revelation (lit., "Torah from heaven"), and reward and punishment. It is incumbent on every follower of a divine law to believe in these, and failure to believe any of them constitutes heresy. However, they are not prerequisites either for divine law in general or Mosaic law in particular. Albo thus diverges from Maimonides, who considers creation *ex nihilo* to be a fundamental and necessary principle of the Law, presumably any divine law. In this Albo follows his teacher Crescas.

Albo also appears to diverge from Maimonides on the question of what Menachem Kellner has called "inadvertent heresy."[3] According to Maimonides, failure to affirm any one of his thirteen fundamental principles of the Law in the *Commentary on Mishnah* constitutes heresy; ignorance does not constitute a valid excuse. Albo, in at least one significant passage, defends scholars whose research and investigation have led them to affirm heretical doctrines, provided that their intentions are pure. Writing at the end of three centuries of philosophical discussion on the principles of Judaism, where there was much disagreement over what constituted a principle, Albo adopted a more tolerant approach than Maimonides.

Albo's project to axiomatize Judaism, or "divine law in so far as it is divine" had no followers, even among those fifteenth-century rabbis who wrote on Jewish dogma. The project was famously criticized by Isaac

---

[3] *Dogma in Medieval Jewish Thought from Maimonides to Abravanel* (Oxford: Littman Library, 1986), p. 199.

Abravanel, who wrote disparagingly of scholars who had copied the ways and customs of the gentile scientists by positing first roots and principles upon which the Torah is based. According to Abravanel, the entire Torah, with all its beliefs, is completely true; there is no reason to posit some as more fundamental than others. This position was later used both to defend an orthodox approach to scripture, as well as the claim that Judaism knew of no dogmas, i.e., articles of faith.

In any event, the attempt to construct "systematizations" of Jewish belief would not return in a sustained way until the nineteenth century.

Chronology

1188–90	*Guide of the Perplexed*, composed by Maimonides in Egypt
1198	Death of philosopher/jurist Ibn Rushd (Averroes) in North Africa
1204	*Guide of the Perplexed* translated into Hebrew by Samuel ibn Tibbon in Provence; other Hebrew and Latin translations of the *Guide* follow
1204	Death of Maimonides in Egypt
1232	*Guide of the Perplexed* allegedly burned, perhaps at the instigation of anti-philosophical Jews
13th–15th cents.	Translation of (mostly) Arabic and Latin scientific, philosophical, and medical texts into Hebrew
c. 1232	Death of translator/philosopher/exegete Samuel ibn Tibbon in Provence
1270	Death of exegete/kabbalist Moses Nahmanides in Palestine
1270s	Emergence of Zoharic Literature and Kabbalah in Spain
1288	Birth of Levi Gersonides in Southern France
c. 1295	Death of translator/philosopher Shem Tov Falaquera in Provence or Northern Spain
late 13th cent.	The *Emendation of the "Opinions"*, composed by Isaac Albalag
1305	Ban pronounced by R. Solomon b. Adret against anybody younger than twenty-five studying Greek science and metaphysics
1329	*The Wars of the Lord* completed by Gersonides in Southern France
1330s	Death of philosopher/exegete Joseph ibn Kaspi in Southern France
1340	Death of philosopher Jedaiah ha-Penini
1340	Birth of Ḥasdai Crescas in Spain
1344	Death of Gersonides in Southern France
1361	The *Treatise on Choice*, composed by Moses of Narbonne (Narboni) in Souria
1362	Death of Moses of Narbonne (Narboni) in Souria

c. 1366	Death of Alfonso de Valladolid (Abner of Burgos) in Spain
1410	*The Light of the Lord*, composed by Ḥasdai Crescas
1412	Death of Ḥasdai Crescas in Spain
1413–14	Religious disputation at Tortosa between Geronimo de Santa Fé and prominent rabbis, including Joseph Albo
1444	Death of philosopher Simeon ben Zemaḥ Duran in Algiers
1425	*The Book of Principles*, composed by Joseph Albo in Souria
1444	Death of Joseph Albo in Souria
1460	Death of philosopher/exegete Joseph ben Shem Tov in Castille
1492	Jews and Muslims expelled from Spain
1492	Death of philosopher/translator Abraham Shalom
1494	Death of rabbi/preacher Isaac Arama in Naples
1509	Death of philosopher/exegete Isaac Abravanel

Further reading

Translations

Saadia Gaon's *Book of Beliefs and Convictions* is available in a complete English translation as *The Book of Beliefs and Opinions*, Samuel Rosenblatt, trans. (New Haven CT: Yale University Press: 1948); see also Alexander Altmann's 1946 abridged and annotated transation, which has been re-edited with a new introduction by Daniel H. Frank (Indianapolis, IN: Hackett Publishing Co., 2002). A good translation of the *Source of Life* into English is a scholarly desideratum; the most accessible one is the French translation by Jacques Schlanger, *Solomon ibn Gabirol: Livre de la source de vie (Fons Vitae)* (Paris: Aubier Montaigne, 1970). *The Wars of the Lord* was recently translated by Seymour Feldman in three volumes (Philadelphia: Jewish Publication Society, 1984–99) with very helpful notes. Maimonides' *Guide of the Perplexed* and Albo's *Book of Principles* are available in good, if dated, translations by S. Pines and I. Husik; see the "Note on the texts and translations" below for references.

Several anthologies of medieval philosophy have selections of Jewish philosophy in translation. See Arthur Hyman and James Walsh, eds., *Philosophy in the Middle Ages* (2nd edition, Indianapolis: Hackett, 1983), Richard N. Bosley and Martin M. Tweedale, eds., *Basic Issues in Medieval Philosophy* (2nd edition, Peterborough, ON; Orchard Park, NY: Broadview Press, 2006), and Ralph Lerner and Muhsin Mahdi, eds. *Medieval Political Philosophy* (Ithaca, NY: Cornell University Press, 1963). A new expanded edition of the Lerner and Mahdi anthology, edited by Joshua Parens and Joseph MacFarland, will include additional selections of Jewish political philosophy, some of which can also be found in Michael Walzer, Menahem

Loeberbaum, Noam J. Zohar *et al.*, eds. *The Jewish Political Tradition* (New Haven, CT: Yale University Press, 2003–). A representative sample of medieval Jewish philosophy appears in Daniel H. Frank, Oliver Leaman, and Charles H. Manekin, eds., *The Jewish Philosophy Reader* (London and New York: Routledge, 2000), pp. 165–302.

For translations of Jewish philosophical exegesis of scripture see Lenn Evan Goodman, trans., *The Book of Theodicy: Translation and Commentary on the Book of Job by Saadiah ben Joseph al-Fayyūmī* (New Haven, CT: Yale University Press, 1988), and Menahem Kellner, trans., *Commentary on Song of Songs by Levi ben Gershom (Gersonides)* (New Haven, CT: Yale University Press, 1998).

Secondary literature in English

The most comprehensive history of medieval Jewish philosophy is Colette Sirat, *A History of Jewish Philosophy in the Middle Ages* (2nd edition, Cambridge: Cambridge University Press, 1990), which is arranged chronologically. Steven Nadler and Tamar Rudavsky, eds., *The Cambridge History of Jewish Philosophy: From Antiquity through the Seventeenth Century* (Cambridge: Cambridge University Press, forthcoming), is arranged topically; Daniel H. Frank and Oliver Leaman, eds., *The Cambridge Companion to Medieval Jewish Philosophy* (Cambridge: Cambridge University Press, 2003) is quite valuable. There is a large section devoted to medieval Jewish philosophy in Daniel H. Frank and Oliver Leaman, *History of Jewish Philosophy* (London and New York: Routledge, 1997). Still useful, if somewhat outdated, are J. Gutmann, *Philosophies of Judaism* (rept. New York: Schocken, 1964) and I. Husik, *A History of Medieval Jewish Philosophy* (rept. Boston, MA: Adamant Media, 2005).

Pre-Maimonidean philosophy is often influenced by the Muslim Kalām, by neoplatonism, and by neoplatonized Aristotelianism. Monographs devoted to thinkers of this period include Henry Malter, *Saadia Gaon: His Life and Works* (rept. New York: Hermon Press, 1969); S. Stroumsa, *Dāwūd ibn Marwān al-Muqammis's Twenty Chapters ("Ishrūn Maqāla)* (New York: Brill, 1989); Alexander Altmann and S. M. Stern, *Isaac Israeli: A Neoplatonic Philosopher of the Early Tenth Century* (Oxford: Clarendon Press, 1958), and T. Fontaine, *In Defense of Judaism: Abraham Ibn Daud: Sources and Structures of Emunah Ramah* (Assen: Van Gorcum, 1990). Translations include Jacob Haberman, trans., *The Microcosm of*

Joseph Ibn Saddiq (Madison, NJ: Fairleigh Dickinson University Press, 2003), and Norbert Samuelson, trans., *The Exalted Faith of Abraham ibn Daud* (Rutherford, NJ: Fairleigh Dickinson University Press, 1986).

The figure of Maimonides dominates medieval Jewish philosophy and its scholarship; there is even a journal, *Maimonidean Studies*, devoted to this thinker. Most of his writings have been translated into English; a convenient anthology is still Isadore Twersky, ed., *A Maimonides Reader* (New York: Behrman House, 1976). For short introductions to Maimonides' philosophy, see Kenneth M. Seeskin, *Maimonides: A Guide for Today's Perplexed* (West Orange, NJ: Behrman House, 1991), and Charles H. Manekin, *On Maimonides* (Belmont, CA: Wadsworth, 2004). Recent monographs include Herbert A. Davidson, *Maimonides: The Man and His Works* (Oxford: Oxford University Press, 2005); Kenneth M. Seeskin, *Searching for a Distant God: The Legacy of Maimonides* (New York: Oxford University Press, 2000); *Maimonides on the Origin of the World* (Cambridge: Cambridge University Press, 2005), and Howard Kreisel, *Maimonides' Political Thought: Studies in Ethics, Law, and the Human Ideal* (Albany, NY: State University & New York Press, 1999). The most recent scholarly anthology in English is Kenneth M. Seeskin, ed., *The Cambridge Companion to Maimonides* (Cambridge: Cambridge University Press, 2005). The octocentenary of Maimonides' death was in 2004, and several more anthologies are in the planning stage at this time.

Post-Maimonidean Jewish philosophy is mostly European, or at least originated around the Mediterranean basin, but special mention should be made of the Jewish philosophical tradition in Yemen, which lasted until the twentieth century. For Yemen's golden age of medieval Jewish philosophy, see Y. T. Langermann, *Yemenite Midrash: Philosophical Commentaries on the Torah* (San Francisco, CA: Harper San Francisco, 1996). For thirteenth-century Europe there is Steven Harvey, *Falaquera's Epistle of the Debate: An Introduction to Jewish Philosophy* (Cambridge, MA.: Harvard University Press, 1986), which is highly recommended for beginners in the field, and Steven Harvey, *Medieval Hebrew Encyclopedias*, Amsterdam Studies in Jewish Thought (Dordrecht: Kluwer Publishers, 2000). While there is still no monograph devoted to late medieval Jewish philosophy, the influence of scholastic philosophy on Jewish philosophy is studied in Mauro Zonta, *Hebrew Scholasticism in the Fifteenth Century: A History and Source Book*, Amsterdam Studies in Jewish Thought (Dordrecht: Springer, 2006).

Philosophical biblical exegesis is dealt with in Robert Eisen, *Gersonides on Providence, Covenant, and the Chosen People: A Study in Medieval Jewish Philosophy and Biblical Commentary* (Albany, NY: State University of New York Press, 1995) and *The Book of Job in Medieval Jewish Philosophy* (New York: Oxford University Press, 2004). Maimonides' philosophical exegesis has been studied by James A. Diamond, *Maimonides and the Hermeneutics of Concealment: Deciphering Scriptures and Midrash in the "Guide of the Perplexed"* (Albany, NY: State University & New York Press, 2002).

Much of medieval Jewish philosophy is indebted to Islamic philosophy, and hence readers are advised to consult Muhammad Ali Khalidi, *Medieval Islamic Philosophical Writings*, Cambridge Texts in the History of Philosophy (Cambridge: Cambridge University Press, 2005), and the recommendations for secondary literature found on pp. xli–xlvi. Special mention should be made of Harry A. Wolfson, *The Philosophy of the Kalām* (Cambridge, MA: Harvard University Press, 1976); Herbert A. Davidson, *Alfarabi, Avicenna, and Averroes on Intellect* (Oxford: Oxford University Press, 1992), and *Proofs for Eternity, Creation, and the Existence of God in Medieval Islamic and Jewish Philosophy* (Oxford: Oxford University Press, 1987); Dimitri Gutas, *Avicenna and the Aristotelian Tradition: Intoduction to Reading Avicenna's Philosophical Works* (Leiden: E. J. Brill, 1988), Gerhard Endress and Jan A. Aertsen, *Averroes and the Aristotelian Tradition* (Leiden: E. J. Brill, 1999), and Majid Fakhry, *Averroes* (Oxford: One World, 2001).

Finally, the online *Stanford Encyclopedia of Philosophy* is in the process of adding articles on major and minor figures in medieval Jewish philosophy. The *Encyclopedia Judaica* (which is now available in a second edition) is still the standard source for contemporary scholarship on these figures; the online *Jewish Encyclopedia* of 1906 is an invaluable resource for nineteenth-century scholarship in medieval Jewish philosophy.

Note on the texts and translations

There are very few critical editions of the principal texts of medieval Jewish philosophy in Hebrew, not even one of Maimonides' *Guide of the Perplexed*. Still, the texts translated for this volume are based on scholarly editions, and most have been prepared by academically trained scholars of Jewish philosophy.

I have not indicated the page numbers of the original editions in the translation, but readers who wish to consult them will have no difficulty finding the appropriate passages. Where the translation does not follow the edition, or where it follows a variant reading in the edition's apparatus, a note is given. Additions to the text are indicated in square brackets, but only those additions which are not clearly implied by the sense. For example, medieval philosophical Arabic and Hebrew rely very heavily on pronouns; at times I have taken the liberty of replacing them with what I consider to be their antecedents without noting this. On the other hand, I omit the honorific benedictions, e.g., "may He be blessed" or "of blessed memory" when their repetition becomes tedious. This is mentioned in the notes. References to scriptural verses, and translations based on textual emendations not cited in the notes, are enclosed within square brackets.

In the translation of Moses of Narbonne's *Treatise on Choice* I have proposed a number of alternate readings, not because M. Hayoun's edition is unsatisfactory, but because it is based on the single manuscript of this work (Paris, Bibliothèque Nationale de France, héb. 403/2) which is very defective. Some of these readings are already proposed by Hayoun in his edition.

Some of the texts have been translated before, a few more than once. Between the extremes of using unmodified existing translations, and of translating everything anew, I have taken the middle path of revising translations (when they exist) to achieve uniformity of terminology and of translation practice. Only the selections from Maimonides and from Albo are presented here with relatively slight terminological revisions and updating; the others are either newly translated or significantly revised.

Saadia Gaon, *The Book of Beliefs and Convictions*. Editions: *Kitāb al-amanāt wa'l-i'tiqādāt*, ed. S. Landauer. Leiden: E. J. Brill, 1880; J. Kafih, *Kitāb al-mukhtār fi l-amānāt wa'l-i'tiqādāt.* Jerusalem: Sura Institute, 1970 (Arabic). *Sefer Emunot ve-De'ot*, trans. Judah ibn Tibbon (Hebrew). The basis of the translation here is that of Samuel Rosenblatt *The Book of Beliefs and Opinions* (New Haven, CT: Yale University Press: 1948), which has been substantially revised, beginning with the title.

Solomon ibn Gabirol, *The Fountain of Life. Excerpts by Shem Tov b. Joseph Falaquera*. Edition: *Mélanges de philosophie juive et arabe, renfermant des extraits méthodiques de la Source de vie de Salomon ibn-Gebirol (dit Avicebron)*, ed. S. Munk (Paris: A. Franck, 1853*)*. I also consulted the text in *Fons vitae = Meqor Ḥayyim*, ed. and trans. into Italian by R. Gatti. Genova: Il melangolo, 2001.

Moses Maimonides, *The Guide of the Perplexed*. Editions: *Dalalat al-Ḥa'irin*, ed. S. Munk, with variant readings by I. Joel. Jerusalem: J. Junovitch, 1930/1 (Arabic); *Moreh Nevukhim*, trans. Samuel ibn Tibbon, ed. Y. Even-Shmuel. Jerusalem: Mossad Harav Kook, 2000 (Hebrew). I have also consulted the new Hebrew translation by Michael Schwarz. Tel-Aviv: TAU Press, 2002. The present translation is a slightly revised version of Moses Maimonides, *The Guide of the Perplexed*, trans. S. Pines. Chicago: University of Chicago Press, © 1963 by the University of Chicago. Permission to use this edition has been granted by the University of Chicago Press.

Isaac Albalag, *The Emendation of the "Opinions."* Edition: *Sefer Tiqqun ha-De'ot*, ed. G. Vajda. Jerusalem: Israel Academy of Sciences and the Humanities, 1973.

Moses of Narbonne, *The Treatise on Choice*. Edition: "L'Epitre du libre arbitre de Moïse de Narbonne (ca. 1300–1362)", ed. and trans. M. Hayoun, *Revue des études juives* 141 (1982): 139–67.

Levi Gersonides, *The Wars of the Lord*. Edition: *Milḥamot ha-Shem*, ed. Charles Touati. (I am indebted to Gad Freudenthal and Professor Touati's family for enabling me to use Professor Touati's unpublished edition of Book III.)

Ḥasdai Crescas, *The Light of the Lord*. Edition: *Sefer Or Adonai*, ed. S. Fisher. Jerusalem: Sifre Ramot, 1989.

Joseph Albo, *The Book of Principles*. Edition: *Sefer ha-ᶜIkkarim: The Book of Principles*, ed. I. Husik. Philadelphia: The Jewish Publication Society of America, 1929. The present translation is a slight revision and updating of Husik's translation. Permission to use this edition has been granted by the Jewish Publication Society of America.

Saadia Gaon, from *The Book of the Beliefs and Convictions*

Introduction

1   The author opened his work by saying:

Blessed be the Lord, the God of Israel – the True, in the sense of evidently true, who verifies for rational beings the existence of their souls with certain truth, through which they find their sense perception to be sound, and know their knowledge to be accurate. As a result, errors are removed, and doubts are eliminated; arguments are clarified and proofs established. May He be extolled over the highest and most genuine praise.

2   Now that we have opened with a brief praise and tribute of our Lord, I will preface this book, which I intend to write, with a report of the causes of errors that beset some people in their investigations, and how these errors can be eliminated, so that the people can fully attain the object of their investigations; moreover, why some errors have taken hold of people such that their thought and fancy affirm them as true. May God help me to uncover such errors in my own mind so that I may achieve the state of obedience towards Him, even as His pious one requested that He might grant him perfection, saying, "Uncover mine eyes, that I may behold the marvels of your Law" [Ps. 119:18].

I have resolved to make these introductory statements, and indeed those of the entire book, easy and accessible, rather than difficult and remote, by citing the fundamentals of the proofs and arguments and not their detailed implications, so that readers may find their way about without too much difficulty. By making their study straightforward, they will attain their object, which is justice and truth, even as the pious one said with regard to wisdom when placed within easy grasp: "Then you will

understand righteousness and justice, and equity, yea, every good path"
[Prov. 2:9].

I shall first report the causes of error that beset some men. I say then that
intelligibles are based upon sensibles.[1] Now doubts may arise concerning
things apprehended by sense through one of two causes: either because
the person who is inquiring has an inadequate idea of the object of the
investigation, or because he is casual and perfunctory in his observation
and research. Take the case of a person who is looking for someone called
Reuben ben Jacob. He may be in doubt whether he has found him for one of
two reasons: either because his knowledge of Reuben is inadequate, since
he never met him before and therefore does not know him, or because he
may casually assume that some other person that he sees is Reuben. By
taking matters lightly, and neglecting to make proper inquiries, he seeks
him half-heartedly and with little application. He will never recognize
him.

We can say the same for the things apprehended by our intellect. Here
again doubts arise from one of two causes: either because the person who
seeks intellectual knowledge is unfamiliar with the methods of demonstration – he judges a bad proof to be correct, and a good one, incorrect –
or he knows the right methods of investigation, but he treats the
matter lightly and carelessly, rushing to a conclusion about some object of
knowledge before having completed the art of investigation concerning
it. The case is worse when both deficiencies are combined in the same
person, that is to say, when the person is not acquainted with the art of
investigation and, in addition, lacks patience to achieve what he can truly
know about his object of inquiry. He will remain far removed from that
object, and will despair of attaining it. Of the first of the two kinds of
persons we have mentioned, the pious one says, "Everyone that knows,
understands" [Neh. 10:29]; of the second, "They know not, neither do
they understand" [Ps. 82:5].

The case is still worse when we add to these deficiencies a third, namely,
that the inquirer has no clear idea as to what he really wishes to know.
Then he is so removed from attaining true knowledge that, even if the

---

[1] Intelligibles [Arabic: *maᶜqulāt*; Hebrew: *muskalot*] are the eternal concepts or true propositions
acquired by the intellect, e.g., the correct concept *triangle*, or the true proposition that the angles
of a plane triangle add up to 180°. Each bit of intellectual knowledge is called an intelligible, since
it is both object and content of the intellect. By contrast, the sensibles [Arabic: *maḥsusat*; Hebrew:
muḥashot] are the objects and content of our senses, e.g., the sensible image of a triangle.

truth should chance upon him, he would not notice it. He resembles a man who is unacquainted with the art of weighing, with the shape of the scales and weights, and with the amount of money owed him by his debtor. Even if his debt is paid it will not be clear to him that he had received the full payment; and if he took less than was owed him, he might think that he had cheated his debtor. The person who claims money from his adversary is similar to the person who wishes to weigh money for himself, but is ignorant of the scales and the amount weighed. Or they are similar to the person who exchanges coins without knowing how to appraise them, and, as a result, frequently exchanges good coins for bad, or, somewhat similarly, to the person who knows how to appraise coins but does not examine them well. Scripture has already compared the appraisal of the words of righteousness to the appraisal of money when it says, "The tongue of the righteous is as choice silver; the heart of the wicked is of little worth" [Prov. 10:20]. Those who have only little knowledge in the art of appraising coins, or are impatient, are considered as wicked because they wrong the truth, as it is said: "The heart of the wicked is little worth." In contrast, the expert appraisers are considered righteous on account of their knowledge and patience, as stated in the preceding words, "The tongue of the righteous is as choice silver." The wise are to be praised and their doubts removed only if they patiently engross themselves in all aspects of their art after they have gained insight in it, as the pious one says, "Behold, I waited for your words, I listened for your reasons, until I searched out what to say" [Job 32:77], and as has been said by another wise man, "Take not the final word of truth out of my mouth" [Ps. 119:43].

What led me to make these opening[2] remarks was my observation of the manner of many people's convictions and beliefs. Some have arrived at the truth and are in a state of knowledge and joy concerning it; of them the prophet says, "Thy words were found, and I did eat them, and Thy words were unto me a joy and the rejoicing of my heart" [Jer. 15:16]. Others have arrived at the truth, but are in doubt concerning it and, not being convinced, fail to hold onto it; of these the prophet says, "Though I write for him ever so many things of My law, they are accounted as strangers" [Hosea 8:12]. Still others "confirm" what is false, thinking that it is true. They hold on to falsehood and abandon what is correct; of them it is said, "He will be misled by falsehood, and falsehood will be his recompense"

---

[2] Reading *at-taṣdīr*, with Munich ms.

[Job 15:31]. Still others conduct themselves according to a certain procedure[3] for some time and then reject it after finding within it a certain defect. They then shift to another procedure for a while and drop it because of finding something odd; then they shift to yet another and leave because of some corrupt opinion. Such people vacillate all their life. They are like a person who wants to go to a town but does not know the road that leads to it; he travels a parasang on one road, becomes perplexed, and returns; then he travels a parasang on another road, becomes perplexed and returns, then again for a third and fourth time. Of him Scripture says, "A fool's labor wearies him, for he doesn't know how to get to a town" [Eccles. 10:15].

When I considered these principles and their evil consequences, my heart grieved for my species, the human species, and my soul trembled on account of our own people Israel. For I saw that in our time many of the faithful lack pure convictions and possess mistaken convictions, while many of the deniers boast of their corruption and act haughtily towards the men of truth, although they are themselves in error. I saw men sunk, as it were, in a sea of doubts and covered by the waters of obscurity, and there was no diver to bring them up from the depths and no swimmer to grasp their hands and bring them to shore.

But as my Lord has provided me with some knowledge that I can use for their support, and endowed me with some capacity to be of help to them, I saw that I was bound to assist them, and that it was my duty to guide them aright, as the saint says: "The Lord God gave me a skilled tongue, to know how to teach something. Morning by morning He rouses, He rouses my ear to give heed like disciples" [Isa. 50:4], although I am aware that my science falls short of perfection, and I admit that my knowledge is far from being complete – regarding my ability and intellectual accomplishments I am no wiser than any of my generation, as the saint says, "But as for me, this secret is not revealed to me for any wisdom that I have more than any living" [Dan. 2:30]. Nevertheless, I beseech Him (exalted be He) to grant me success and sustain me in accordance with what he knows to be my aim and purpose in my quest, and not in accordance with my gifts and abilities, as has been said by another saint: "I know, God, that you search the heart and desire uprightness" [1 Chron. 29:17].

---

[3] *madhab*.

In the name of God, the Creator of the universe, I adjure any learned man who peruses this book and finds in it a mistake, to correct it, or if he finds in it a doubtful term, to replace it with a better one. That it is not his book should not deter him, nor that I preceded him in clarifying matters that he found obscure. For the wise have compassion on wisdom and feel a longing for it as close relatives feel a longing for each other, as is said: "Say unto wisdom: thou art my sister" [Prov. 7:4]; the ignorant have likewise compassion on their ignorance, and do not forsake it, as is said: "Though he saves it, does not let it go, holds it inside his mouth" [Job 20:13].

In the name of God (exalted be He) I implore further all seekers of wisdom who examine my book to read it without prejudice, to make my aim their own, and to abandon partisanship, haphazard conjecture, and confusion, so that they may derive the most benefit and profit through the power of Him who has taught us wherein consists our benefit, as the saint said: "I the Lord am your God, instructing you for your own benefit, guiding you in the way you should go" [Isa. 48:17]. If both the scholar and the student conduct themselves in this manner when they read this book, then whoever is certain will have his certainty increase, and whoever is in doubt will have his doubt vanish; the believer on the basis of tradition will become a believer on the basis of speculation and understanding; the sophist will be silenced; the obstinate and the arrogant will be ashamed; and the righteous and upright will rejoice, as is said: "The upright see it and rejoice; the mouth of all wrongdoers is stopped; the wise man will take note of these things, he will consider the steadfast love of the Lord" [Ps. 107:42–3].

In this way men's inner being will be made to resemble their outward behavior. Their prayers will be pure, as there will be deep in their heart something warning them about sin, and summoning them to right conduct, as the prophet says: "In my heart I treasure your promise; therefore I do not sin against You" [Ps. 119:11]. Their faith will show itself in their dealings with each other; jealousy between them in matters of this world will diminish; all will turn towards the Master of Wisdom and not to anything else. He will be for them salvation, mercy, and happiness, as God (praised and sanctified be He) has said: "Turn to Me and be saved, all the ends of the earth, for I am God, and there is none else" [Isa. 45:22]. All this will result from the disappearance of doubts and the removal of errors. The knowledge of God and His Law will spread in the world like the spreading of water in all parts of the sea, as is said: "For the earth shall be full of the knowledge of the Lord, as the waters cover the sea" [Isa. 11:9].

3 Now someone may ask: "Why did the Creator (exalted and magnified be He) permit these uncertainties and doubts to remain among His creatures?" To this question we answer that the very fact of their being creatures necessitates their entertaining uncertainties and illusions. That is to say: by the plan of creation, they require for every act they perform a span of time within which to complete that act step by step. Cognition, therefore, which is one of these activities, obviously depends upon a like condition. Now the process of knowing on the part of men begins with things that are at first jumbled, obscure, and ambiguous. However through their rational faculty they continually refine and purify their idea over the course of time until the uncertainties depart, and the idea emerges dissociated from any doubt.

Now, since all human arts consist of stages, if men were to stop in their endeavors before these stages were completed, the operation in question, such as sowing or building or weaving or other tasks, that can be brought to completion only by the patience of the worker to the last stage, would never be completed. In like manner the art of cognition requires that one start in it at the beginning and proceed step by step until its end. At the initial stage, for example, there may be ten problems, which at the second are reduced to nine, and at the third to eight. Thus each time that man's reasoning and reflection are applied to them these problems decrease, until at the last of these stages, the sole object of his quest is extracted and left removed from all ambiguity or doubt . . . [some text omitted].

It has been shown, then, that the person who speculates begins with many things that are all mixed up, from which he never ceases to sift nine out of ten, and then eight out of nine, and then seven out of eight, until his object has been refined from all perplexities and doubts with only the pure essence remaining. If, therefore, he were to cease in his speculation upon reaching the fifth or the fourth or any other stage, the number of doubts resolved by him would be in proportion to the number of stages he had completed, and he would still be left with a number proportionate to the stages before him. Should he retain what he has achieved, there is hope that he may come back to it and complete it. If, however, he does not retain it, then he will be compelled to repeat the entire speculation from the beginning. It is on this account that many people remain in error and reject wisdom, some of them not knowing the way to wisdom, others because they began their journey but fail to complete it. They are of the ruined, as the verse says: "A man who wanders from the way of intellect will rest in the company of ghosts" [Prov. 21:16]. The sages among the Israelites have said of a person who does not complete his studies: "When the disciples of Shammai and Hillel who had not sufficiently served their masters increased, so did dissension." This saying teaches us that had their disciples completed their studies, there would not have been either dissension or controversy.

Let not the vexed fool ascribe his sin to the Creator (exalted and magnified be He) by saying that it was He who had imposed the doubts in him. Rather it was his own folly or his vexation that plunged him into these doubts, as we have shown. For it is impossible that a one–time act on his part should remove all uncertainties, for then he would not be subject to the laws governing creatures – and yet he is one! Even if one does not ascribe his sin to his master, yet wishes God to provide him with indubitable knowledge, he asks to become His equal. For one who knows without a cause is the Creator of All, blessed and sanctified be He, as we shall show below.

But created beings cannot acquire knowledge except by the mediation of a cause; that is, by the process of research and speculation, which requires time, as we have shown. This is why they remain in doubt from the first period of time to the last, as we have explained. The praiseworthy will wait patiently until they have refined the dross from the silver, as Scripture states: "The dross having been refined from the silver, a vessel emerges for the smith" [Prov. 25:4]; or, until they have distilled the [milk of the] art and extracted its cream, as Scripture says: "As milk under pressure brings forth butter" [Prov. 30:33] or, until their seed has grown so it can be harvested, as Scripture says: "Sow righteousness for yourselves, reap the fruits of goodness" [Hos. 10:12]; or, until the fruit has ripened on the trees and has become fit for food, as Scripture says: "It is a tree of life to those who hold on to it" [Prov. 3:18].

4   Now that we have concluded what we wished to mention concerning how to resolve uncertainties and doubts, we should explain the meaning of conviction.[4] We say that it is a notion that arises in the soul

---

[4] *I'tiqād*. Another common translation is "belief." The term denotes a cognitive attitude of assent and is neither limited to religious conviction, nor opposed to rational knowledge.

regarding the actual state of the object of knowledge. When the cream of speculation emerges, when it is embraced and encompassed by the minds and, through them acquired and digested by the souls, then the person becomes convinced of the truth of the notion he has thus acquired. He then deposits it in his soul for a future occasion or for future occasions, as the wise say: "The Wise store up knowledge" [Prov. 10:14]. Scripture says also: "Accept instruction from His mouth; lay up His words in your heart" [Job 22:22].

Convictions are of two kinds: true and false. A true conviction consists in believing a thing to be as it really is; namely, the much as much, the little as little, the existent as existent, and the nonexistent as nonexistent. A false conviction, on the other hand, consists in believing a thing to be the opposite of what it actually is, such as that much is little, and little is much, and white is black, and black is white, and that what exists is nonexistent, and what is nonexistent exists.

The praiseworthy wise man is he who makes a principle of the truth of things and bases his convictions thereon. Notwithstanding his wisdom, he relies only on what is deserving of trust and is wary wherever caution is in order. The reprehensible fool, on the other hand, is he who makes a principle of his own conviction and assumes that the truth of things results from his convictions. Notwithstanding his ignorance, he trusts in what should be shunned and shuns what is deserving of trust. All this is borne out by Scripture, which says: "A wise man fears and shuns evil, but a dullard rushes in confidently" [Prov. 14:16].

Regarding this observation I should express my surprise at certain people who, being slaves, yet believe that they have no master, and who are confident that whatever they deny must be non-existent and whatever they affirm must exist. These individuals are so sunken in folly as to have reached the very depths of perdition. For if they are correct, then let him among them who has no money take it into his head that his coffers and chests are filled with money, and see what it would profit him. Or let him believe he is seventy years old, when he is only forty years of age, and see what good it would do him. Or let him assume that he is sated when he is hungry, or that his thirst is quenched when he is thirsty, or that he is covered up when he is naked, and see what would happen to him. Or let one of those fools who has a vicious enemy believe that his enemy has died and departed, with the result that he no longer takes precautions against the latter. How quickly will he be overcome by the misfortune for which he did not sufficiently prepare.

Now it is utter folly for people to imagine that, if they do not believe in God's sovereignty, they will be exempt from His commandments and prohibitions, and from his promises of reward and threats of punishment and other such things. Of such individuals the Scripture says, "Let us break the cords of their rope" [Ps. 2:3]. Thus some Hindus learn to endure fire, although it burns them whenever they touch it. Other individuals feign youthful heroics and learn to endure the blows of the cane and the whip, although when struck by them they are in pain. How much more serious should be the case of those who embolden themselves against the Creator of the universe! Despite their folly they will not escape what His wisdom has decreed for them, as Scripture has indeed said: "Wise of heart and mighty in power – who has challenged Him, and prospered?" [Job 9:4].

5   Now that we finished what we saw fit to add to our first statement, we ought to mention the principles that lead us to truth and are conducive to certainty, the principles of all science and the mainspring of all knowledge. We will discuss them as much as befits the aim of this book.

We say that there are three such conducive principles. The first is observational knowledge; the second, intellectual knowledge, and the third, knowledge obtained from necessary inference. We shall explain each of these principles separately.

We say that observational knowledge is that which a man apprehends with one of his senses, i.e., sight, hearing, smell, taste, or touch. Intellectual knowledge is that which arises solely through the human intellect, such as the approval of truthfulness and disapproval of mendacity. Knowledge obtained from necessary inference is that which, if not accepted as true, entails the impossibility of a sensible or intelligible. Since there is no way to reject either of these, the individual is compelled to regard the matter as being correct. Thus we are forced to affirm that man possesses a soul, although we have not seen it, in order not to deny its manifest activity. Now we find that there are many people who deny these principles. A small minority of them reject the first principle. Of these we shall give an account in the first treatise of this book, together with a refutation of their opinion. By rejecting the first principle, they have rejected the second and the third, since the latter two are based upon the first. More numerous than this group are those that acknowledge the validity of the first but reject the second and the third [principles]. Of their thesis, too, we shall make mention in the first treatise and refute it. Most numerous of all, however, are those who acknowledge the validity of the first two principles [of knowledge] and reject the third. The reason for the divergent number of adherents lies in the fact that the second [type of] knowledge is more profound than the first, and likewise the third more so than the second, and that whatever is invisible can more readily be denied than what is visible.

Again there are people who reject the validity of [inferential] knowledge in some instances and recognize it in others, each sect among them affirming what its opponent negates. They argue that necessity compelled them to draw a certain conclusion. Thus there is one who affirms that all things are at rest. That one consequently denies the reality of motion. Another, again, affirms that all things move, and thereby denies the reality of rest. They consider the proofs cited by their opponents doubtful and unconvincing.

As for ourselves, the community of monotheists, we accept these three principles of knowledge to be true. To them, however, we add a fourth conducive principle, which we have derived by means of the other three, and which has thus become for us a further principle, namely, the validity of authentic tradition. For it is based upon sense knowledge and intellectual knowledge, as we shall explain in the third treatise of this book. Here we say that this knowledge (I mean the religious tradition and the prophetic books) confirms for us the first three principles of knowledge. Thus Scripture enumerates the senses when it denies them of idols, bringing their total to five and adding an additional two. It says, namely: "They have mouths that do not speak; eyes that do not see; ears that do not hear; a nose that does not smell; hands that do not touch; feet that do not walk; nor do they utter anything with their throat" [Ps. 115:5–7]. The first five are the senses themselves, while one of the additional two ["feet that do not walk"] refers to motion. Through motion we become conscious of heaviness and lightness. Thus a person is hindered from moving about on account of his heaviness, but not on account of his lightness. For this reason, indeed, certain people thought to add to the number of the senses, for they asked: "How [else] can the sensation of lightness and heaviness be experienced?" Our answer is: "By means of the sense of motion, according to whether the latter is found to be easy or difficult."

The other one is speech [implied in the statement: "Nor do they utter anything with their throat"], i.e., speech in general, which includes individual nouns, connectors, propositions, and proofs, as we have previously explained.

Then again, Scripture confirms for us the validity of intellectual knowledge, when it commands us to speak the truth and not to lie: "For my mouth shall utter truth, and wickedness is an abomination to my lips. All the words of my mouth are in righteousness, there is nothing perverse or crooked in them" [Prov. 8:7, 8]. It also confirms for us the validity of knowledge obtained by necessary inference, for whatever implies the rejection of what is perceived through the senses or intellectually cognized is absurd.

Then again, Scripture refutes the rejection of sense-perception when it states: "You who tear yourself in anger, will the earth be abandoned because of you, or shall the rock be removed out of its place?" [Job 18:4]. It also refutes the rejection of what is cognized intellectually, the distinction of the true from the false, when it remarks: "Who can refute me and consider my speech worthless?" [Job 24:25]. Afterwards, it informs us that all the sciences are based on sense-perception, from which they branch out and proceed. Thus it says: "Hear my words, wise men; and lend me your ears, possessors of knowledge. For the ear examines words as the palate tastes food" [Job 34:2, 3]. Moreover Scripture confirms the validity of reliable reports when it says: "I will speak up, so hear me; I will declare what I have seen – what wise men have transmitted from their fathers, and have not withheld; to whom alone the land was given, no stranger passing among them" [Job 15:17–19]. We have already explained the conditions of the various principles in our commentary on these verses in their proper place.[5]

Now that we have mentioned these four origins [of knowledge], we ought to explain what sorts of inferences are to be drawn from them:

Sense-knowledge. We say that whatever is perceived in our healthy senses on account of the connection existing between us and the object should be believed to be truly as we have apprehended it. No doubt arises here as long as we are experienced in detecting illusions and not led astray by them, unlike [a] those who believe that the image that they see in

---

[5] See *The Book of Theodicy: Translation and Commentary on the Book of Job by Saadiah ben Joseph al-Fayyūmī*, trans. L. E. Goodman (New Haven, CT: Yale University Press, 1988), pp. 264–5.

the mirror is an image that has really been created there, when in fact it is only a property of polished bodies to reflect the outline of objects facing them; or [b] those who regard the figure that appears reversed in the water as possessing a true reality that was created at that [particular] time, not knowing that the cause of that [illusion] resides in the fact that the water is deeper in measurement than the length of the figure. So long, then, as we guard ourselves against such illusions and the like, our conviction of what is perceived with the senses will be correct, and we will not be led astray by such an illusion as reported by Scripture: "The Moabites saw the water from a distance as red as blood" [II Kings 3:22].

Intellectual knowledge. We say that whatever is conceived in our intellect free of all defects is to be regarded as true and indubitable knowledge. This assumes that we know how to reason, and that we complete our process of reasoning, watching out for dreams and illusions. For some people accept dreams as realities that have originated in the visible forms. They are forced to do so in order not to reject what they have seen with their eyes. But they do not realize that some of what they see is a result of the affairs of the previous day passing through their mind, of which Scripture says: "For a dream comes through a multitude of business" [Eccles. 5:2]. Others are the result of the food that has been consumed, i.e., its being warm or cold, a lot or a little. Of this Scripture says: "A hungry man dreams that he is eating" [Isa. 29:8]. Others are the result of the humor that has exceeded its proportion in the mixture [of the elements composing the body]. So heat and moisture produce images of mirth and gaiety; cold and dryness produce images of sadness and sorrow, as the pain-wracked invalid says: "When I say, 'My bed shall comfort me . . .'; you scare me with dreams and terrify me through visions" [Job 7:13, 14]. Of course there is also apt to be mingled with these dreams a flash of heavenly light in the form of a hint or a parable, as Job says: "In a dream, in a vision of the night; when deep sleep falls upon men, in slumberings upon the bed; then He opens the ears of men" [Job 33:15, 16].

Knowledge obtained by necessary inference. When our senses perceive and become persuaded of some thing, and when we can possess a conviction of that thing only in our soul if we possess concomitant convictions of other things, then we must possess all those convictions, be they few or many. For what we have perceived does not exist except through the others' [existence]. Now there may be one, two, three, four, or more concomitants, however numerous they may be. For since there is no escaping that sense-perception, there is no escaping any of its concomitant convictions.

An example of a single [inferred] thing: Let it be supposed that we see smoke, but do not see the fire from which that smoke originates. We must in that case believe in the existence of the fire because of the existence of the smoke since the one can be effected only by means of the other. Likewise if we hear the voice of a human being from behind a wall, we must believe in the existence of that human being, since a human voice can emanate only from an existing human being.

An example of more than one [inferred thing]: When, for instance, we see whole food descend into the belly of a living thing and waste-products emerge from it, we must assume four things, or else what we have perceived will not be produced. There must be a faculty that attracts the food into the interior; a faculty that retains it until it has been digested; a faculty that digests and breaks it down, and a faculty that expels the waste to the exterior. Now inasmuch as what has been perceived by the senses could be effected only by means of these four things, we must believe that the four are real.

Occasionally our conviction concerning what we have observed cannot be fully realized unless we have created a science that confirms it for us. We may even be compelled to resort to many such sciences. Once, however, it is realized that the object sensed depends upon them, we must affirm all of them in order for the object to be established. Thus, for example, we see the moon rise upon the earth and set again at different moments of the night and the day. It does this by following either a long or a short route: in the short route it does not reach one of the twenty-eight stations that we have apprehended and designated by name, whereas in the long route it passes by the latter.[6] We note, furthermore, that at one time it travels to the south and at another to the north. From this we infer that, if it had only one motion, it would not have varied its course or its direction. From the fact, therefore, that we observe both these variations we infer that the moon has many motions and that these multiple motions can be due only to multiple bodies, since one body cannot be endowed with two different motions at one and the same time, let alone three or four motions. We also infer that when a multiple number of bodies equal in

---

[6] According to Arab astrologers, the moon passes through twenty-eight stations (or mansions) in its monthly orbit. See Al-Biruni, *Book of Instructions in the Elements of Astrology*, trans. R. Wright (London: Luzac, 1934), p. 81.

form intercept each other, they thereby diminish or increase the speeds of their respective motions.

Now all this is demonstrable only by means of the art of geometry, which shows us how one figure is subsumed under others through construction, after we have known the simples from which they are composed. After points and lines we begin with simple figures, such as the triangle, the square, the circle, the concentric, the tangent, and the secant, until we get to know the properties of the intercepting [spherical] figure,[7] and which of its segments are impossible and which are possible. This finally enables us to recognize that the figures of the heavenly orbs are spherical or circular, and that some are located within others. Once these sciences have been thoroughly mastered, it becomes clear to us that the moon's course is a composite of five motions. We must, therefore, accept all these sciences as correct, for only then can our conviction in the variations of the moon's course be established according to a natural description.

Now that we have explained the character of knowledge obtained by necessary inference, we must note the ways that it may be preserved from corruption. For most of the controversies of men, and the opposing inferences they draw, depend on necessary inference, or are due to it. We say, then, that when someone says: "I believe such and such a thing in order not to deny a sensible," we must investigate whether this sensible may obtain without that conviction [being true]. For if it may obtain, then his conviction will be nullified.[8] Thus, for example, some believe that the Milky Way had formerly been circled by the sphere of the sun because they have observed it to be white. However, when we examine their remarks, we find that the phenomenon may be due to an ascending mist or a permanent particle of fire, or a concentration of little stars, or some other thing. [If an alternate explanation is possible] then their conviction will be nullified.

If someone were to say: "I believe such and such a thing in order not to deny an intelligible," we must investigate whether this intelligible may obtain without that conviction [being true], for in that case, his conviction will be annulled. Thus, for example, some maintain that there exists another earth besides this one. Their proof for this is that fire is thereby located in the center, since whatever is highly prized is kept in

---

[7] "until . . . figure" – added by Ibn Tibbon and the Munich ms.
[8] Lit., "is negated," i.e., for lack of warrant.

the center. However, that distinction has been granted by us to man, who dwells on the earth, which is the center of the universe. So the inference they drew collapses.

If someone were to say, "I believe such and such a thing by way of analogy with the sensible," and that conviction denies another sensible, then in that case one must decide in favor of the stronger of the sensibles and what it entails. Thus, for example, there are those who claim that all things were created from water because living things originate from the humid element. They neglect, however, water's observed tendency to be unstable and flowing. It is, therefore, impossible that it should be the origin of all things, since it is not stable in itself. When two such [conflicting] arguments are encountered, it is proper to learn from the stronger of the two.

If someone were to say: "I believe such and such a thing by way of analogy with a certain sensible," but some of his words contradict others, then his argument is annulled. Thus, for example, some claim that the good is that which gives us pleasure, because that is how they feel it to be. They do not recall, however, that their being killed would please their enemies just as much as the killing of their enemies would please them. That would involve something being good and evil at the same time, which are opposites.

If someone were to say: "I believe such and such for such and such a reason," but after investigation we find that this reason implies something else that he does not believe, then he has annulled that reason. Thus, for example, the eternalists[9] declare: "We believe that all things have existed since eternity because we do not assent to anything that is not apprehended by our senses." But their not assenting to anything that is not apprehended by the senses prevents them from believing in the eternity of things – because they cannot apprehend the eternity of eternal things.

Occasionally you hear somebody saying: "I reject this because of that," and yet you find him adopting a more difficult position than the one he avoids. Thus, for example, some monotheists avoid saying that God is unable to bring back yesterday in order not to ascribe to Him impotence. They thereby adopt something worse by ascribing to God an absurdity, as we shall note in part [thirteen] of the second treatise of this book, if God (exalted be He) is willing.

---

[9] I.e., the proponents of the eternity of the world.

In short, if we seek to establish the truth of [a conviction] through the knowledge obtained by necessary inference, we must preserve it from the five notions that corrupt it: [a] the sensible's truth cannot be established through another conviction [besides ours]; [b] the knowable's[10] truth cannot be established through another conviction; [c] the conviction cannot annul another truth; [d] some convictions cannot oppose others; [e] certainly one should not accept a conviction that is worse than the conviction one avoids. All these precautions should be taken after [f] the sensibles and the intelligibles have been carefully supervised using the methods we outlined.

If we add [to our list] [g] "perseverance until the process of reasoning has been completed," then these seven notions of ours will produce the truth in the correct fashion. Should somebody, therefore, approach us with a proof in the realm of knowledge obtained from necessary inference, we shall test his thesis by means of these seven notions. And if, upon being tested and weighed by them, it turns out to be correct and acceptable, we shall make use of it. We ought likewise to proceed with the matters of authentic tradition – I mean the books of prophecy. However, this is not the place for explaining the types of these books, something that I have already done for an extensive portion of this subject in the introduction to my commentary on the Torah.[11]

6   If one asks, "How can we trust ourselves to study and investigate the knowables, to the extent that we believe them, in a precise and established manner? There are people who censure such an occupation on the grounds that speculation leads to unconviction and is conducive to heresy." We say that that such a view is held only by the common folk, just as you see the common folk of this country thinking that whoever goes to India becomes rich, or you hear that certain commoners of our own nation believe that something like a serpent swallows the moon, and that is the eclipse, or that some of the common folk of the Arabs think that whoever does not have a she-camel slaughtered on his grave is brought to the last judgment on foot. There are many other ridiculous stories of this sort.

But if one objects, "The foremost of the sages of the children of Israel forbid this sort of occupation, and in particular, speculation about the beginning of time and place, saying: 'Whoever looks into the following

---

[10] *Maᶜalūm*. In our context the term appears synonymous with *maᶜqūl*, 'intelligible'.
[11] This part of the commentary is not extant.

four matters would have been better off had he not been born; namely: "what is below and what is above, what is before and what is behind?'" [Hagigah 2:1], we shall reply – seeking the support of the Merciful One – that it is simply impossible for them to have forbidden us to engage in genuine speculation. For our Creator Himself commanded us to do this very thing, together with authentic tradition, as when the prophet said: "Do you not know? Do you not hear? Has it not been told you from the beginning? Have you not understood the foundations of the earth?" [Isa. 40:21]. And one of the saints remarked to the others, "Let us choose for ourselves what is just; let us know among ourselves what is good" [Job 34:4]. Wide-ranging statements on this subject were moreover made by the five persons figuring in the Book of *Job* – I mean, Job, Eliphaz, Bildad, Zophar, and Elihu.

What the sages forbade was to set aside the books of the prophets and to accept any opinion that might occur to an individual about the beginning of place and time. For whoever speculates in this manner may either hit the mark or miss it. Until he hits it, however, he is without religion, and even after he has hit it and holds it firmly, he cannot be certain that he will not lose it again because of a doubt that occurs to him and corrupts his convictions. We all agree that someone who does this is a sinner, even though he be a man of speculation. But we, the congregation of the children of Israel, engage in research and speculation in a different way. It is this method of ours that I wish to describe and demonstrate with the help of the Merciful One.

Know, then, and may God direct you aright, you who study this book, that we have two goals when we investigate and speculate into the matters of our religion. One is to verify in actuality the knowledge we have received from God's prophets. The other is to respond to any one who argues against us in regard to matters pertaining to our religion. For our Master, blessed and exalted be He, has inculcated within us everything that is necessary in regard to religious matters through the medium of His prophets. He did this after he verified their prophecy through signs and marvels. Then he commanded us to believe these matters and observe them. Then he informed us that when we engage in speculation and diligent research, this will produce for us in each instance the complete truth, the same as what he had informed us through the speech of His messengers. He gave us the assurance that the heretics will never be in a position to offer a proof against our religion, nor the doubters an argument against our creed. This comes from the statement in which God informs us that all things have an origin, and that He is the Creator who originated them, and that He is one, having no associate with Him: "So says the Lord, the King of Israel, and his Redeemer, the Lord of hosts: 'I am the first, and I am the last, and beside Me there is no God'" [Isa. 44:6].

He tells us immediately thereafter that whatever He has commanded or forbidden us to do, or has informed us about, was and will be. "Who like Me can proclaim it – let him declare it and set it in order for Me – since I appointed the ancient people? And the things that are coming, and that shall come to pass, let them declare" [Isa. 44:7]. Next He calms our fear of those who disagree with us, stating that they will not be able to prevail against us in argument, nor be successful in producing convincing proof against us. That is the meaning of His subsequent remark: "Do not fear, do not be shaken! Have I not predicted this to you for a long time? I told you, and you are My witnesses. Is there a God beside Me? There is no other Rock that I know" [Isa. 44:8]. When He says: "Do not fear," He means the numerical and physical might of your adversaries, or their other qualities, as He says elsewhere: "You are afraid continually all day because of the fury of the oppressor" [Isa. 51:13]. The expression *ve-al tirhu*, is the same as *ve-al tire'u* [Do not fear], for it is customary to substitute the letter *he* for *aleph*. He means thereby that [we must not fear] the proofs or the claims of our adversaries. This is borne out by what He says elsewhere: "You, son of man, should not be afraid of them, neither be afraid of their words" [Ezek. 2:6]. In a similar vein it is said: "He feared the word of the Lord" [Exod. 9:20].

God's statement, moreover, "Have I not predicted this to you for a long time?" [Isa. 44:8] refers to the prophetic revelations concerning the future. His remark "I told you" refers to the prophetic revelations concerning the past, as He also says there: "The former things, what are they? Tell them that we may consider, and know the end of them; or predict for us the things to come" [Isa. 41:22].

When, furthermore, He says: "And you are My witnesses" [Isa. 44:8], He alludes to the marvelous signs and the manifest proofs witnessed by the [Jewish] people, these being many, such as the visitation of the ten plagues and the cleaving of the [Red] Sea and the assembly at Sinai. In my opinion, the sign of the manna is the most amazing of all miracles, because something that occurs continually is more wondrous than something that does not. For no stratagem is conceivable whereby a people numbering

18

close to two million can be nourished for forty years with nothing else than food produced for them in the air by the Creator. For had there been any possibility of coming up with a stratagem to achieve something of this sort, the ancient philosophers would have done so to nourish their disciples. They would have taught its wisdom to them, thus enabling them to dispense with working for a livelihood or seeking assistance. It is also inconceivable that the ancestors of the children of Israel would conspire to lie in this matter. That condition suffices for every authentic tradition. Moreover, if they had told their children: "We lived in the wilderness for forty years eating manna," and there had been no basis for that in fact, their children would have answered them: "Now you are lying. Is not this your field, Mr. So and So?" or: "Is not this your vineyard, Mr. So and So, from which you always derived your sustenance?" This is something that the children would not have accepted from them.

His statement, again, "Is there a God beside Me?" [Isa. 44:8] means: "Perhaps you suspect that some of the things about which I have told you that they had come to pass or some of those concerning which I have told you that they would come to pass, are not true; [that fear on your part might be justified] if some thing besides Me had participated in creation. In that event I may perhaps not have known everything that he was making. But inasmuch as I am One, My knowledge embraces everything that I have made and that I will make."

Finally, His statement, "There is no rock [*zur*] that I do not know" [Isa. 44:8] refers to the superior people and their sages. For the expression "*zur*" may be applied to superior men. Scripture says, "Look to the rock [*zur*] you were hewn from, to the quarry you were dug from. Look back to Abraham your father, and to Sarah that bore you" [Isa. 51:1, 2]. It says also: "You have turned back the blade of the sword, and have not sustained him in battle" [Ps. 89:44]. He means by these verses that "there is no wise or superior man that I do not know. Hence it is impossible that he should be able to produce an argument against you in the matter of your religion or do injury to your creed, because My knowledge is all-embracing and I have imparted it to you." In this manner [may God show mercy to you] we conduct our speculation and inquiry, in order to actualize what our Master has informed us about through revelation.

We cannot avoid considering another question that is connected with the foregoing discussion: Inasmuch as investigation and correct specula-tion can establish the religious matters concerning which our Lord has informed us, where was the wisdom in God's transmitting them by way of prophecy and supporting them by means of visibly miraculous proofs, rather than the intellectual ones? We shall reply to this question fully, with the help of God. We say [that] the All-Wise knew that the problems studied by the art of speculation could be thoroughly mastered only over a period of time. If He had directed us to that art alone for our knowledge of religion, we would have remained without religion until we had completed this art and ceased occupying ourselves with it. Perhaps many would never complete the art because of some inborn defect, or they would not finish occupying themselves with it because of some annoyance which had overcome them. Or because they had been beset with doubts that perplex and confuse them. For these reasons God, may He be magnified and exalted, liberated us from all these burdens by sending us His messenger, who transmitted them to us in a [public] announcement. He thus made us see with our own eyes the signs and the proofs that support them indubitably, as He said, "You yourselves have seen that I have talked with you from heaven" [Exod. 20:19]. Furthermore He addressed His messenger in our presence, and made it an obligation to believe forever, as He said: "That the people may hear when I speak with you, and may also believe thee forever" [Exod. 19:9].

Thus we were obligated immediately to accept our religion, together with all it contained, because it had been proven by the testimony of the senses. Anybody to whom it has been transmitted is also obligated to accept it because of the indications of reliable tradition, as we shall explain. Now God commanded us to take our time with our speculation until the arguments in favor of it have become convincing for us, and we feel compelled to acknowledge God's religion [that has already been authenticated] by what our eyes have seen and our ears have heard. So even if it should take a long time for those of us who speculate to complete their speculation, this is of no concern. He who is held back from engaging in such an activity by some impediment will, then, not remain without religion. Furthermore women and young people and those who have no aptitude for speculation can thus also have a perfect and accessible faith, for everybody is equal when it comes to sense-knowledge. Praised, then, be the All-Wise, the Governor. Accordingly you see Him include often in the Torah the children and the women together with the fathers whenever miracles and marvels are mentioned.

To explain the matter further I say that one might compare the situation to that of a person who, out of a total of 1,000 dirhams, weighs out twenty to each of five men,[12] 16 2/3 to each of six, 14 2/7 to each of seven, and 12 1/2 to each of eight, and 11 1/9 to each of nine, and who wishes to check with them quickly on how much money is left. So he tells them that the remainder amounts to 500 dirhams, supporting his statement by the weight of the money. Once, then, he has weighed it quickly and found it to be 500 dirhams, they are obligated to believe his statement. Then they have the time to find out the same answer by way of calculation, each one according to his understanding and the effort he can put into it and the obstacles he might encounter.

One might further compare this case to that of a person who, upon being informed about an illness accompanied by certain states, immediately characterizes it by a natural symptom, until the searcher is able by means of speculation to find the answer to his problem.

We also should believe that even before the time of the children of Israel God never left His creatures without a religion fortified by prophecy and miraculous signs and manifest proofs. Whoever witnessed the latter in person was convinced of their authenticity by what he had perceived with his sense of vision. Whoever received the transmission was convinced by what his sense of hearing had apprehended. Thus the Torah says about one of these: "For I have known him, to the end that he may command his children" [Gen. 18:19].

[Some text omitted]
8   And now that our remarks have reached this point, I should mention the design of the book, and the number of treatises. Afterwards I shall commence with the explanation of each treatise, prefacing my remarks with what the prophets have said on the subject, and then supporting them with rational proofs, as I stated previously.

I say that I have composed in the book ten treatises:
The first treatise: that the world and everything within it is originated.
The second treatise: that the Creator (magnified be His greatness) is one.
The third treatise: that He (exalted be He) lays down commands and
     prohibitions.

---

[12] Following Landauer's emendation.

The fourth treatise: obedience and rebellion.

The fifth treatise: good and evil deeds.

The sixth treatise: the soul, the state of death, and what comes afterwards.

The seventh treatise: the resurrection of the dead.

The eighth treatise: the salvation of the children of Israel.

The ninth treatise: reward and punishment.

The tenth treatise: what is good for man to do in this world.

I shall begin each treatise with what our Lord has made known to us, and what the intelligible confirms of it. Afterwards I shall bring each view that differs from mine, from what I have heard of it. I shall mention what can be said in its favor as well as against it. I shall then conclude with the prophetic proofs pertaining to the subject of that treatise. I ask God to be a facilitator for me and for anyone who examines my book, and to enable me to realize my aspiration on behalf of His nation and its pious. He listens and is near at hand.

Solomon ibn Gabirol and Shem Tov b. Joseph Falaquera, *Excerpts from "The Source of Life"*

Introduction

Shem Tov ibn Joseph (blessed be his memory) ibn Falaquera said: I examined the book composed by R. Solomon ibn Gabirol called *The Source of Life*, and it seemed to me that he followed, in his doctrines, the view of the ancient philosophers mentioned in *The Book of the Five Substances* composed by [Pseudo-]Empedocles.[1] That book is based on the view that all spiritual substances have spiritual matter. The form comes from above and the matter accepts it from below, that is, the matter is the substratum, and the form is predicated of it. I found that Aristotle wrote in Book Lamda of the *Metaphysics* that the ancients had attributed matter to eternal things.[2] He said that whatever has matter is composite and possesses possibility, and that, of necessity, only things that are generated and corrupted have material foundations. Such things change into other things. I have collected excerpts of [Gabirol's] discussion that encompasses his entire view.

Excerpts from Treatise One [The Knowledge of Universal Matter and Form]

1   The knowing part of man is the most worthy; hence, he must seek knowledge, and the knowledge he seeks should be of himself, so that

---

[1] Fragments of this neoplatonic work were published by D. Kaufmann in *Studien über Salomon Ibn Gabirol* (Budapest, 1899).

[2] Both Munk (p. 4, n. 1) and Gatti (p. 248, n. 3) take this to refer to *Metaphysics* (1069b 24–26), but an Arabic recension may be more pertinent.

through such [self-knowledge] he will achieve knowledge of other things beside himself. For his essence encompasses and penetrates all things, and these things are subsumed under his faculties. Together with this [knowledge] he should seek the knowledge of the final cause for the sake of which he exists, in order that he achieve his happiness through this [knowledge]. For there is a final cause for the sake of which man exists, since everything is subsumed under the will of God (blessed and exalted be He).

2   Will[3] is a divine faculty that creates and moves everything; nothing can possibly be bereft of it. Through knowledge and action the soul attaches[4] itself to the supernal world, for knowledge requires action, and action distances the soul from its contraries that corrupt it, and returns it to its nature and substance. In general, I say that knowledge and action liberate the soul from nature's prison, and purify it from its opacity and its obscurity. Then it returns to its supernal world.

3   There are only three things in existence: (a) matter and form, (b) First Substance, and (c) will, which is an intermediary between the two extremes. The reason why there are only three things in existence is that there cannot be an effect without a cause, nor without an intermediary between the extremes. The cause is First Substance, the effect is matter and form, and the intermediary between them is will. Matter and form can be likened to man's body and its form, that is, the constitution of its limbs. Will can be likened to the soul. First Substance can be likened to the intellect.

4   The worthiest and most beneficial subject of study, after one knows the art of demonstration, is the study of the essence of the soul, its faculties, its accidents, and everything that belongs to it and is attached to it. For the soul is the substratum of cognitions, and apprehends all things with its faculties that penetrate everything.

When you study the science of the soul you will recognize its higher rank, its permanence, and its comprehensiveness, so that you will be astonished at its essence, for you will see it as the subject of all things, in a certain manner. Then you will feel yourself encompassing everything that you know of existing things, and that they subsist within you, in a certain

---

[3] Translators of Gabirol often capitalize 'will' as a proper name of God. In our translation, capitalization of Divine names and attributes is reserved for terms that are accompanied (at least once) by an honorific phrase, e.g., "blessed be He."

[4] Or conjoins.

manner. Then you will feel yourself encompassing the entire world in the blink of an eye. You could not do this were it not for the fact that the soul's substance is both subtle and strong, and hence permeates everything, and serves as the abode for everything.

5   The knowledge at which human existence aims is the knowledge of the All, and particularly the knowledge of the First Substance, which supports[5] and moves it. Knowledge of the true reality of [Its] essence, abstracted from the actions that are generated from it, is impossible. Knowledge of the existence described by the actions that are generated from it is possible. The knowledge of the true reality of the essence is impossible because it is above everything and is infinite.

6   If there is a universal matter in all things, it follows that it will have the following properties: *existent, self-subsistent, one in essence, supporter of diversity, that which gives everything its essence and name*. *Existence* is attributed to [universal matter] because nonexistence cannot be the matter of what exists. *Self-subsistence* is attributed to it because it cannot proceed to an infinite regress, which it would do if matter were subsistent in something else. *Oneness* is attributed to it because we desire to seek one matter for all things; *supporter of the diversity*, because diversity occurs in forms, and forms are not self-subsistent, and *that which gives everything its essence and name*, and because it exists in everything, it follows that it gives everything its essence and name.

7   Diversity among apparent existing things results from[6] the apparent forms; likewise diversity among internal existing things from the internal forms. Hence diversity results from the forms of entities. However their internal essence [that supports] the forms, that is, the universal first matter, is one, lacking diversity. This may be likened to a bracelet, an earring, and a nose-ring made from gold. Their forms differ, yet the matter that supports them is one, its essence not differing from one another. Similarly, existing things differ through their forms, but the matter that supports them is one.

8   Our saying that matter exists [is true] when we join to it the spiritual form. By itself it is not worthy of the same existence that it is worthy of when the form is attached to it, that is, actual existence. However, although it cannot [actually] exist without [the form], it is worthy of another existence, that is, potential existence.

[5] Lit.: 'bears.'   [6] Lit.: 'falls within.'

9   Matter (and likewise form) is divided into four species: particular artificial matter, particular natural matter, natural universal matter that supports generation, and the matter of the sphere. Each of these matters has its form predicated of it.

10   These species of matter and forms, although they differ from each other in sensibles,[7] accord with each other with respect to the notion of matter and form. There is nothing within the natural sensibles, universal or particular, besides matter and form.

Excerpts from Treatise Two [On the substance that supports the corporeity of the world]

1   The method of arriving at the knowledge of the existence of corporeal matter, that is, the substance that supports the corporeity of the world, is by reasoning from what was previously mentioned concerning [the different kinds of] matter. For if the world is a corporeal substance, then, just as body is a substance possessing figure and color, from which follows that body is the matter for the forms that it supports, such as figures, colors, and other accidents, and that these things will be forms for it – it will also follow that there will be another thing, that is, the matter for the corporeity, and for which corporeity will be its form. Thus the relation of the corporeity to the matter that supports it is like that of the universal form, that is, the figures and colors, to the corporeity that supports them. Hence it follows that there will be a matter for the sensible[8] that supports corporeal form.

I will give you a general method for arriving at the knowledge of forms and matter. Represent the classes of existing things, some of them superordinate, encompassing, and supporting others, and let two extreme [classes] encompass [the existing things], one from above, one from below. The upper extreme that encompasses everything, the universal matter, is matter that only *supports* [form]. The lower extreme, the sensible form, will be form that only *is supported* [by matter]. As for what lies midway between the two extremes, the higher and finer serves as matter for the lower and the coarser, whereas the lower and the coarser serves as the form for it. From this it follows that the corporeity of the world, which is external matter for the form it supports, must be the form that is supported by

---

7 Reading with the mss. *be-muḥashim*.   8 Latin: a non–sensible matter.

the internal matter, of which we spoke above. Through this reasoning, matter will be the form for what follows it, until the thing arrives at the First Matter that encompasses everything.

2   Merely the name "body" is a proof for the existence of matter that supports corporeity. For if you describe something as 'corporeal,' you affirm a description and that which is described. Thus when you describe 'body' as being colored or possessing figure you thereby affirm the description as well as what is described. When you define ['body'], you say that it is the long and the wide and the deep, and you thereby affirm a thing that is long and wide and deep.

3   Particular artificial matter is supported by particular natural matter, which in turn is supported by universal natural matter, which in turn is supported by the spherical matter, which in turn is supported by the universal corporeal matter, which in turn is supported by the universal spiritual matter. [It follows from this that the sphere, with everything in it, subsists in spiritual substance, and that spiritual substance supports it.][9]

4   It follows that the particular natural forms exist in the universal natural form, which in turn exists in the universal spherical form, which in turn exists in the universal corporeal form, which in turn exists in the universal spiritual form.

5   If the substance of the intellect knows itself, then it follows that the form of the true will be supported by that substance. This is why the intellect apprehends that form in an indubitable fashion, because that form is supported by [intellect] itself, and is not something remote from it. Hence, the substance of soul apprehends the form of the true at times, because of its proximity to the form of intellect, that is, the proximity of the former's nature to the latter's, and because of their similarity. The vital soul does not apprehend this form perfectly but rather according to imagination, because of its remoteness from the intellect, that is, the remoteness of the former's nature from the latter's. This is analogous to sight. For when one is remote from the sensible (*muḥash*), one is doubtful of the form and cannot confirm it. Now if the matter is as we have said, that is, that intellect apprehends the form of the true by its substance, because of that form's being supported by that substance – and if its apprehension and knowledge of things implies that it encompasses

---

[9] Following the Paris ms.

and includes them – then it is impossible for the intellect to apprehend what is ordered above its rank. This [impossibility] must be qualified, for the intellect can apprehend what is arranged above it insofar as it exists within it, that is, the effect's apprehension of the cause. If the intellect could apprehend all the substances, then it follows that it would be higher than them. And were it higher then it follows that it would encompass them, and from this follows that all of them would be encompassed within it.[10]

6   The more subtle a thing and the purer its substance, the stronger its reception and its apprehension of things. Now the reception of the intellect is strong, as is its apprehension of things below it. Hence it follows that its substance is more subtle and purer than any of the substances below it.

7   As the intellect does not possess a form proper to itself, but rather always apprehends all the forms, it thereby follows that the forms of all things are the forms of its substance. And as all the forms are the forms of the substance of the intellect, and yet they are distinct with respect to the intellect, it follows that they are distinct in themselves.

8   Moreover, all the forms of existing things that are encompassed by the sense and the intellect are distinct in themselves because they are distinct with respect to the sense and the intellect, even though they are not distinct in existence, since all existing things are united and combined. The distinctness of substances and accidents as intellected, and their variety in themselves, despite their being united in existence, is analogous to the distinctness of sensed bodies and their accidents, despite their being united in existence, like the color and figure of body. For each is distinct in itself from the other, although both are united in existence. The same applies to quantity and the substance that supports it; for quantity is distinct in itself and as intellected from the substance that supports it, yet they are united in existence. Thus the unity of quantity with substance is analogous to the unity of color and figure with quantity. Their distinctness from substance in themselves and with respect to intellect is analogous to the distinctness of color and figure from the quantity of substance in themselves and with respect to sense, even though they are not distinct in existence.

---

[10] Omitting, following the Latin, the last phrase, *ve-yithayyev she-yihyeh masig otam*. If the phrase remains, then the argument is circular.

9   Quantity in general is supported by substance, and indeed, all the substances that are intellected are supported, some of them by others, such as the supporting of color and figure in quantity, and the supporting of quantity in substance.

10   All forms are in first matter in a manner similar to how color and figure, and other accidents like them, are supported within quantity, and as quantity is supported within substance. From here it will become evident that the most external existing thing is the likeness of the most internal existing thing. Then you find evident that all existing things in first matter are parts of it. You will see that first matter encompasses all of them and that some of these things are parts of others to such an extent that first matter, that which supports, will seem to you like a book written and inscribed. Then you will consider your intellect to encompass all things and [look over them], in accordance with human capacity.

11   The substance that supports the nine categories is the starting-point for the speculation of what is more concealed than the sensibles, for it occupies a level that is closest to sensible things. Moreover, the substance that is conceived through the nine categories illustrates the proof of what is concealed.

I will give you a general consideration that will suffice for what follows: The soul is devoid of the knowledge of secondary substances and accidents from the time it is connected with the body; it acquires them subsequently when it views the primary substances and accidents, examines and appraises them. Now from this it follows that the primary substances and accidents, that is, the natural world, are engraved within the soul, and the senses are prepared for them so that the former are apprehended by the soul to such an extent that, when the soul apprehends them, it apprehends through them the secondary substances and accidents. Therefore, whatever knowledge man has acquired of the sensibles from the time of his birth has increased his intellect, which has passed from potentiality to actuality. For the sensible forms are impressed within the [sense-]organs, which they resemble, and the impressed sensible forms are further impressed in the faculty of imagination in a more subtle and simple way than they are impressed in the sense-organs. Then the relation of sensible forms to the soul is that of a written book to a reader: when sight perceives characters and signs, the soul will remember the meaning and verification of those signs. This proves that the substance that supports the nine categories is the likeness that serves to prove what is concealed.

12   I will give you a [principle] on which you may rely: When we are aiming at the knowledge that ascends from the lower extreme of existing things to the upper extreme, and inasmuch as everything in the lower extreme comes from the upper extreme, we should treat whatever is in the lower extreme as a proof of, and as analogous to, whatever is in the upper extreme. For the lower is the likeness of the higher from which it emanates, and since the former emanates from the latter, it follows that the former will be a likeness for the latter. (We shall explain later how the lower emanates from the higher.) This being the case, and considering the resemblance between the extremes, knowledge of the concealed is clarified by virtue of [knowledge of] the visible. Now, because our aim is to ascend to the upper extreme of what exists, that is, the universal matter that supports all things, and the universal form that is supported in it, which are the limits of what exists from our perspective, and which are their principles from the perspective of the Creator (exalted and praised be He), we find that when we examine the lower extreme, that is, the matter that supports the nine categories, it corresponds and is equal to the other [loftier matter]. Similarly, we find that the form of quantity that is supported by this substance corresponds to the universal form, that is, the form of the intellect that is supported in the universal first matter. The upper extreme is like the body of the sun and the lower is like its rays that shine on the terrestrial globe.

13   You see how these two extremes correspond one with the other when you examine the properties of universal matter, for you find [the properties] also in the lower matter, such as self-subsistence, unity, and the supporting of diversity, and other of its properties. The same is true of the correspondence between the two forms. For just as first form, when it attaches to the higher matter, creates the species of intellect and constitutes its essence, so too the form of quantity, when it attaches to the lower matter, creates the species of body and constitutes its essence. Hence, the form of quantity corresponds to the form of intellect. Now the elucidation of this is as follows: [1] The form of intellect is a simple unity, and the form of quantity is a multiplicity of complex unities. [2] Just as the form of the intellect is not distinguished from the upper matter, so too the form of quantity spreads through the entire essence of the lower matter. [3] Just as the form of intellect covers and encompasses the upper matter, so too the form of quantity covers and encompasses the lower matter. [4] Just as the form of intellect supports all the forms, and all the forms

are supported in it, so too the form of quantity supports all the bodily forms and accidents, which exist in it. [5] Just as figure is the end of the bodily form and the definition that encompasses it, so, too, knowledge is the end of the intellectual form, and the definition that encompasses it. The knowledge that the intellect possesses is [like] a figure for it because it is the end that encompasses it, similar to the figure that encompasses the body. [6] Just as the body, when it comes into contact with another body, attaches itself to that body's shape, so too the intellect, when it comes into contact with another intellect, attaches itself to that intellect; the contact and attachment, however, are via that intellect's knowledge. [7] Just as the form of quantity resolves itself into point and unity, so too the form of intellect resolves itself into matter and unity.[11] [8] Just as the form of quantity, when it is examined by the intellect, will be found to be the highest of forms, all others being subordinate to it, and the closest to substance, so too the intellect, when you examine its essence, you find that essence to be the highest of forms, all others being subordinate to it, and the closest to matter. [9] Just as matter possesses some forms necessarily and inseparably, such as the forms of the intellect and the simple substances, as well as those it possesses not necessarily, such as the forms of the elements, so too substance possesses some forms not necessarily, such as color, figure, and other accidents that belong properly [to a given substance] – and those that belong necessarily, such as quantity, which belongs necessarily to substance [in itself]. [10] Just as the forms of matter come into contact with intellect, so too the forms of substance come into contact with sense. There are other similarities between the two extremes.

14 In order to achieve the knowledge we seek concerning matter and form, you do not need to know anything of the categories besides their genera, their species, their differentiae, their properties, what they share in common, and what distinguishes them; and the knowledge that all these genera are forms of the substance that is their substratum. But take care to investigate the substance that supports them, and employ your intellect diligently concerning it, for it is intelligible and not sensible, and the knowledge of it precedes all intelligible substances. Still, even though this substance is intelligible, its rank is not that of the other intelligibles

---

[11] Universal intellect is the principal form of universal matter and is placed immediately after it; see 5.17 and 5.18, below (Munk, p. 21 n. 1)

because it is arranged at the lower extremity of the substances, and it is the recipient of action, whereas all other substances are agents. The proof that this substance is the recipient of action, and is not an agent, is that every agent besides the First Agent needs for its action a substratum that can receive it. But there is no further substance that underlies this one. For this substance is at the utmost limit of the lowest being, and serves as the center point for the other intelligible substances. Moreover, quantity impedes the movement of [this substance], and keeps it embedded so as to prevent the parity [between the two]. Thus [this substance] is like a flame dimmed by dampness surrounding it that impedes its quick movement, or by a foggy atmosphere that impedes the penetration of light. Thus the impression of substance is more visible when its admixture is finer and disposed to receive such impression (by 'impression' I mean the impression that the penetrating intelligible substances make upon it), and when it displays the action that spiritual substances exercise upon the body, through their penetrating and breaking through them, like the sun, when it breaks through the clouds.

But aside from quantity impeding it and preventing it from acting, this substance itself is deprived of movement because of its distance from the source and principle of movement, and because it does not receive any motive power [of its own] from the active power that moves things. Consequently, it remains unmoving, even though it is moved, that is, is acted upon. The proof that quantity prevents the substance that supports it from moving [can be seen from] body, which becomes heavier and more difficult as its quantity increases.

15 This thing is sometimes called 'substance' and sometimes called 'matter', and the distinction between the term 'substance' and the 'matter' is that the former applies to the thing that is disposed to receive form and that has not received it, whereas the latter applies to matter that has received a certain form and, by virtue of that form, becomes a particular substance.

16 This substance is the thing that supports the form of quantity. The nature of this substance emanates from another higher essence, namely, the substance of nature,[12] and [the former's] essence emanates from the substance of nature. If you wish, say that it is the lowest rung of nature, or the lowest of its powers. Now whenever one thing comes from another,

---

[12] See below 3.42 and *passim*, for the gradations of being.

there must be a certain likeness between those things. So since this substance is from the substance of nature, it follows that there must be a certain likeness between substance and nature.

17   When a person knows the 'what' of this substance, he will know its 'wherefore,' for the latter belongs to the former.[13] The discussion of the 'wherefore' of existents is part of the science of the will, for the 'wherefore' implies the [final] cause for the sake of which every one of the genera, species, and individuals, passes from the potential to the actual.

18   Now since the will is the mover of all forms supported by matter, and makes them penetrate to the utmost extreme of matter – because the will penetrates and encompasses all, and the form is consequent and subordinate to it – it follows that the parts of the form, that is, the distinctions that constitute and differentiate the species, will be impressed and imprinted upon matter, according to will.

19   This testifies to a great secret, namely, that all existent things are retained by and dependent upon the will, because it is through will that each of their forms is impressed within matter, and imprinted there equally. By 'equally' I refer to the opposition of forms within matter and their equibalance, for will retains them and determines the limits and extremes at which they stop, and through will the forms are properly disposed and equibalanced, inasmuch as they are subordinate to it and retained by it. An example of this is the division of substance into simple and complex, and the division of the simple into intellect and soul, and into form and matter, and the division of the composite into the vegetative and the non-vegetative, and into the living and the non-living, and into the other differentiating oppositions that divide and constitute matter.

20   But you cannot understand the secret of the will until after you have cognized the universality of matter and form, for the will is the agent and mover of matter and form. The superiority of the doctrine of the will over that of matter and form is the same as the superiority of the doctrine of the intellect over that of the soul; the superiority of the doctrine of the intellect over that of the soul is the same as the superiority of the doctrine of matter and form over that of the intellect.[14]

---

[13] That is, when we know its quiddity, we shall know its purpose.

[14] Latin: "The superiority of the doctrine of the will over that of matter and form is the same as the superiority of the doctrine of the soul over that of the body, the superiority of the doctrine of the intellect over that of the soul, or the superiority of the doctrine of matter and form over that of the intellect."

21   If you ask *how* this substance exists, and *in what place* you may represent its existence, know that not everything requires a corporeal place for it to subsist. For whatever is a simple substance and incorporeal subsists through its cause that supports it. It follows that this cause must also be simple and similar. This substance is not in itself a body that has place, but rather it is the place for quantity, in which the true reality of place is found. And if you object, "Granted that place is in quantity, still, how is your comment that substance is the place for quantity compatible with place's requiring the conjunction of the surface of a body with the surface of another body? This substance does not in itself have a surface through which it conjoins with quantity, for it is incorporeal!"

22   Our response is that in conceiving the true reality of things, you must not exchange the forms of lower things with those of higher things. So when you find a certain attribute[15] of individuals, or species, or genera, do not suppose that you find this attribute in the individuals, species, or genera, of higher things. For although the attributes belonging to lower things emanate from the higher things, they do not exist in the lower things in the same form that they exist in the higher things. This is a universal principle that applies to everything that follows from the higher to the lower.

23   There are nine degrees of the subsistence[16] and the continuing existence of existing things: The first is the subsistence of all things in the knowledge of the First (praised be He); below that is the subsistence of universal form in universal matter; below that, the subsistence of some of the simple substances in other simple substances; below that, the subsistence of quantity in substance; below that, the subsistence of planes in solids, and the subsistence of lines in places, and the subsistence of points in lines; below that, the subsistence of colors and figures in planes; below that, the subsistence of some homogeneous parts of bodies in others; below that, the subsistence of some bodies in others, which is what is generally known as 'place.' Whatever descends from simples to composites is coarser and denser; whatever rises is finer and more subtle.

24   Now you should not doubt our comment that substance is the place for quantity, for we said that in order to let you know that substance supports quantity, and the latter subsists and exists continually within it. For it is not impossible to say of an incorporeal substance that it is the place

---

[15] Latin: *forma*.   [16] Or "the being sustained, and the continuing existence."

for body when such a substance supports it, just as it is not impossible to say of a body that it is the place for something incorporeal, such as colors, figures, lines, and planes, and other accidents of body, even though the common notion of place requires the conjunction of two bodies, and those accidents are not bodies.

25   Indeed, there are two species of place: spiritual and corporeal. When you wish to conceive how a simple substance subsists in another simple substance, and how one is the place of the other, you should represent the subsistence of colors and figures in planes, and the subsistence of planes in solids, and, more subtle than this, the subsistence of simple accidents in simple substances, like the accidents that are supported in the soul, for these accidents subsist in the soul, and the soul is the place for them. Recall the principle that we posited in this manner, that visible things are the likenesses of concealed things. From this principle follows that the external lower place is the likeness of the internal higher place, and similarly for the rest of what is between the two extremes.

26   The first unity, which is unity in itself, causes the unity that is beneath it. Now since this [lower] unity is originated from the true first unity – a unity without beginning or end, alteration or diversity – it follows that the unity that is the impression [of the first unity] possesses beginning and end, alteration and diversity. Hence it is not like the Perfect Unity in its true reality because of the multiplicity, diversity, and alteration that accrue to it. It also follows that this unity is divisible into diverse degrees, and that the nearer a unity is to the first unity in its true reality, the simpler and more cohesive the matter conceived within it is. By contrast, the farther a unity is from the first unity, the more multiple and composite it is.

That is why the unity that constitutes the matter of the intellect is one and simple, and not essentially divisible or capable of being multiple, although it is coincidentally divisible. This unity is more simple and united than the rest of the unities that pertain to the other substances because it is at the uppermost extreme, near the first unity that causes it. This is why the substance of the intellect apprehends all things by means of the unity of the essence that constitutes it, for its unity encompasses all unities that constitute the essences of every thing. This is so because all the unities are multiplied and rendered manifold after [their descent from] the first *created* unity; the latter constitutes their substances, and the substances of the multiple unities subsist from the substance of the single unity. Hence the single unity is found with them, subsisting in them; this is why the forms of all things are found within the form of the intellect, which supports and brings them together. For its simple unity brings together in its substance all the unities, and the forms of all things are nothing but the multiplied unities.

The proof is that any intelligible or sensible must be either one or many, and since the unity that is supported in the matter of the intellect is unique and simple, as we mentioned previously, it follows that the unity that is supported in the matter of the soul will be multiplied and rendered manifold, for this unity is ordered below the rank of the unity that is supported in the matter of the intellect. It also follows that the unity will be multiplied and rendered manifold, and will endure alteration and diversity, in the other degrees of matter that support it, according to the descent of the degree of the matter to the lowest place and its distance from the highest, until it reaches the matter that supports quantity, that is, the substance of this world, where [these unities] are rendered manifold, divided, augmented, and densified in the matter that supports them, for they are subordinate to the causative unity. As a result, substance becomes denser, corporeal, and is retained within itself. This lower substance, with its density and coarseness, stands in opposition to the higher substance, with its simplicity and subtlety, for the latter substance is the abode of the principle and beginning of unity, whereas the former substance is its terminus and utmost limit. Now the terminus cannot be similar to the beginning because the terminus must be the end and termination of the power of the principle.

27 What I have mentioned concerning the simplicity of substance in its descent to nature, and its becoming corporeal when it moves from nature to the center,[17] can be illustrated by the example of flowing waters, some of which are deeper than others; for some are light and subtle, whereas others are dense and dark;[18] or by the example of a piece of forged lead when removed from the furnace, for some of it is finely molten and penetrates one's eyesight, whereas some of it is the opposite. Our eyes can see the diversity of unities in the matter that supports [things]: that the parts of fire exist in the utmost unity, simplicity, and homogeneity, so

---

[17] Nature is the last of the simple substances and their limit; from nature to the center of the earth (and of the universe) lie the various gradations of the substance that supports the categories.

[18] That is, rivers that flow from a pure source and collect in a deep pool.

that its form appears to be one thing lacking multiplicity, that the parts of air and water are more disparate and divided, so that their parts and unities can be apprehended by sight. [These illustrations] enable us to understand the aforementioned point about how the quantity supported by substance is constituted by the combination of manifold unities. Of this we can say, "The composition of the world was made by the writing of number and letters in the air."

28   Each of the forms of simple substances is one, admitting no division, for how can it receive division and remain one? Unity is divisible into quantity because of the substance that is its substratum. Do you not see that all the unities into which quantity divides agree with respect to the form of unity, and differ only with respect to their substratum? The proof is that it is unity that constitutes matter and through it becomes specific, and this unity retains it. And when matter is simple and subtle, remote from being dispersed and separated, the unity will conform to it, and will agree with it, and the unity and they will become one thing, indivisible in act. But when matter is dense and weak, the unity will not conform to it, and it will be too weak to unite it and bring together its essence.

29   You should reason analogously from the subsistence of the body in the soul to the subsistence of the universal corporeal substance in the universal spiritual substance. Just as the soul encompasses the body and supports it, so too the universal spiritual substance encompasses the universal body of the world and supports it. And just as the soul is in itself separate from the body and yet is attached to it, without being in contact with it, so too the spiritual substance is separate in itself from the body of the world, and yet is attached to it, without being in contact with it.

30   One can get at the idea of the attachment of spiritual substance in corporeal substance, and in general, the attachment of some spiritual substances in others, and the subsistence of some in others, from the attachment of light or fire in air, and the attachment of color and figure in quantity, and the attachment of quantity in substance, and the attachment of spiritual accidents in spiritual substances. For since the exterior of things must be the likeness of their interior, it follows that the attachment of such parts of corporeal substances like color, figure, quantity, and substance, some in others, and the subsistence of some in others, will be like the attachment of some spiritual substances in others, and the subsistence of some in others.

31   In things that are intellectually cognized, whether universal and particular, there is nothing besides matter and form.

Excerpts from Treatise Three [On the Existence of Simple Substances]

1   We need to explain demonstratively that there is an intermediate substance between the First Agent (praised be He) and the substance that supports the categories. In this regard let us posit the following principle: If the first existing thing is the First Agent, with no other [prior] agent, and the final existing thing is the final recipient of action, with no other [subsequent] recipient of action, then there is an essential and actual distinction between the first thing and the last. For if there were no distinction then the first would be the last, and the last would be the first. This distinction means the removal of likeness, and the removal of likeness means the removal of attachment, because the attachment is through likeness.

2   The proof of the existence of simple substances is very difficult. We shall provide first the demonstrations that indicate the existence of an intermediate substance between the First Agent and the last recipient of action.

Demonstration. The First Agent is the first thing, and the first thing is separate from the last thing. The substance that supports the nine categories is the last thing. Hence, the First Agent is separate from the substance that supports the nine categories. Let us place this conclusion as a premise: the First Agent is separate from the substance that supports the nine categories. Now, concerning any two separate things, if there is a distinction between them, then there is an intermediary between them; otherwise they would be the same thing and not separate. Hence, there is an intermediary between the First Agent and the substance that supports the nine categories.

3   The soul is separate from the body, and were it not for the spirit that is intermediate between them, neither of them would be attached to the other.

4   Were the First Agent to be separate from the substance that supports the categories without there being an intermediary between them, they could not become attached. And were they not attached, then substance would not exist for a second.

Demonstration. The First Agent (blessed be He) is the true One in which there is no multiplicity, whereas the substance that supports the categories has the utmost multiplicity; there is nothing after it that has a more powerful multiplicity. Now every composite multiplicity is reducible to the one. Hence, there must be intermediaries between the true One and the composite multitude.

Demonstration. Every agent causes what resembles it, and the simple substance is similar to the First Agent. Hence, only the First Agent causes the simple substance.

5   The more a substance descends, the more it becomes multiple; and the more it ascends, the more united it becomes. Now whatever becomes multiple in descending and united in rising necessarily reaches true unity.[19] Therefore it is necessary that a multiple substance arrive at the substance truly united.

6   The microcosm [i.e., man] is like the macrocosm [i.e., the world] with respect to order and construction. Now the substance of the intellect, which is the most subtle, simple, and noble of all substances of the microcosm, is not attached to the body, for the soul and the spirit are intermediaries between them. One may reason analogously to the order of the macrocosm, that is, that the simple and noble substance is not attached to body, that is, the substance that supports the categories.

7   *Demonstration.* The movement of the substance that supports the categories is in time. But time is subsumed under sempiternity,[20] and the First Agent is above sempiternity. Hence, sempiternity is intermediate between [the First Agent] and substance. But the sempiternal is sempiternal only for a thing [of this sort]; it is measure for that which is measured. Therefore there is something intermediate between the First Agent and the substance that supports the categories, the sempiternal and duration. Therefore the substance that supports the categories is not conjoined to the First Agent.

8   The coarse attaches to the subtle only through an intermediary that resembles both extremes, and it receives its impression only through an

---

[19] Following Munk's suggested emendation on the basis of the Latin (although it is a bit odd that his emendation has terms with different roots, that is, "*ya'aleh*" and "*silluq*," where the Latin has "*ascendit*" and "*ascendendo*").

[20] *dahr* (Latin translation: *sempiternitas*; the Arabic is left untranslated by Falaquera). In this context the term appears to signify the property of sempiternity (everlastingness) for incorruptible things and finite duration for corruptible things. In any event, God does not possess it, for God is above time.

intermediary. This is like the human body, which receives the impression of the rational soul only through the intermediary of the animal spirit, or like man, who receives intellect only through the intermediary of the rational soul, or like the sense of sight, which attaches to bodies only through the intermediary of the pupil and the subtle air, or like the universal soul, which attaches to bodies only through the intermediary of the sphere that is midway between spirituality and corporeality. Through these analogies we have shown again that there are intermediary substances between the First Agent and the substance that supports the categories.[21]

9 Some bodies are more noble than others, the higher being more noble than the lower. It follows thereby that the extreme of the higher existents is the noblest and strongest, and the extreme of the lower existents the worst and the weakest. The relation of the highest extreme of the sensibles to the highest extreme of the intelligibles will be the same as the relation of the lowest extreme of the sensibles to the highest extreme of the sensibles.[22] Through this you will know that simple substances are intermediary between the First Agent and the substance that supports the categories.

10 Simple substances themselves are not transmitted, rather it is their powers and their rays that are transmitted and extended. For the essences of all these substances are retained and limited and not extended to infinity. However, their rays are transmitted from them and cross their borders, because they depend upon the first emanation that is transmitted from will. This is like the light that is transmitted from the sun in the air, for this light transcends the limit of the sun and is extended together with the air, while the sun in itself does not go outside its limit; or, like the vital faculty that is transmitted from the rational faculty (whose abode is the brain) into the nerves and the muscles – for this faculty penetrates and spreads in all parts of the body, while the substance of the soul in itself does not spread and does not extend – so every simple substance extends its ray and its light and spreads them on that which is lower, although the substance retains its rank and does not cross its boundary.

11 Since the lower substances emanate from the higher substances as a force issues from something strong, and not as essence issues from essence, it follows that the essences of the higher substances do not

---

[21] Munk reconstructs this paragraph and a few others on the basis of Falaquera's commentary on the *Guide of the Perplexed*; see *Moreh ha-Moreh*, ed. Y. Shifman (Jerusalem: WUJS, 2001), p. 244.

[22] The Latin has: "to the lowest extreme of the intelligibles."

diminish when the lower substances come into being. It likewise follows that these powers, I mean the lower substances, are not separated from the essences of the higher substances, although they are transmitted from them. Thus the heat of fire does not diminish and is not separated from fire, although the latter produces heat in the air that is near it, and this heat is not the same as that of the fire because the fire can be withdrawn while the heat remains in the air, because the two subjects are different, and because the heat supported in the air differs in strength from that of the fire. Similarly, when this light of the sun spreads over the earth, the light that is supported by the sun in itself is not diminished, although the former light is transmitted from it, and the light that spreads over the earth is not the same as the light that is supported by the sun in itself. The proof of this is that both subjects[23] differ in strength and weakness, as do both lights.

12   In general, the first emanation, which embraces all substances, necessitates the emanations of some substances into others. This is like the sun, which emanates [its influence] by itself, that is, without mediation, and transmits its rays on account of the same cause, namely, because all are subsumed under the first emanation, and all are subordinate to it. Moreover, since the form is more subtle than matter, and since it is the custom of what is subtle to penetrate and permeate whatever faces it, it follows that every form penetrates and permeates whatever faces and is present to it.

13   Corporeal substance is prevented from emanating its essence because of the density and obscurity of quantity, even though quantity emanates its shadow upon the bodies that are before it, so that when it meets a polished body, it transmits its form to that body. This argument implies *a fortiori* that a spiritual substance, free from quantity, should emanate its essence and its force and its light.

14   Now when you reflect that simple substance is infinite; when you consider its force; when you examine how it penetrates and permeates the thing it encounters that is disposed to receive it; when you weigh the difference between it and corporeal substance – you find that corporeal substance cannot be in every place, and is too weak to penetrate things, whereas simple substance, that is, the substance of universal soul, penetrates and permeates throughout the entire world. You also find that

---

[23] The sun and the earth.

the substance of intellect penetrates and permeates through the entire world. This is caused by the [different] subtlety, force, and light of each substance. Hence the substance of intellect permeates and penetrates to the innermost core of things. This argument implies *a fortiori* that the force of God (sanctified and blessed be He) penetrates and encompasses all things, and acts upon all things timelessly.

15   Because this substance[24] is a sensible and compound body, it follows that the impression of the spiritual substance within it should be sensible also. However, this impression is not corporeal absolutely nor spiritual absolutely, but is intermediary between the two extremes, like [the phenomena of] growth, sensibility, motion, colors and figures, which receive, in the compound substances, the impressions of simple substances. For these impressions are not corporeal absolutely nor spiritual absolutely, since they are perceived by the senses. This point implies that all the sensible forms in corporeal substance are impressions from intelligible spiritual substance. These forms are sensible only because the matter that receives them is very close in its nature to corporeality; and these sensible forms are more simple in the intelligible spiritual substance than in matter.

This transmission of the form from the simple spiritual substance, and its impressions in corporeal matter, may be likened to the light transmitted from the sun, which permeates and penetrates the air, but is not visible, on account of its subtlety, until it encounters a hard body like earth. Then the light is visible to sight because it cannot penetrate the parts of this body and be dispersed through them; rather, the light stops on the surface of the body, and its essence is condensed so that it becomes more clearly visible to sight. Similarly, the lights of the simple substances penetrate and are transmitted through each other without being visible, on account of the subtlety and the simplicity of these substances. But when the lights have penetrated to matter, then the light becomes visible to sight on account of the density of the corporeal matter.

Through this example one can ascend to the knowledge that all forms supported by universal matter exist in the essence of the faculty that gives it, that is, the will, more simply than in the first matter that receives it. Yet as the first matter differs in its nature from the essence of the will and in its relation to will resembles the body, it follows that the will's

---

[24] The substance of the sublunar world.

impression in matter should be perceptible, as the impressions of the intelligible substances are perceptible in body. It also follows that will should bring forth what it has in its essence and give it to the matter, just as the intelligible substances effect the bringing forth of what they have in their essence and give it to the body: except that the will acts without [recourse to] time, motion, instrument, and space, while the intelligible substances do the very opposite. That is why the simple substances and, in general, all active substances[25] perform their actions because of the first action[26] that moves all and penetrates all. In this manner one achieves knowledge of the penetration of the first power and the first action in all things. For if the power of the simple substances and, in general, the power of all existing things is transmitted, permeates, and penetrates throughout everything, then certainly the power of the First Agent (may He be blessed and exalted) does likewise. On account of this we say that the First Agent (may He be blessed and exalted) exists in everything, and that nothing is devoid of Him.

16   Every action derives from a spiritual faculty, and every reception derives from a corporeal faculty. Now were a substance to act from the aspect of its being a receiver, it would be spiritual and corporeal simultaneously. And were part of it to act, and part of it to receive, then part of it would be spiritual and part of it would be corporeal. The substance that supports the categories is entirely corporeal; hence, no order of action can proceed from it.[27]

17   *Demonstration*: Every spiritual substance possesses a form; every spiritual substance is subtle; every subtle thing has its form transmitted and emanated from it. Therefore, spiritual substance has its form transmitted and emanated from it. Then let us place this conclusion as a premise: Spiritual substance has its form transmitted and emanated from it. Now whatever has its form transmitted and emanated from it will have that form reflected in what faces it, which receives the form. We conclude that spiritual substance has its form reflected in what faces it, which receives the form. Let us combine with this conclusion the statement, "Whatever has its form reflected in what receives it, will have that form

---

[25] That is, causally.

[26] Reading *po'al* rather than *po'el*, 'agent', because no honorific phrase qualifies the term. Munk, who adopts the former reading, refers it to the divine will.

[27] The forms of the substance that supports the categories (i.e., corporeal substance) also exist in the spiritual substances, from which they are transmitted. This will be demonstrated in the following paragraphs.

penetrate and encompass the recipient, if the [emanating] substance is subtle." We conclude that spiritual substance has its form penetrate and encompass the substance that supports the categories. Now, the form which is supported by the substance that supports the categories penetrates and encompasses it. We conclude that the form that is supported by the substance that supports the categories is the form of spiritual substance.

18   *Demonstration*. Whatever receives many forms does not possess its own proper form. Simple substance, e.g., intellect, soul, nature, and matter, receives many forms. Hence, none of these possesses a soul proper to it.

19   *Demonstration*. The intellect and the soul know everything, and "knowledge" is the subsistence in the soul of the intellect of the form of that which is known. Hence the form of everything subsists in the intellect and the soul. Now the form of everything subsists in them by virtue of the union [of each form]. Hence, all the forms are united in the intellect and the soul, and this union is through likeness. Hence, all the forms are like the intellect and the soul.

20   *Demonstration*. Sensible things exist in the soul simply; that is, their forms are found there without their matters. The forms of things exist in the intellect more simply, and their existence is more universal. It follows that all the lower forms exist in the higher forms, rank after rank, until the universal form is reached in which exists all forms. But the latter forms are not in place, while the former forms are in place; the higher forms are united through the union of spiritual substance, whereas the lower forms are divided by the division of corporeal substance.

21   You may ask: If the lower is the likeness of the higher, and the lower exists in the higher, how is it possible for the ten corporeal genera to be in the simple spiritual substance? [We reply:] Look at the lower extreme of existing things, i.e., each of the ten genera, and investigate also the higher extreme in comparison to it. You find that, for each of the ten genera belonging to the lower extreme, there exists something corresponding[28] to it at the upper extreme. Corresponding to *substance* you find universal matter. Corresponding to *quantity* you find the form of intellect, as well as the unities that exist in the forms of substances. Corresponding

---

[28] Lit.: "facing it."

to its seven species[29] you find the number of the seven simple substances: [universal] matter, [universal] form, intellect, souls,[30] and nature, as well as the number of the faculties of each of these substances. Corresponding to *quality* you find the divisions of these substances and their forms. Corresponding to *relation* you find their being causes and effects. Corresponding to *time* you find sempiternity. Corresponding to *place* you find the degrees of these substances, which are prior and posterior to each other. Corresponding to *situation* you find [the relation of] supporting. Corresponding to *agent* you find the substance that makes impressions, the originator and the producer. Corresponding to *patient* you find the recipient of the impression of the substance that makes impression, the recipient of benefit. Corresponding to *habit* you find the existence of the universal soul in universal matter, and the existence of each of the forms of the simple substances in the matter that supports them, and the existence of the faculties that are proper to each one of these substances. This indicates that the forms of composite substance are transmitted from the forms of simple substances.

22   If these forms become corporeal, they do so because of their attachment to corporeal substance. They are like a pure and fine transparent garment, which, when attached to a black or red body, takes on that color, and is perceived to have altered, even though it has not done so essentially.

23   It is the way of form to be attracted to matter when it is imprinted upon it, and when it receives its shape. Since matter is in itself corporeal, it follows that the form that is reflected in it from the spiritual substance will also be corporeal. Moreover, it is the way of form to penetrate and permeate the matter that receives it, when the latter is disposed to receive it because of the first form, which collects all the forms, penetrates and permeates the first matter. If the matter is dense, the form is too weak to penetrate and to spread within it, and the essence of the form contracts and does not disperse, so that it becomes sensible because of its contraction; for when the essence of a thing contracts, this thing becomes corporeal and is shown to the senses: and, by contrast, when the essence of a thing

---

[29] The seven species of quantity are: number, word, line, surface, body, time, and place. See *Categories*, ch. 6.

[30] Universal soul is divided into three, corresponding to the three faculties of the human soul: the vital, the natural, and the intellectually cognizing. See below 5.13.

disperses, it becomes more subtle and concealed from the senses. Use this analogy when you reason: the reflection of the spiritual forms on the corporeal forms, [causing] the appearance of the corporeal forms in the corporeal matter is [like] the reflection of light on bodies, [causing] the subsequent appearance of colors.

24   As the soul is intermediary between the substance of the intellect and the senses, it follows that when it inclines towards the sense, it is deprived of the apprehensions of the intellect. Similarly, when it inclines towards the intellect, it is deprived of the apprehensions of the senses, for each of the extremes is distinct from the other, and when the soul turns to one, it withdraws from the other.

25   The 'subsistence of the sensible forms in the form of the soul' means the unity of all those forms in its form. That is to say, the form of the soul, by its nature and its being, is an essence that collects essentially every form, because all forms are united in the idea of form. For all of them are forms, and they participate in the idea of the form. And the idea of the form is united with the form of the soul, since both are forms. The particular forms, that is, all the sensibles, are united in the universal form, that is, that which collects all the forms, and these forms are united in the form of the soul, because the universal soul that collects [all of] them is united with the form of the soul.

26   These forms, in the essence of the soul, are intermediary between the corporeal forms supported by composite substance and the spiritual forms existing in the substance of the intellect. And the proof of this is that the substance of the intellect apprehends being in all things, that is, the unitary simple form, namely, the genera and the species, while the substance of the soul apprehends what is other[31] [than being], that is, the [specific] differences, the properties, and the accidents that the senses attain. That is why, when the soul wants to know the quiddity of the thing, it attaches to, and unites with, the intellect so that the latter may provide it with simple being. And when the soul attaches to the intellect, the form of the intellect assimilates to that of the soul, for the genus is being, and the difference subsists in the form of the soul, for the difference is other [than being]. One assimilates to the other, that is, the genus that subsists in the intellect assimilates to the difference that subsists in the essence of the soul. Then the soul perceives the quiddity of the thing, because

---

[31] *Ha-zulat*; the Latin has *non esse* [i.e., non-being].

46

the simple elements of the essence, that is, the genus and the difference, attach to the essential part of the soul; thus it knows perfectly the quiddity of the thing, that is, its definition.[32]

27 Forms do not pass through the soul in the nonessential way that light passes through air, as many think. For if the forms were not essential in the soul, they would not unite with it, and would not become actual. This is indicated by the fact that the substance of the soul receives in a dream the intelligible form in a psychic, that is, imaginative, manner, and later views it in the waking state as corporeal and material. One reasons in the same way from the lower to the higher [levels of reality] until one reaches the first matter which supports all. The lower substances wear the light of the higher substances, and everything wears the light of the First Agent (may He be blessed). The impression made by the higher substances on the lower ones is visible in the growth, nutrition, and reproduction of vegetables; the impression one apprehends as belonging to nature is attraction, alteration, retention, and expulsion; the impression one apprehends as belonging to the vegetative soul is reproduction and growth.

28 The action of nature is inferior to that of the vegetative soul for the vegetative soul moves the body in its entirety, whereas nature does not. And the impression one apprehends as belonging to the animal soul is sense and movement. [The animal soul] moves the body in its entirety, and moves it locally from place to place in its entirety. The vegetative soul only moves parts of the body.

29 The animal soul is superior to the vegetative soul in that it attaches itself to the forms of bodies that resemble it with respect to subtlety, and divests them of their corporeal forms; whereas the vegetative soul attaches itself to the bodily substances that resemble it with respect to density, proximity, and contact.

30 The actions of the animal soul are: perception of the forms of the dense bodies in time, local movement, and production of sound and voice without an order that signifies meaning.[33] The actions of the rational soul are: perception of the subtle forms of the intelligibles, timeless and

---

[32] A (real) definition is composed of specific difference and genus. Thus, *rational animal* is the (real) definition of man. According to Gabirol, the soul apprehends the difference, and the intellect the genus; when soul attaches to, or conjoins with intellect, it brings together the difference and the genus, thereby cognizing the definition.

[33] Latin, "*qui significat intellectum*" [which signifies understanding].

non-spatial movement among intelligibles, production of sound and voice with an order and coherence that signifies meaning. Finally, the action of the intellect is the timeless, non-spatial, and effortless perception of all intelligibles, without any requirement save the intellect itself, for it is completely perfect.

31   What you need to know is that the investigation of simple substances, and the determination of what can be known about them, provide the greatest repose and pleasure for the rational soul. The ability to know sovereignty, that is, divinity, and to become attached to it, is commensurate with the ability of the soul to know and to be familiar with them, to determine their forms and properties, and to recognize their impressions and activities. Make a supreme effort to examine the simple substances, most certainly the substance of soul and intellect, for they are the supporters of everything, and within them is the form of everything.

32   The more the simple substances descend, the coarser they become, until they become corporeal and retained. You find the same description true of composite substances. How can the divine power weaken, change, and become material, with the activity of the First Agent (may He be sanctified) more visible in some substances than in others – given that it is the highest degree of power, perfection, and ability?

33   It is impossible for the divine power to weaken. Rather, all the powers yearn for it and ascend to it, thus leaving the lower world in shadow. Matter receives form from the active power according to its readiness for it. Were it ready to receive a single perfect form, without any distinction, then the power would not be too weak to do this. There is no need to attribute the alteration in power to the power's essence; attribute it instead to the essence of the things that receive its action. Matter is more receptive of action when it is closer to the source than when it is more distant.

34   If you wish to represent this, ascend immediately from the lower to the higher. For then you will see a more subtle, simple, and united existent, be it matter, form, or motion. Take what is visible as proof of what is concealed, and reason from the compound to the simple, from the effect to the cause. For if you do this, you will achieve your desire regarding this subject.

35   Liken [the simple substances] to the absolute universal body. This is a true likeness because the lower is the likeness of the higher. For if you

consider the composition of the absolute body and the order of its parts, your conception of the relation of the simple substances and their orders will be facilitated.

36 Assume first matter to correspond to the substance that supports all the forms of body, since matter supports all forms. Assume the substance of intellect to correspond to quantity, for since the intellect has two faculties, it is subject to division. Assume the substance of soul to correspond to the figure that encompasses quantity. And assume the substance of nature to correspond to color, which is the last of the parts of the body, as nature is the last of the simple substances, and color is originated from nature. The more sight passes beyond color and focuses[34] upon figure, [then] quantity, and [finally] substance, the more the [corporeal] existent is concealed from it, and disappears because of its subtlety. Conversely, the more it returns from substance and leaves it for quantity, quantity for figure, and figure for color, the coarser the existent becomes for him, and because of its density, the more manifest. So, too, the more that the intellect focuses upon that which is after the substance that supports the categories, that is, the spiritual substances, until the [first] matter is reached that is the counterpart to [corporeal] substance, the more the [spiritual] existent is concealed from it, and disappears because of its subtlety. Conversely, whatever returns from matter and leaves it for the closer substances, the existent will become more visible and manifest because of its density. The comparison I have made facilitates your conception of the relation of spiritual substances to their degrees.

37 I say in general that if you wish to represent these [spiritual] substances, and how your essence may spread and comprehend them, you need to raise your mind up to the last intelligible, to purify and clean it from the filth of sensible things in order to release it from the prison of nature. By the power of your intellect you will arrive at the limit of what can be apprehended of the true reality of intelligible substance – as if you were to strip your substance of sensible substance and not to know anything about it. Then your substance will encompass the entire corporeal world, and you will place it in one of the corners of your soul. For if you do this, you will realize the smallness of the sensible when compared

---

[34] Lit.: 'permeates.'

with the intelligible. Then the spiritual substances will be placed within your hands, right before your eyes, and you will see them encompassing and rising over you. You will consider yourself to be identical with them; sometimes you will think that you are [only] a part of them on account of your connection with the corporeal substance; other times you will think that you are the entirety of these substances and that there is no distinction between them and yourself, because of the union of your essence with their essences and the attachment of your form with their forms. If you ascend the different ranks of the intelligible substances, you find the sensible bodies extremely trivial and minor, and you will view the entire corporeal world roaming about them as if it were a ship in the sea or a fowl in the air.

38   And if you lift yourself up to [the rank of] universal matter, and you are protected by its shadow, you will see there the most wondrous things. Apply yourself diligently to realize this goal, for the human soul aims to this end, wherein is its overwhelming joy and great happiness.

39   [Divine] will, the faculty that activates these substances, is finite from the aspect of its action, but infinite from the aspect of its essence; as such its action has a terminus. If will is finite from the aspect of its action, it is because action has a beginning. The opposite is the case for the substance of intellect, for since it is originated it has a beginning, but since it is simple and timeless, it lacks an end.

40   Look at the attachment of light with air, soul with body, intellect with soul, and the parts of the body with each other, that is, figure color, quantity, and substance, and their mutual arrangement. You may reason analogously that there is a proof of the union of some spiritual substances with others in the union of accident in body, accident in soul, and soul in body. There is additional unity as the body becomes more subtle, which is an additional proof.

41   These simple substances are called spheres and circles because some are higher than others and some encompass others. The meaning of 'encompassing' here is like the encompassing of the subject by the predicate, the cause by the effect, and the knower by the object known.

42   Examine the natural faculty and you find that it encompasses the body because it acts on it, and the body is activated by it. Examine also the vegetative soul: you find that it acts on nature and rules it, and you find that nature is retained within it, and receives its impression. Likewise, the

intellect and the rational soul: you find that both of them encompass all the substances that are beneath them, that they know them, penetrate and rule them, and more than any, the substance of the intellect, on account of its subtlety and its perfection. From these particular substances you may fashion a proof that some universal substances encompass others and that all of them encompass the composite substance in a manner akin to how soul encompasses body and intellect encompasses soul. For the lower substance among them exists in the higher substance because the latter supports it and represents it. And universal soul supports the entire corporeal world, represents and sees all that is in it, as our particular souls support our bodies, represent them and see all that is in them: and, even more, universal intellect, according to its perfection, its extension, and the nobility of its substance. One can show thereby how the First Agent (may He be blessed and exalted) knows all existents and how all things exist in his knowledge.

43   Hence it is evident that the meaning of the phrase "spiritual substance encompassing corporeal substance" is the subsistence and retention of corporeal substance in spiritual substance, like the subsistence and retention of all bodies in the body of the celestial sphere. The return of the spiritual substance unto itself, in perpetuity and everlastingness, is like the return of the sphere unto itself in local movement and revolution.

44   If you wish to represent the structure of the universe, i.e., of the universal body and the spiritual substances encompassing it, look at the structure of man, for it will give you an analogy. This is so for the counterpart of man's body is universal body; the counterpart of the spiritual substances that move it are the universal substances that move universal body. The lower of these substances serves and obeys the higher, until you arrive at the movement of the substance of the intellect. There you find that intellect governs and rules them, and you find that all the substances that move man's body are consequent upon intellect, and subservient to it, and that intellect rules and judges them. A noble matter and great secret is thereby revealed, namely, that the movement of the lower of the universal substances results from the movement of the higher and that, for this reason, the lower serve the higher and obey them, until we arrive at the motion of the highest substance, which is obeyed and served by all the substances [beneath it]. They follow intellect and act at its behest. And I think that the governance of the particular soul follows the governance

of the universal world. This is the way to arrive at perfect happiness, and the attainment of true pleasure, which was our intention.

Excerpts from Treatise Four [On the investigation of the knowledge of matter and form in simple substances]

1   If the lower is transmitted from the higher, then whatever is in the lower must be in the higher, i.e., the corporeal spheres correspond to the spiritual spheres from which they are transmitted. Now since the corporeal spheres possess matter and form, it follows that the spiritual spheres possess matter and form. The proof is that spiritual substances have matter in common and differ in form. For since the activities of the substances differ, undoubtedly their forms are different. The matters of these substances cannot differ because they are all simple and spiritual, and because difference lies within form, and simple matter in itself has no form.

2   You should represent the spiritual forms as one form. They do not differ from each other in themselves because they are completely spiritual. Diversity occurs on account of the matter that supports them. If the matter is close to perfection it is subtle, and the form supported by it is absolutely simple and spiritual; the converse is true as well. The simile you should use is the light of the sun: although the light is one, it looks completely different when it passes through thin air or fetid, impure air; likewise with form.

3   That simple substances, which are higher than composite substances, are composed of matter and form, can be shown as follows: The lower come from the higher, and the lower are the likenesses of the higher. Now if the lower comes from the higher it follows that the degrees of the corporeal substances correspond to the degrees of the spiritual substances. Now just as there are three ranks of corporeal substance – dense body, subtle body, and the matter and form from which [corporeal substance] is composed – so too there are three ranks of spiritual substance: the first is the spiritual substance that comes immediately after corporeal substance, then the spiritual substance that is more spiritual, and then the matter and the form from which [spiritual substance] is composed.

4   The proof that the higher exists within the lower is that the higher bestows upon the lower their names and definitions, and furthermore,

intellect abstracts the forms from corporeality, and this is a proof that the forms supported in composite substance are transmitted from the simple substances.

5   If it is not impossible that the composite is simple, it is not impossible that the simple is composite, since the composite is simple for what is lower than it, and the simple may be composite for what is higher than it.

6   From the fact that particular intellect is composed of matter and form, it follows that universal intellect is composed of matter and form. For we judge that universal intellect exists because of the existence of particular intellect. But since we showed that each one of the simple substances is composed of matter and form, we thereby showed that the intellect is composed of them. Hence we should examine further how the matters of these universal substances are connected, and compare them with each other, and we should likewise examine how the forms of these substances are connected and compare them with each other. We should compare the matters and forms of sensible substances so that we may compare the matters and forms of intelligible substances, and the parts of spiritual matter will become united for us. We shall then examine the connection of spiritual matter with corporeal matter, and the connection of spiritual form with corporeal form. After this has been done, the different parts of universal matter and universal form will become united. And when the union of the universal matter and the universal form is completed, we will examine each of them separately.

7   Matter cannot exist bereft of form, for existence pertains to a thing by virtue of its form. The proof of this is as follows: An existent is either a sensible or an intelligible. Now, intellect and sense attach only to sensible and intelligible form because sensible and intelligible forms intervene between the forms of the intellect and the soul and the matters that support the sensible forms, or those that support the intelligible forms. For this reason these forms [of the sense and the intellect] do not attach to the matters but rather to the forms, for they meet each other, and certainly because they are similar to each other and fall under the same genus.

8   Let us return to our investigation, namely, that nothing exists in intelligibles save matter and form.[35] We say that we have already shown

---

[35] I.e., intelligibles possess only matter and form, and nothing else.

in what preceded that the lower is transmitted from the higher, and hence that the sensible spheres are transmitted from the intelligible spheres, and hence that the intelligible spheres are composed of matter and form, as are the sensible spheres. We have also shown that a spiritual substance cannot be solely matter or solely form but must be composed of both. This can also be shown from the consideration that spiritual substances agree with one another in a certain respect and differ in another. It follows thereby that they agree with respect to matter and differ with respect to form. This can also be shown as follows: The Creator must be solely unique, and it is also necessary that the Creator differ from creatures. Now if he had created a being that is solely matter or solely form, that being would be similar to the One, and there would be no intermediary between them, for two is subordinate to one.[36]

9   This can also be shown from the consideration that things do not differ in all aspects or agree in all aspects; from the consideration that every intelligible thing divides into two, i.e., the description and the thing described; and from the consideration that intellect apprehends only matter and form. The proof for [the latter consideration] is that the final apprehension achieved by the intellect is of genus and difference, which proves that matter and form are the end of things. Moreover, when a thing is known by the intellect, it is comprehended from the aspect of its having a limit. Now something has a limit by virtue of its form, for whatever has no limit has no form by virtue of which it is defined and differentiated from another. This is why eternal substance has no limit, since it has no form.

10   We sum up this section as follows: since a part possesses [the nature of] the whole, then indubitably all parts of a thing in their entirety [possess that nature]. Accordingly, since the part is [composed] of matter and form, the whole is also [composed] of matter and form.

11   A further proof of the point that all things are composed of matter and form is that the matter which is ordered at the lowest extreme [of the world] is composed of matter and form, i.e., it is a body possessing three dimensions. Now if everything that exists forms a continuum reaching from the highest extreme to the lowest extreme, and the latter is composed of matter and form, we have shown thereby that everything that exists

---

[36] Assume that the first created thing is one, i.e., unique. Then the first created thing has to follow without any mediation from what is unique, in which case that creature must resemble what is unique, which is absurd.

from the highest extreme to the lowest extreme is composed of matter and form.

12   Assume that there are three matters: the simplest spiritual matter, which does not wear form; the most composite corporeal matter; and the matter that lies midway between them. The point of my saying that first matter does not wear form is [to distinguish it from] the matter that wears form which, though simple spiritual matter, nevertheless is other than the matter that does not wear form, as Plato said.[37]

13   Corporeal matter, i.e., the quantity that supports the form of figure and color, is not form for the body that supports it, as quality, i.e., figure and color, is form for it. And just as abstract body, which is simpler than body possessing qualities, is a quality-supporting matter, so too it follows that it is a form for another simpler matter into which it resolves, this resolution proceeding until it arrives at the truly simple matter.

14   Each inferior substance is the form for its superior, and each superior substance is the matter that supports the inferior, until one reaches the first matter which is truly simple. It follows from this that the first matter that supports everything is one. From our having demonstrated that a substance that serves as matter for its inferior serves as form for its superior, it follows that all substrata, though they serve as material substrata in a certain respect – the more subtle substance as substratum for the coarser substance – also constitute the forms that are supported in the first matter. You also know that one must assume a first matter that supports all things, because all finite things aim towards one end, and hence it is thereby demonstrated that first matter that supports everything exists, i.e., the first universal matter that we investigated above. We thereby show that the cause for the diversity among substances lies in the form and not in the matter, for there are many forms, whereas matter is one.

15   The first matter, which supports everything, is one by virtue of it combining the sensible and intelligible matters in one matter for all of them. Now since all of them have one matter, it follows that its properties are found in all. And indeed, when you investigate all substances, you find that the properties and impressions of first matter are found in them. For you find that body is a substance that supports many various forms.

---

37 For a discussion of Gabirol's references to "Plato," see Gatti, pp. 84–106. When Gabirol speaks of matter without form, he has in mind potentially existing matter. Matter never actually exists without form; cf. 4.17 and 5.31 below.

This [generalization applies] even more to nature and vital souls, for they impress the forms within the body; and even more to the rational soul and the intellect, for all forms are found within them. In general I say that the higher the substances, the more permanent and comprehensive of forms they are, and the more similar they are to the first matter that supports all forms than the other substances below them. For when you look at the phenomenon from this aspect, i.e., how the properties penetrate, subsist, and extend throughout substances, and how their fit with substance is in accordance with their level and proximity to the upper limit, it is thereby demonstrated that the properties are emanated from above, and that they derive from the universal first matter, which includes and encompasses all, and which bequeaths to them its name and definition. And when you consider further that all the multitude of things seek to unite, it is thereby demonstrated that the matter that is the supporter of everything is one. For the multitude of particulars would not seek to become one unless the all which retains them, and subsists in them, is one.

16   Now since all existents differ in form, and whatever differs in form must agree in matter, it follows accordingly that the matter of existing things is a single matter. You should draw an analogy from the one universal matter to the one universal form and know that it is the universal form that constitutes the essence of universal matter. This being the case, the essence of each one of these substances is necessitated through the necessitation of each of the others.

17   The essence of matter is never devoid of form, and the essence of form never subsists for an instant without matter. This constitutes a strong proof that the essence of the one is necessitated through the necessitation of the essence of the other. Consider the properties of unity, and you find them attached to form. For unity sustains and retains multiplicity, endows it with existence, encompasses it, and is found in all its parts. Unity is supported by its substratum and superior to it. These properties exist [also] in form, since form sustains the essence of that in which it subsists, endows it with existence, retains and encompasses it, subsists in all its parts, and is supported by the matter that serves as its substratum. Form is above matter, and matter below it.

18   It is incorrect to say that unity is the root of everything, since unity is solely form, and everything is not solely form, but rather form and matter. Rather, it is correct to say that *three* is the root of everything, in

so far as *one*[38] corresponds to form and *two* corresponds to matter. I have already shown you that the properties of *one* belong to form, i.e., form sustains the matter for which it is form, and encompasses it, and subsists in all its parts, and is supported by the thing that serves as its substratum. I will now tell you how the properties of *two* belong to matter. I say: *two* is placed below *one*, and *one* above *two*; similarly, matter is placed below form, and form above matter. Moreover, form is *one*, and *two* is a divisible multiplicity; likewise matter is multiple through division. For this reason matters are a cause of the multiplicity and divisibility of things, for the substratum is of the rank of *two*.

Moreover, there is one property of form, namely, sustaining essence. But there are two properties of matter; the first is to support the form, which complements the form's property, for the essence of everything is sustained, and its nature perfected, through matter supporting form and form sustaining the essence of matter. This property belongs to matter from the first *one*, which complements the *one* of form. By '*one*' I mean a half of the *two* which we placed corresponding to matter. The second property of matter is divisibility and multiplicity, for form divides and becomes multiple in matter. This property belongs to matter from the second *one*, i.e., the second half joined with the first *one*, and through this conjunction, they become *two*. Multiplicity and divisibility arise from the existence of *two*. Moreover, matter first divides into two parts corresponding to the nature of *two*, i.e., into the matter of the simple substances and the matter of composite substances. In this respect they achieve the property of *two*. Hence, we have demonstrated that form is at the level of *one*, and matter is at the level of *two*. This being the case, and since matter and form are the root of everything, it is obvious that *three* is the root of everything.

19   The form of the intellect resembles the form of the *one*, since it apprehends a single proposition. The form of the soul resembles the *two* since it moves from the premises to the conclusion, from the same thing to something else. The form of the vital [sensible] soul resembles the *three* since it apprehends a body possessing three dimensions by means of three things: figure, color, and movement. The form of nature resembles the *four* because nature possesses four faculties.[39] In general I say that

---

[38] Gabirol refers to "the one," which poses a problem for translators. Rather than use terms like 'unit' or 'monad,' I adopt Munk's practice in his French translation of italicizing the number.

[39] The attractive, retentive, transformative, and expulsive. See *Fons Vitae* III, 47.

if you look at all existing things, you find them ordered and constituted according to the nature of number, and you find them all subsumed under the form of the intellect, which is unity, since all number is subsumed under unity; this is why the form of the intellect and its essences collect everything and encompass everything.

20 It follows from this that universal form is the impression of the veritable One (blessed be He), spreading throughout all matter and encompassing it. For since the first unity is truly one and self-acting, i.e., not acting by virtue of another, it follows that there is a unity that is subsequent to it, the first of the numerical unities. This is the universal form that constitutes the essence of the generality of species, i.e., the universal species that gives to each [particular] species its very essence; all species participate in its notion. For no species, whether of simple or complex substances, can fail to possess a form that constitutes its very essence. The notion that constitutes all things is the universal form, i.e., the unity that is subsequent to the agent. Hence we say that form retains matter and sustains it, for form is unity, and unity is what retains all things and sustains them, since it brings together and unifies the essence in which it exists, preserving it from becoming separate and multiple. This is why we say that unity includes everything and belongs to everything.

21 The totality of form spreads through the totality of the essence of matter, permeating all its parts. It resembles light, which permeates the totality of substance of the body into which it penetrates, and quantity, which spreads through the substance into which it penetrates.

22 The diversity and division that occurs in forms is not because of the form itself, but because of the matter that supports it. For if there is an absolute first unity that is indivisible and self-acting, it follows that there is a subsequent unity that is hylic and divisible, which is the universal form that is supported in universal matter. It follows that this [subsequent] unity is multiple and divisible because of the matter that supports it, even though it itself is unity. Now it follows that this unity is hylic because it is subsequent to the absolute first unity, i.e., it was originated by it. And since this unity, i.e., the universal form, is hylic, it is divisible because of the matter that supports it, and not because of itself. This may be explained as follows. Form is pure light, and its division and multiplication, as it spreads through matter, causes it to become weak, opaque, and dense (and, generally speaking, causes its middle to be altered from its beginning, and

its end from its middle). But there is nothing here besides matter and the light that spreads through it, i.e., the form. So this shows that the weakness, density, and opacity, and generally, the obscurity, that befalls light spreading throughout matter arises because of the matter and not because of the light in itself.

For this reason some substances are more perfect and knowing than others, because of the opacity and density of matter, and not because of the form itself. For knowing and cognizing pertain to form and not to matter. Form is pure light and matter is its opposite. The more subtle and elevated matter becomes, the more knowing and perfect in the intellect and the soul substance becomes, because of the penetration of light. By contrast, as matter descends, it becomes denser because of its distance from the light that spreads through it. This resembles air, because the more air becomes distant from sight, the more it cannot be penetrated by sight. Sight cannot apprehend the visible forms behind air because of the redoubling and multiplication of the atmospheric regions; the air materializes[40] and forms a barrier between sight and the visible. By contrast, as something approaches, the faculty of sight permeates and rends it. Such is the case with light spreading throughout matter. For matter materializes as it descends, preventing air from permeating it completely.

One can say the same thing about all parts of matter, i.e., that light cannot permeate its lower parts just like its higher parts. The truth is that when a thing is pure it preserves its species in a greater fashion; it is stronger and more visible. Whatever mingles with it acts upon it and alters its purity and clarity. One can say the same thing about form that spreads through matter: its strength and perfection is in accordance with how pure and free of matter it is. It preserves its species better, and is stronger and more permanent, when it is mingled with a purer part of matter than with a denser part. This indicates to you that the alteration that occurs to the light as it spreads through matter is because of matter and not because of the light itself. This resembles the light of the sun when mingled with the darkness, or a thin white garment when worn on a black body, for in the latter case, the white is not seen because the black overwhelms it. This also resembles a light that permeates three

---

[40] *Yitgashem,* i.e., 'corporifes.' Matter is more or less "material" (refined or dense) according to its place in the hierarchy of being.

glass panes, for the light is more diminished in the second pane than in the first, and more diminished in the third than in the second. Now it is evident that this does not result from the weakness of the light itself but because of the panes, which are partitions that present the permeation of the light, for they are dense and corporeal. Analogously, the deficiency of the forms of substance, and their division, is not on account of the light itself but because of matter, which is corporeal in relation to form. This being the case, it is evident that light is a single thing in itself, but opacity can accrue to it, just as it accrues to light spreading through glass panes, and to the light of the sun extending through impure air.

23   All the lower forms exist in the upper forms, and the more substance is elevated and pure, the more forms it encompasses and brings together – as substance, which is subtle, supports quantity and whatever is in it of figure and color; or as sentient soul, which is purer than substance, receives the forms of sensible things and supports them because of their subtlety and the subtlety of its essence; or as rational soul supports substance with all its forms; or as intellect supports all the forms below it; or as universal first matter supports the form of everything without qualification.

24   The corporeal and composite world is the likeness of the simple and spiritual world, and the lowest of the simple worlds is the likeness of the highest of them, until one reaches the truly simple world. An example of this may be drawn from some of the corporeal forms that are visible when awake, for those corporeal forms are the likeness of the psychic forms that are apprehended in dreams. Similarly, the psychic forms apprehended in dreams are the likeness of the internal intellectual forms.

25   It thus follows that the lower forms are transmitted from the higher forms such that the form of corporeal substances is found in that of nature, and the form of nature is found in that of soul, and the form of soul is found in that of intellect.

26   That sensible forms are concealed in intelligible forms is proved from [the consideration that] figures and colors appear in animals, vegetables, and minerals by means of the impression that soul and nature make upon them; similarly, representations, [colors] and figures, and in general, all artificial forms, come from the rational soul. If one were to object, "Perhaps these forms are originated in composites by means of a combination of elements according to a certain proportion, and not by

means of the impressions made by simple substances," then I would reply: "if these representations and figures were originated from the elements, then they would always exist the same way in objects composed out of them, and composites would not differ in representation and figure, as they do in receiving the impressions of substance."

27   All lower forms exist in the upper forms with a simple and more subtle existence. For example, bodies and their forms subsist in the faculty of imagination, one of the psychic faculties, although they are concealed from sense. More [elevated] than this is the subsistence of all forms in the intellect.

28   The form of the intellect apprehends and cognizes all forms. The form of the rational soul apprehends and cognizes some of the intellectual forms, moving and passing among them, which resembles the activity of the intellect. The form of the vital soul apprehends and cognizes the corporeal forms, moving entire bodies in their places, which resembles the activity of the rational soul. The form of the vegetative soul apprehends the essences of bodies, moving their parts in a [single] place, which resembles the activity of the vital soul. The form of nature activates the combination, attraction, repulsion, and conversion of parts, resembling the activity of the vegetative soul. Since these activities resemble each other, it follows that the forms that produce these activities resemble each other.

29   We have already said that the perfect and strong substance is the cause of the deficient and weak. Just as the forms of simple and composite substances spread through the essences of these substances, and encompass them in their entirety, some forms generated from others, the lower from the higher, and [just as the forms] are ranked uniformly from the upper extreme to the lower extreme, so too the [universal] form spreads through the forms, as light spreads through air, extending continuously from the upper to the lower, and replenishes and encompasses matter, leaving none of its parts empty, and none of its bare places unclothed. However, the degrees of form change in matter: At the upper extreme the light which emanates from it is complete and pure, and the substance that supports it is spiritual and subtle; at the lower extreme the line that emanates from it is dark, shadowed, and concealed, and the substance that supports it dense and corporeal. Between these two extremes one finds the intermediaries [ranked] according to the alteration of the light and the density of matter, depending upon which [of the extremes] is

closer and which is farther away. If you examine the form from this aspect, you will see that it begins complete and spiritual, and then, degree after degree, it becomes more and more dense, until it arrives at the last extreme. You will see movement cease there, and the indwelling form stop.

30   Since first form is the second unity,[41] the object of the action of first and active unity, and since first unity does not act like numerical unity, it follows that the unity which is the object of [first unity's] action is like numerical unity. I mean to say that it follows that it must be multipliable and divisible. This entails that the first form will multiply and become altered,[42] and as it multiplies and becomes altered, the number of forms will increase, and the forms will become altered. The cause of this [multiplication] is form's mingling with matter, and its distance from the source of unity.

31   The light that spreads through matter is transmitted from another light which is above matter, i.e., the light that is found in the essence of the agent faculty, namely, the will, which brings the form from potentiality to actuality. In the will, the entire form is actual with respect to the agent; it is said to be potential with respect to the recipient of the action. When you examine the faculty of will, and what forms it possesses in itself, you see that what universal matter receives from it (all the forms that are supported by it according to their light and multiplicity and their greatness[43]), compared with what it possesses in itself, resembles what air receives from sunlight. For the degree of light that spreads through the air is quite small compared with the light found in the sun itself. This is the comparison of material form with that of will. But the second light is called form rather than the first,[44] because the second is supported by matter, and is form to it, whereas the first is not supported by anything, hence is not form for anything.

32   It follows that forms are threefold: first, the form existing in the essence of will, which, even though we call it 'form,' we do so only to give

---

[41] The first unity appears to be an attribute of God, cf. 2.25 above; that it is not God may be seen from the fact that the honorific 'blessed be He' is never used in conjunction with it; the second unity is universal created form.

[42] Gabirol assumes here a version of the classical principle of plenitude: Whatever *can* happen *will* happen. Otherwise it is difficult to see how he gets from first form as a enumerated unity, hence multipliable, to its actually multiplying. The cause of its actual multiplication appears in the last sentence of the section.

[43] Reading, with Munk, *'ozmam* rather than *'azmam*.   [44] I.e., will

it a name and designation. Strictly speaking it is not form, because it is not supported [by matter]. But because its essence is other than the essence of the form supported by matter, it should be set apart and designated by a name. For it is inadmissible that the form of intellect existing in the essence of will *before* it has been emanated from the essence of will and attached to matter, should be [considered] like the form *after* it has been emanated and attached to matter. The second form is the form that is actually attached to matter, which is the form of universal intellect. The third is the imagined form removed from matter, [yet] attached to matter potentially. The other forms, however, are those that are contained in the universal form. Hence, you need not doubt Plato's division of form, for he divided the form in three species: (1) the form in potentiality, abstracted from matter; (2) the form in actuality, attached to matter; (3) the form of the elements, i.e., the first four qualities.[45]

33   If will is an efficient cause then the form of everything is in its essence, for the form of every effect is undoubtedly in its cause, or rather, the effect exists in its cause through the form it possesses. Things exist in the essence of will only inasmuch as they are its effects.

Excerpts from Treatise Five [On universal matter and universal form in themselves]

1   He said: the aim of this treatise is to discuss universal form and universal matter abstracted from each other, to make known the essence of each of them, as well as the notions that can be apprehended about them, so that this knowledge may [serve] as a stepping stone from which we ascend to the knowledge of will, and that of the First Substance.

2   Intellectual knowledge occurs when the form of the intellect attaches to the intelligible form and unites with it. When the form of the intellect is with this form, it knows by itself that this form cannot exist without the matter that supports it, and that form is something other than the matter that supports it. To clarify this point let us take for example the substance of the intellect. When it has been demonstrated for you that the substance of the intellect is something other than its form, it will likewise be demonstrated for you that the matters of the simple substances and those of the composite substances are something other than

---

[45] I.e., Hot, cold, dry, moist. For the reference to Plato, see above, p. 55, n. 37.

their forms. Through this you know that universal matter is something other than the universal form.

We say, therefore, that the intellect knows in itself that it possesses form, since the form of the intellect knows itself [and hence it knows other forms that are other than it. Now inasmuch as the form of the intellect knows itself and that it is supported by matter that is other than it, you know thereby that it possesses a matter that supports it, and you also know that it differs from the matter that supports it, because it knows itself and that its essence is other than the matter that supports it. Since the form of the intellect knows itself][46] it follows likewise that it knows matter and that matter is other than it.

3   Represent the essence of matter as a self-subsistent spiritual faculty that lacks form, and represent the essence of form as an existent light that endows its characteristic[47] to that in which it exists, and provides it with the notion of the species and the form. In general, I say that matter and form should be represented like all the spiritual things, i.e., as intelligibles rather than sensibles, and not as informed, hylic entities. For if you attempt to represent hylic matter abstracted from form, you will not apprehend it – because matter in itself is other than that which possesses form and because it is at the highest extreme, soul being intermediate between both extremes. Similarly, if you attempt to represent form in itself, you will find that task difficult because the faculty of conception is one of the psychic faculties, whereas the essence of form is simpler than that of soul.

4   You should represent the distinction between matter and form like the distinction between body and color: liken matter to body and form to color, and liken also the way sense distinguishes between color and body by apprehending the form of color in itself to the way intellect distinguishes between matter and form by apprehending form in itself. You may more easily represent [the distinction between matter and form] when you represent the distinction between body, soul, and intellect despite their union, or, generally, the distinctions between spiritual substances despite their union, or the distinction between substances and the accidents they support. When you represent this, and when you grasp its image within your soul, you find it easier to represent the distinction between matter

---

[46] There appears to be a homoiteleuton in the Falaquera mss.; at any rate, the material in brackets is a translation of the Latin.

[47] *To'ar*, lit.: 'attribute' or 'description.'

and form, which resembles the distinction between body and soul, and the distinction between soul and intellect. For form relates to matter as soul relates to body and intellect relates to soul.

5   If you wish to know the distinction between matter and form in every spiritual substance, and, generally, the distinction between universal form and universal matter, take as an example the essence of intellect; for when you have judged the distinction between the matter and form of intellect you will be able to judge the distinction between the matter and form of each of the simple substances and its form, and, generally, the distinction between universal matter and universal form. For this reason I say that whoever wishes to know the principles [of things], and, generally, the knowledge of everything, will have to investigate assiduously the essence of intellect, and set it before him in all inquiries. This is truly the case, for since the essence of intellect is the specificality of everything, i.e., the form of everything, it follows that everything exists in the essence of intellect. And from the latter follows that whoever knows the essence of intellect knows everything.

6   To examine the distinction between universal matter and universal form in light of the examination of the essence of intellect, you should grasp by yourself the form that is proper to intellect, i.e., the essential difference that constitutes its essence (the notion through which you judge that something is what it is), and then you should examine how, through this form, the essence of intellect is differentiated from other things. This manner of examination will lead you to think that intellect knows by itself that it possesses form, and that, through this form, it is differentiated from other things. Now to grasp the form of the intellect, and to know that this form is distinguished from other things, you will need the existence of matter that supports this very form. It is as if you touch the essence of matter by the form of your intellect, and you feel it, just as sense feels the thing sensed.

7   Represent form's attachment to matter like light's attachment to air, or sound's attachment (i.e., movement's[48] attachment) to voice. For each one attaches to its matter respectively [though they are] without limits. I say in general that the representation of the attachment of form to matter is like the representation of the attachment of some spiritual forms to others, and the attachment of spiritual substances to spiritual

---

[48] I.e., tonality.

accidents and to corporeal substances. Take as illustrations intellect and soul, or soul and body, as we explained above: [the attachment of form to matter] will be analogous to the attachment of intellect to soul, and to the attachment of the soul to the accident supported by it, and to the body with which it is linked; and, what is more subtle and concealed, the attachment of the intellect to the intelligible and the senses to the sensible. By means of this illustration, the manner in which the Creator (blessed be He) brings forth form in matter from nonexistence to existence is analogous to how intellect transmits its essence to the intelligible and how sense [transmits its essence] to the sensible.

8   If we examine all substances and forms, we shall not find a form more perfect, or inclusive of all the forms, than the form of the intellect. For we find that this form, by itself, knows every form, and that it unites, by itself, with every form. From this we learn that all the forms are in its essence. Moreover, we have found that the essence of intellect by itself apprehends the forms of things, which proves that these forms unite with its essence, and that its essence is none other than one thing, namely, the totality of these forms, for all these forms unite spiritually within its essence. It follows that the form of the intellect is a *unitive* form, which brings together in its unity, the unity of every form. Moreover, we find that intellect does not apprehend hylic matter by itself, but through the intermediary of soul and senses, since it is outside of itself. It follows that intellect apprehends the forms because they are not outside itself, and since they are not outside itself, they are in its essence.

9   Just as the preponderance of forms exist within the particular intellect, since the particular intellect apprehends by itself every form and finds in itself every form, it follows of necessity that the forms of all things exist in the form of the universal intellect.

10   If you ask, "How can all the forms exist in the particular intellect?" Recall how the soul thinks, and how it becomes what is in the intellect, and how it represents the forms of things by the faculty of imagination when awake, and how it represents them in veridical dreams such that it knows them.

11   The proof that the essence of intellect contains all the forms of things goes as follows: The form of the intellect apprehends all the forms which unite in its essence, and everything in whose essence all the forms unite contains all the forms in its essence. Hence, the essence of intellect contains all the forms [of things].

12   The proof that the existence of a thing is on account of its form goes as follows: An existing thing must be either sensible or intelligible. Sense and intellect do not attach to anything save a sensible or intelligible form, for the sensible and intelligible form intervenes between the form of the intellect and the soul, and between the matters that support sensible forms and those that support intelligible forms. This is why forms attach only to forms, since only they meet each other.[49] Moreover, intellect and soul apprehend only their [respective] forms, and forms attach only to forms, because of their likeness, and [their belonging to a] common genus. This is why the intellect, in its perception of hylic things, needs the intermediary of forms because of the likeness between its form and those forms. Now since something exists only by virtue of its form, it is impossible for matter stripped of form to exist in an unqualified sense. If, however, existence must be predicated of such matter, then one may say of it that it exists potentially, i.e., when it assumes the form, it passes into act and exists actually.

13   We do not say that all things are in the intellect, or that all things are intellect, because of things that possess matter. Rather we say that the spiritual intelligibles are in the intellect and that they are intellect. But the corporeal sensibles are not in the intellect nor are they intellect, for they are external to its essence. Hence intellect does not apprehend things that possess hylic matter except through the intermediary of sense, which resembles its nature, since it is intermediate between the spirituality of intellect and the corporeality of hylic matter. The reason why intellect is prevented from apprehending hylic things is that the intellect apprehends a thing when its form attaches to and unites with the form of the thing intellected. Now since intellect is subtle, and sensibles are coarse, and the subtle cannot attach to the coarse, it follows that intellect does not apprehend sensibles except through the intermediary of sense. For the sensing subject resembles both extremes, i.e., it is intermediary between the spirituality of the intellect and the corporeality of the sensible forms.

Here is the explanation: Since knowledge occurs when the form of the knower unites without an intermediary with the form of the object known (the union of these two forms being in proportion to their likeness and proximity), and the intellectually cognizing soul does not resemble the corporeal forms (the soul being spiritual and the sensible forms

---

[49] See 4.7 above.

corporeal), it is thereby impossible that the form of the intellectually cognizing soul attach to the corporeal forms without an intermediary that resembles both extremes. Moreover, since the vital and natural soul is midway between the intellectually cognizing soul and the body, it is impossible that the intellectually cognizing soul attaches to the form of the body, and unites with its essence, without an intermediary. Analogously, sensing substance apprehends sensible forms through the intermediary of organs and air, because organs and air resemble the two extremes, i.e., the sensing substance and the sensible forms.

14   [Hence,] when we say that everything is in intellect, and that everything is transmitted from intellect, we do not mean thereby that everything is composed of intellect, or that some of the simple substances are composed from others. For if something is composed of something else, then this entails the actualization of the composition. But intellect is not like that, for its essence is simple, i.e., everything exists simply within it in such a way that its essence is every form and, and the forms of things are united *knowingly and essentially* within its essence, not corporally and accidentally.

15   Since the form of the intellect entails the knowledge of the form of everything, it follows that all forms attach to it, and exist within it, for all forms are created by it, i.e., they are united within its essence in a spiritual and essential unification. Hence, the form of the intellect includes all the forms, and this being so, it follows that this form[50] is the one that gives form and quiddity to everything, just as it gives substantiality to everything.

16   The sages agreed that intellect does not have a proper form, and they spoke rightly. For if intellect had a proper form, that form would prevent the apprehension of all other forms. Their expression, "a proper form," means a particular form. They did not deem impossible intellect possessing a universal form. For a universal form entails the apprehension of all forms. Now when you examine the cause of the forms' apprehending substances, you will grasp the truth of what we have said, that the form of intellect is universal, and you will know that this form apprehends, by itself, all the forms.

17   There is no doubt that the more subtle and simple substance is, the more capable it is of receiving many diverse forms, and the straighter and

---

[50] I.e., the form of the intellect.

fairer the forms in it are, and vice-versa. This is so because composition within an object prevents the permeation of all the forms into it, for it interposes between its essence and the forms. Simple substance, by contrast, lacks something that interposes between it and the forms and prevents their permeation. It follows thereby that as the simple substance becomes purer and more elevated, the more forms it receives, and it becomes the recipient of every figure and form. Were the simple substance to receive only one figure and to concentrate upon it, there would be no difference between it and composite substance. This being the case, it follows that the sensible substance, due to its coarseness, does not receive the variegated forms.[51] Rather it concentrates upon one form.

It follows that as an intelligible substance becomes purer and more elevated, the more capable it becomes to receive forms, and the collection of forms within it becomes greater and clearer than the one in the lower [existents], such as in nature or in soul. This principle continues until one arrives at the purest and simplest substance, the substance of intellect. It follows that this is the strongest substance with respect to receiving forms, and the strongest in collecting them in its essence and its unity. Moreover, since the substance of intellect is ordered at the highest extreme, opposite the substance of body, which is ordered at the lowest extreme and is receptive of only one form, it follows that the substance of intellect receives all forms and supports them. It also follows that, as the substances descend and draw near to body, they become increasingly weak in receiving the forms, and vice-versa: the reception of the forms becomes stronger as the substances ascend until they arrive at the rank of the intellect. This substance is more receptive of forms than all the rest of the substances, and more collective as well.

18   The matter that is proper to the form of the intellect, the highest extreme of universal matter, receives the form of intellect, which supports all forms, from will, which dwells above with the Creator (blessed and exalted be He). The form is in it[52] in a perfect fashion; it is everything, and everything is in it. But matter receives from will according to the receptive disposition that is in matter's essence, and not according to the will's power. What matter receives from the light of will is small compared with what will possesses.

---

[51] Lit.: 'is other than the recipient of variegated forms.'
[52] The antecedent of 'it' is ambiguous in the Hebrew; according to the Latin, the antecedent is will.

19   You should know that this absolute form belongs to will from the standpoint of the agent *actually*, and from the standpoint of the recipient[53] of action *potentially*. Things do not exist in the upper existents in the same manner as they do in the lower ones since the forms are more perfect in the causes than in the effects. For the forms originate in the effects because the causes contemplate their respective effects. It follows accordingly that forms exist in the will in the most perfect and correct fashion. This is true also of everything that approximates will, until one arrives at the lowest limit of substance, where form ends. This is generally what Plato said about these matters. For he considered the origination of forms in the intellect to result from wisdom's contemplation; their origination in the universal soul to result from the universal intellect's contemplation; and likewise their origination in nature and substance to result from universal soul's contemplation. He compared these with the origination of intellectual forms, i.e., thoughts, and their representation in the soul, when [particular] intellect contemplates them.

20   The meaning of 'contemplation' when used in reference to substances, is that some substances face others, and some of their powers and lights influence others because they are retained under the First Substance that influences in itself, i.e., whose influence comes solely as a result of Him.

21   The collection of many diverse forms in one subject would be impossible were they to occupy a place. But since they do not occupy a place, the collection of many diverse forms in one subject is not impossible. And since the forms that are collected in the form of the intellect are not divided, but rather are united in its essence, and since the substance of intellect is simple, it is thereby demonstrated that these forms do not occupy place; on the contrary, they and the place in which they are, i.e., the substance of intellect, are the same thing. Because of this, i.e., because the substance of intellect is a simple substance and the forms supported in it are not divided but rather are united within its essence, the substance of intellect contains everything, and is not restricted to anything, because it supports everything in its unity, i.e., its essence, with a support that is one and essential. You should investigate this matter and examine it with respect to all substances, that is to say, you should relate how one substance supports the forms with how another supports the forms. For

53 Switching *po'el* with *pa'ul* in the Hebrew.

example, when you examine how the forms exist within the intellect, you find it comparable to their existence in the soul, and the existence of the nine categories in substance.

Hence we say that intellect is the place of the natural forms; we say further that just as hylic matter is a faculty that receives sensible forms, so too soul is a faculty that receives intelligible forms. In this way you should compare the existence of all the forms in the first matter, for you shall find all the forms existing in universal matter, and likewise the nine categories existing in substance, and likewise the diverse things existing in the soul, which supports them; their existence is not hindered by the fact that some of them exist in others. For just as the body and its accidents, though diverse and different, are one thing, and the soul distinguishes each one of its parts from another, though they are joined and united; so, too, when all things, though diverse in their essences, are joined and united together, the intellect divides some from the others, and distinguishes some from the others. It follows from this comparison that the relation of the All to first matter is like that of the body to the soul, or, to generalize, like the relation of the forms within the intellect. For if the forms of all things exist in the intellect, they certainly exist in first matter. You should reason analogously for all things that are superior to them.

22   By 'intelligible knowledge' we mean the unity of the intelligible form in the intellect; similarly for 'sensible knowledge.' This particular unity is not like the unity of universal form in universal matter, which is inferior to it, and which we do not call 'knowledge.' Yet although we do not call the unity 'knowledge' this does not imply that the unity of intelligible forms in the intellect is nobler than it. For the notion of the first unity is nobler than that of the second.

23   Regarding this point you should know that form encompasses matter like intellect encompasses soul and like some of these simple substances encompass others. The Creator (blessed and exalted be He) encompasses will and all matter and form within Him [in a manner] that is unparalleled and unique.

24   You should know that although quality is above quantity, this is only with reference to sense perception. In truth, quality and quantity concur, for color and figure are necessary for physical material to be realized; and other *genera* concur within substance. Reason analogously from this case to that of the concurrence of all the forms in first matter. For

the supporting relation[54] between first matter and all forms is comparable to the supporting relation between intellect and soul, and all intelligible forms, and to the supporting relation between substance and the nine categories, and even more clearly, to the supporting relation between quantity and figure and color.

25   The inferior must be hylic to the superior, since the superior acts upon it. Hence the savants have said that only first intellect is the true form, and it is called by them, 'active intellect.'

26   The more a form descends, and becomes corporeal, the more visible it becomes to the sense, like color, which is the closest of forms to the sense. Shape is more concealed than color, corporeality than shape, substance than corporeality, nature than substance, soul than nature, and intellect than soul. This is so because the first form that is attached to the first matter is simple and spiritual, and the last form is corporeal and composite. Between these two extremes are intermediaries that link and attach them. The closer the form is to the first and [most] spiritual form, the more subtle and concealed it will be, and vice-versa – the closer the form is to the corporeal form, the coarser and more visible it will be.

27   The proof that spiritual forms are concealed in corporeal forms is as follows: the soul resides in the body with its faculties, each faculty attaching to the corresponding form in subtlety. The soul first separates the form of quality and quantity from that of substance, then afterwards separates the form of substance from that of nature, the form of nature from that of soul, the form of soul from that of intellect, and the forms of intellect from the first matter.[55] You should know that whoever learns well how these forms are separate, and how to distinguish each substance from another, will achieve the utmost knowledge and pleasure.

28   The impression that first form makes upon everything is existence, for that form constitutes the essence of everything. The form of intellect is the form that encompasses every existent, and the existence of all forms comes from the existence of the form of intellect.

29   To define universal matter and universal form is impossible, because they have no superior genus that could be posited as a

---

[54] I.e., the predicative relation.
[55] Since the forms that the soul's faculties abstract from body are more and more spiritual, this is an argument that spiritual forms are concealed within corporeal ones.

defining principle.[56] But they can be described via the properties that belong necessarily to them. The description of the universal matter taken from its properties is a self-subsistent substance that supports diversity, and is numerically one. It can also be described as a substance that receives all the forms. The description of universal form is a substance that constitutes the essence of all forms; one could also describe it as the essence of perfect wisdom and pure light.

30   Simple substances lack a "whereforeness" external to themselves. Rather their "whereforeness" and their "whatness" are the same, for they are simple unities. This is why we say of first matter, first form, and generally all simple substances, that their coming into existence is caused only by the Creator (blessed and exalted be He). For the fourth cause, the "whereforeness," is external to the effect, and there is nothing external to simple substances besides their Creator (blessed and exalted be He). For this reason we say that they have perpetual existence because of the perpetuity of the Creator (blessed and exalted be He). In this chapter I will give you a sufficient principle that you can adopt for your own use.

I say that what exists is ordered from the highest extreme to the lowest according to four degrees: existence, which is called in Arabic "thatness," "whatness," "howness," and "whereforeness."[57] The Most High is existence not possessing quiddity, quality, or quarity,[58] i.e., Truly One (blessed and exalted be He). Below is the quiddity not possessing quality or quarity, i.e., Intellect. Below is the quiddity possessing quality, i.e., Soul. Below it is quiddity possessing quality and quarity, i.e. Nature and generated things. Each of these is ordered according to numerical order. Existence is ordered on the level of one, for it is simply existence. Quiddity is ordered on the level of two, for quiddity is composed of two things, genus and specific difference. Quality is ordered on the level of three, because it is supported by the essence of quiddity and joined to it. Quarity is ordered on the level of four because it is joined to quality, quiddity, and existence, which is three.

31   What exists can be ordered on more general levels than these, namely: the necessary, the possible, and the impossible. The necessary is

---

[56] Since definitions are comprised of a genus and difference, primitives that do not follow under a genus cannot, strictly speaking, be defined. But they can be described via their properties.

[57] I.e., existence, quiddity, quality, and quarity. Henceforth these terms will be used in the translation.

[58] I.e. an external purpose for the sake of which God acts. For the use of these four terms in theological contexts, including Gabirol, see S. M. Stern in *Isaac Israeli: A Neoplatonic Philosopher of the Early Tenth Century* (Oxford: Oxford University Press, 1958), pp. 13–23.

the One Agent (blessed and exalted be He). The possible is every existent that is acted upon by Him. The impossible is the absence of what exists and its cessation. The necessary is the unchangeable source; the possible is the contrary, and hence it is possible, in my opinion, that what is acted upon is changeable, for that is the nature of what is possible in itself. Whoever called first matter 'possibility' by this reasoning spoke correctly. And since the one is the first agent, it follows that he alone is one. And because that which is acted upon is possible, it follows that it cannot be the same [thing], but must be distinct things, and thus it follows that it must be a supporter and a supported.[59]

32   The changeability of matter and form serve as a proof for will, since it is the way of will to effect something and its contrary.

The reason why form is visible and matter concealed in intelligible things is because of the encounter of the form of the intellect and the intelligible forms. For all forms face each other when in matter, like men in a battle. [The reason for the visibility of form and the concealedness of matter] in sensible things is because the forms are corporeal and matter spiritual in relation to the forms supported by it; also, because matter wears [something], and form is worn; also, because matter is akin to privation and form is akin to existence; also, because matter is potential and form is in act, since it is perfected and exists by virtue of form. Hence it moves first to receive its form, i.e., towards perfection.

33   Because form is the unity that receives the action of the first unity, which retains and sustains everything, and also because it is the way of unity to unite and bind together a thing so that it does not become separate and multiple, it follows that form must retain matter. But because matter's way is to be multiple and divided, it follows that it must be united by unity, and retained and collected by it.

34   In the Creator's knowledge (blessed and exalted be He) form is separate and afterwards combines with matter, but this [occurs] timelessly. The separateness of matter and form in God's knowledge (blessed and exalted be He) may be likened to the spiritual form, which is first conceived [separately] in the soul and afterwards combines with matter and becomes actual; or it is like form which is first in intellect and afterwards exits and unites with soul. Yet the form found in the Eternal's knowledge (blessed and exalted be He) becomes actual timelessly, and hence you will not find

---

[59] Or "a subject and predicate."

form devoid of matter even for an instant. This is not the case with the form that exits from the soul.

35   The attachment of matter and form may be likened to the attachment of light with air, color with body, intellect with soul, sense with the sensible, and intellect with the intelligible. That is why one says that everything exists by virtue of God's knowing, seeing, and encompassing things.

36   It has been said that the substance of intellect has a limit at two extremes. It has a limit at the highest extreme because will is above it; and it has a limit at the lowest extreme because hylic matter is outside of its essence. All the simple substances possess a limit in the upper levels and lack one in the lower levels, because they proceed successively from each other,[60] for they are simple and spiritual. But since hylic matter is corporeal and dense, it is accordingly outside of the essence of intellect. They said that intellect and all the simple substances have a limit from this aspect, i.e., they are distinct from the corporeality that is a feature of hylic matter, and this distinction implies a limit.[61]

37   Matter exists only through form, for existence is due to form. This is why matter moves to receive form so that it may exit from the pain of nothingness to the joy of existence. But matter may exist devoid of some forms, for some matter is devoid of spiritual form – not of the first form that constitutes the essence of first matter, but rather of the second form that constitutes the essences of the simple substance. Likewise one finds that some corporeal matter divests itself of some forms and wears others.

38   Consider matter as possessing two extremes: one ascending to the limit of creation – i.e., the limit of the attachment of matter with form – the other descending to the limit of the cessation [of form].[62] Now represent what is above the heavenly sphere to be spiritual form; the higher one ascends the more united and simple this spirituality becomes, until the limit of creation is reached. And represent what descends from the heavenly sphere to be corporeal form; the lower one descends, the more corporeal it becomes, until the limit of cessation is reached.

---

[60] Lit.: 'some are the edges of others.'

[61] In *Fons Vitae* III, 57 the Master implies that the intellect is limited qua effect and unlimited qua cause. Here, it is suggested that intellect can be considered limited even qua cause, inasmuch as it is distinct from corporeality.

[62] See above, 4.29.

39   Matter is naught but one; diversity [exists] by virtue of form. If you concentrate on representing spiritual substance, you will know that its relation to corporeal substance is like the relation of light to air. If you ask, "How is this [representation achieved]?" then [I answer]: "Turn your intellect away from [representing] corporeal substance and concentrate entirely on spiritual substance until you stop at the limit of creation, i.e., the origin of the conjunction of matter with form. Then reverse your thinking downwards, and you will apprehend conclusively the truth of what I told you regarding the smallness of corporeal substance in comparison with the magnitude of spiritual substance. If you are able to compare created spiritual substance, I mean, the spiritual matter that unites with form, with the source from which the effulgence flows, i.e., will, then you will consider corporeal substance to be even smaller."

Consider as an analogy the relation of heaven and earth. When you train your mind on the first limit of the uppermost heavens overlooking the earth, then you regard the earth, which is actually in the middle of the heavens, as a measureless point in relation to them, even though it really is quite big.[63] Likewise, when you train your intellect on the first limit of spiritual substance, then you regard the relation of corporeal substance to spiritual substance, or rather, of both to will, as the relation of the earth to the heavens. Hence you should not be put off when the higher is beneath the lower, for what is higher and lower exists only for us and in reference to us. They pertain to a discrete atom of existence, i.e., [corporeal] substance. But spiritual substance is a continuous one, some parts of it overlapping other parts, subsisting in God's knowledge (blessed be He) and power, which encompasses everything.

40   I will represent this to you in a brief overview that you should rely on. Train your intellect on the limit of creation, I mean to say, the principle of the unity of matter and form. Then represent a substance that has neither beginning nor end, namely, the substance of the Creator (blessed be He). Now represent that every spiritual and corporeal existent subsists within Him, as you represent certain notions that subsist in your soul. Then you will see that the power of the Creator (blessed and exalted be He) exists in everything, and you will see that the power and essence of a superior entity exists in what is inferior to it, until one reaches the bottommost limit, which is the limit of cessation. In this way you can

---

[63] Cf. *Moreh ha-Moreh*, ed. Shifman, pp. 302–3.

represent how matter and form extend uniformly from the higher to the lower.

41　Matter exists in God's knowledge (blessed be He) like the existence of the earth in the middle of the heavens, and form shines upon and penetrates it, like the sun shines upon and penetrates air and earth. This form is called 'light' because the word from which form flows is called light, i.e., an intelligible rather than a sensible light. Moreover, it is the way of light to reveal [sensible] form and to display form after it had been concealed. Likewise, when form attaches to matter, form displays matter after it had been concealed, and through it matter exists.

42　Matter is said to be the place of form, i.e., matter supports form, which is supported by it. It is also said that will is a place for both of them together. The meaning of this is that each of them needs will for its existence and permanence. But true place is an accident that is originated at the lowest extreme of form.

43　It is impossible for matter to precede form or form matter. How would it be possible for one to precede the other, when they do not exist [separate from one another] even for the blink of an eye, but rather are bound to one another? Moreover, matter does not exist by itself formally, i.e., in act. It exists only through form, from which follows that its existence does not obtain except through form.

44　The thing that binds matter and form together, combines them, and keeps them united, is a unity that is superior to them. For the union of matter and form is the impression left by unity on them. Now just as there is no intermediary between *one* and *two*, so you should know that there is no intermediary between unity [on the one hand] and matter and form [on the other]. The proof that unity is what orders matter and form is the strength of the union of matter and form near the limit of creation, i.e., its origin, existence, and preservation because of its proximity to the source of unity; conversely, its multiplicity, divisibility, separateness, lessened permanence and existence near the limit of cessation, i.e., at the end of substance, because of its distance from the source of unity. This is a proof that unity retains all, and supports all.

45　The force of unity differs with respect to strength and weakness. At the outset it unites the existent to the utmost, and retains it to the utmost; whereas at the end it does the reverse, because of the diversity of matter. The movement of matter to receive its form resembles the movement of the soul which is devoid of knowledge to see and receive that knowledge. When the form of that knowledge attaches itself to the soul, and establishes it, then the soul is knowing. Likewise, when the form attaches itself to matter, the latter is informed through it, i.e., becomes the supporter of form.

46   What causes matter to move to receive form is the yearning of matter to apprehend the good, and the pleasure [it obtains] upon receiving the form. This is true of the movement of all substances, i.e., the movement of all substance is towards the one. The demonstration of this is as follows: every existence wishes to move for the sake of achieving something of the perfection of the first existent. But the movement of existing things differs according to the difference in their degrees of nearness and remoteness. As substance becomes nearer to the first existent, it achieves perfection more easily; as it becomes more remote, it achieves perfection only through slow movement, or through many movements and at many times. If the one adds to the remoteness, the movement stops. Compare this with the heaven and the earth.

47   The proof that whatever moves, moves towards the one, and for the sake of the one, is as follows: Whatever moves, moves to receive form. Now form is nothing more than the impression of the one, which is the good. Hence, the movement of all things is for the sake of the good, which is the one. Another proof is that none of the existent things desires to be many, but rather they desire to be one. Hence, they all desire towards unity.

48   Since the notion of *love* and *desire* implies seeking to be attached to the object of love, and to be united with it, and since matter seeks to be attached to form, it follows that its movement is for the love of form and desire for it. This is true of everything that moves to seek form.

49   You may remark: if the movement of matter to receive form is because of its desire for the first existent, then this implies likeness between them; for there can be desire and attachment only between things that are alike! My response is that there is no likeness between matter and the first existent, except from this aspect: matter receives light from the essence of will, and this brings[64] it to tend towards [the will] and to desire it. It does not move to apprehend [will's] essence, but rather to apprehend the form that [will] originates for it.

---

[64] Lit.: 'carries.'

50   You may remark: What likeness can there be between form and matter, which are two distinct substances, for one supports the other? My response is that there is no likeness between them – except that since matter receives form within itself, and form's influence upon matter is powerful and permeating, it follows that matter moves to receive form, and that form unites with it. This is proof that they are retained under the will, and are subordinate to it, for they are essentially distinct, yet united together.

51   You may remark: When matter moves to receive form because it seeks the good, which is unity, it follows that matter knows the thing that it intends to seek by virtue of itself – and yet we saw above that matter knows something by virtue of form! [My response is:] Know that the closeness of matter to unity entails that matter receives the faculty of apprehension from unity, and that unity flows upon matter. This entails [in turn] the movement of matter towards it in order to receive from it perfection, until it receives the form on account of which it is knowing and perfect. There will be nothing more for it to receive. It may be compared[65] to air that at dawn is mingled with a bit of light: as the sun facing it rises, it fills with light until it is complete and receives nothing further from the sun. Likewise for first matter: its proximity to unity entails that it will be infused with unity's light and power, which is then the cause of its desire for unity, and its movement towards it. A similar sort of response may be given to one who finds objectionable the likeness between the First Agent and matter and other substances: one posits that the movement of these substances is one of desire and yearning, for the proximity of matter to unity entails that matter apprehend some of its power and light, which entails that it desires to tend toward it [the First Agent] in order to receive perfection and to pass from nonexistence to existence – to the point where will infuses it with universal form, with which it unites, and, its nature having been perfected, it becomes intellect.

52   This seeking after the First Agent (blessed be He), and the movement towards Him, spreads through everything. But it varies according to the degree of proximity and remoteness from God. For example, particular hylic matter desires a particular form, like the hylic matter of vegetative and living things, which move, when generated, to receive the form of vegetative and living things. They are the object of action of

---

[65] Lit.: 'on the level of.'

particular form, which act upon them. Likewise, the vital soul desires the form appropriate to it, i.e., the sensible form. Likewise, the rational soul desires the intelligible forms. For the particular soul, which is called "first intellect," is initially like hylic matter that receives form, and when it has received form from universal intellect, which is the third intellect, it passes into act and is called "second intellect."[66] And since particular souls are desirous in this manner, it follows that universal souls are even more so, i.e., that universal soul desires universal [forms]. The same is true of natural matter, i.e., the substance that supports the categories. For this matter likewise moves to receive the form of the qualities, and afterwards, to receive the form of the mineral soul, then the vegetable, then the vital, then the rational, and then the intelligent, until it becomes attached to the form of the universal soul. Reason analogously to the movement of all universal things, and it follows that first matter desires to receive first form for the sake of apprehending the good, which is existence. This is true of all things that are [composed] of matter and form, for matter moves to receive the form of the perfect: as the existent becomes higher, its movements and desires become less, because of its proximity to perfection. For this reason, as the existence becomes higher and closer to the source of unity, its activity becomes more united and enduring, without time. For as a thing becomes more united in itself, its activity becomes more united as a result. And when its activity is united, many things act simultaneously.

53   You may ask: If the union of matter and form at the upper extreme occurs because they seek union, why does separation spread to the lower extreme? Know that as matter descends and becomes dense, it multiplies, divides, and separates; this causes the form to multiply, divide, and separate. Nevertheless, when you look at all the separate things below, you find all of them, though separate, seeking to mingle and unite; this mingling at the lowest extreme corresponds to the union at the highest extreme. I say in general that all separate and distinct things in the upper and lower regions, i.e., individuals, species, genera, specific differences, properties, accidents, and all the contraries and contradictories – yearn for reception, long for agreement, and seek union. They combine despite their separateness, and they agree despite their distinctness, by means of a thing that retains, combines, and makes them agree with each other.

[66] On this tripartite numbering of intellects, see Alexander Altmann and Stern, *Isaac Israeli*, p. 31.

The general principle here is that unity dominates everything, permeates everything, and retains everything.

54   If the existence, quiddity, quality, and likeness of universal matter and universal form have been demonstrated for you, as well as whatever [additional] knowledge may be obtained of them, and if you examine and observe them carefully, you will consider matter as if it were an open book, or a tablet on which lines are traced, and form as if it were the traced figures and letters, arranged to provide their reader with utmost knowledge and wisdom. And when my essence has encompassed them, and I have comprehended their wonders, it is as if I find myself desiring and longing to see the tracer of this wonderful form, and the creator of this noble form.

55   It is impossible to ascend to the first and supreme substance, but it is difficult [though possible] to ascend to what is near it. Hence I say that matter and form are two closed gates that intellect finds it difficult to open and enter through, inasmuch as intellect is below them, and the substance of intellect is composed of them. Whoever possesses a subtle soul, and whose intellect is so pure that it is able to permeate them, and to enter through them, has already reached the end, and has become a spiritual and divine [being], rejoicing in what is near perfection. His movement will cease, and his joy will endure.

56   There are three sources and principles of this science: the first is the science of matter and form; the second is the science of active word, i.e., will; the third is the science of the first substance. Whoever is able to comprehend these three universal sciences has encompassed all things through his science to the best of human intellect's ability. There will be nothing left him to seek in these sciences, for everything falls under them.

57   The difference between movement and word is that the latter is a force that pervades spiritual substances providing them with knowledge and life, whereas the former is a force that pervades corporeal substances providing them with activity and passivity. For word, i.e., will, after having made matter and form, and having become connected to them, like the connection of soul to body, spreads through them, and stays with them. It permeates from the superior to the inferior.

58   The proof that will exists, and that it is something else besides matter and form, is taken from the movement that is in will, as well as its shadow and rays. This movement is found in corporeal substance

and spreads through it. But it does not belong to corporeal substance, having permeated it from the spiritual substances. It is impossible for this movement to be in corporeal substance as it is in spiritual substance for corporeal substance does not possess the receptive power possessed by spiritual substance, because of its distance from the source, as I have told you several times. It is impossible also for will to be in the lower of spiritual substances as it is in the higher of them.

59   Hence, in spiritual and corporeal substances, will has different degrees of permeation and impression, corresponding to the difference in substances with respect to superiority and inferiority, proximity and distance, spirituality and corporeality. The cause of the variations in the activity of will may be attributed to the matter that receives the activity, not to the will itself, as we mentioned several times.[67] From this statement it follows that will produces existence (which is the universal form that supports all) in the material of the intellect *timelessly*. The way universal will produces universal form in the matter of the intellect may be likened to the way particular form, i.e., particular intellect, produces the particular intelligible form. That is to say: intellect infuses this form in the soul and brings it to her timelessly. Likewise, [will] produces life and self-movement in the matter of the soul. It produces local movement and the rest of the movements in the matter of nature and what is below it. All these movements are transmitted from will, and will transmits them. It follows accordingly that all substances, spiritual and corporeal, are moved by will. The way will moves all spiritual substances, and the corporeal substances moved by them, may be likened to the way the will of the soul moves bodies, or to the movement of one of its limbs, like the heart, when the soul judges that the thing needs to move. Thus, if this movement, i.e., the movement that spreads through all substances from will, differs in strength and in weakness, that is because of the diversity of substances that receive it, not because of any difference in itself, as I mentioned.

60   To define will is impossible, but it may be described approximately as follows: a divine faculty that acts upon matter and form by connecting them, and which permeates from the higher to the lower, as the soul permeates and spreads throughout the body. It is the mover of everything, and it governs it.

---

[67] See 5.18 above.

61   Matter and form are like body and air in the soul and the light. Will joins itself to them and connects them, and permeates in them, like soul in body, light in air, and intellect in soul. For when will permeates in the matter of the intellect, spreads through it, and penetrates it totally, then by means of it this matter knows and apprehends the forms of everything. And when will permeates in the matter of soul, spreads through it, and penetrates it totally, then by means of it this matter lives and moves, and apprehends forms according to its ability and degree [of closeness] to the source of Truth and origin of form. And when will permeates further in the matter of nature and corporeal matter and penetrates it, each one of these receives power, movement, figure, and form, according to its capacity.

62   Active will may be likened to[68] a writer, the produced form to writing, and the matter that is their substratum to tablet and page. Now since will is a spiritual faculty, indeed, above spirituality, it doubtlessly spreads through matter and encompasses it at the same time as does form. You should compare this with the manner in which the psychic faculty, i.e., the faculty of sight that resembles light, spreads through the air and unites with sunlight. Will may be likened to this faculty, form to light, and matter to air. For this reason we say that the Creator (blessed and exalted be He) exists in everything, for will, which is His faculty, is transmitted to everything and enters everything, and nothing is empty of it. For through it everything exists and is sustained. Do you not see that everything is sustained through matter and form, and that matter and form is sustained by will, which produces, combines, and retains them? Even though we say that form retains matter, we say this metaphorically, because form receives from will the faculty by which it retains matter. The explanation of this is as follows: form is the impression made by unity, the faculty of retention belongs to unity, and will is the faculty of unity. Therefore, the faculty of retention belongs to will. But will retains matter through the intermediary of form; accordingly, we say that form retains matter, for form is intermediate between matter and will, and it receives from will and provides for matter. Therefore, just as will permeates [everything] and is transmitted from the First Source, matter and form permeate [everything] at the same time. It and they are found in everything, and nothing is empty of them.

---

[68] Lit. 'is of the rank of,' here and throughout the paragraph.

63   Will permeates everything without movement and acts on everything timelessly because of its great force and unity. To understand this
more easily, represent how intellect and soul acts without movement or
time, and represent also how light suddenly permeates without movement or time, although it is corporeal and sensible. Now since matter is
dense and remote from the source of unity, it is too remote to receive the
impression of the will that acts immediately, without movement and time.
It follows accordingly that matter moves as a result of will in time.

64   Will is the source of the form of intellect, which is the perfect
form. And will is the agent of everything, and the mover of everything.
The way in which the Creator (blessed and exalted be He) creates things,
I mean to say, the way in which form emerges from the first thing, i.e.,
the will, and flows into matter, may be likened to the way in which water
gradually flows from its sources on what is near to it. The former, however,
is without interruption and cessation, without time and movement. One
can liken the way in which form, when it proceeds from the will, makes an
impression upon matter, to the way that a spectator makes an impression
upon a mirror. For matter, according to this simile, receives the form
from the will in the way that a mirror receives the form of the spectator,
i.e., without matter receiving the very essence of that which provides him
the form. One can liken it to the way that sense receives the form of the
sensible without receiving its hylic matter, for sense receives the form of
the sensible without receiving its hylic matter, just as intellect receives
the form of the intelligible without receiving its hylic matter – and just as
everything acts upon something else through the form the agent impresses
upon the recipient.

65   You may ask: Why is the soul so deprived of wisdom's impressions
that it must instruct itself and remember? Know that the soul is created
with true wisdom, from which it follows that it possesses, by virtue of itself,
its own, proper knowledge. But when the soul unites, mixes, and mingles
with [corporeal] substance, it becomes too remote to receive those impressions. These impressions are now concealed within it – for the shadows
of substance cover it and dim its light; its substance becomes dense. It is
like a transparent mirror whose reflection[69] becomes murky, and whose
substance becomes dense, when it comes into contact with a murky and
dense substance. That is why the Creator (blessed and exalted be He)

---

[69] Lit.: 'light.'

formed substance, i.e., the world, and let it run as He had established it. He prepared soul with senses so that through them it apprehends sensible figures and forms to such an extent, that it also apprehends intelligible figures and forms, and it emerges from the potential to the actual. Hence we say that the ascent to the knowledge of secondary substances and accidents is by way of the knowledge of primary substances and accidents.[70] From this follows the proposition that sense-knowledge leaves no impression on the soul except what we have mentioned, and that the soul, when it apprehends the sensible, resembles a man who looks at things in order to see them: when he turns from them, nothing remains except the sight of the image and the thought.

66   The profit that accrues to the soul when it connects to the sensibles consists in its purity, clarity, and emergence from the potential to the actual in the manner that I discussed previously, i.e., the knowledge of secondary substances and accidents by way of the knowledge of primary substances and accidents.

67   Matter corresponds to [First] Substance, I mean that the former is created by the latter. Form corresponds to an attribute of substance,[71] I mean, wisdom and unity, although [strictly speaking, first] substance is not described by an attribute that is other than its essence. That is the difference between the agent and the acted upon. For the agent is one substance, and the acted upon is two substances, namely, matter and form. The explanation of this is as follows: First Substance (blessed be He) and His attribute are a true unity without any variation. But matter and form are variable, for they are at the farthest reach of the impression of unity. By "farthest reach" I mean the beginning of its action, for they are the first things that follow it. You can infer this also from the multiplicity that befalls form as substance moves away from the source of unity. Allow me to explain: intellect's matter is more strongly united with form and more simple than soul's matter, which is more strongly united with form and more simple than the nature's matter, and this continues until one arrives at body, where there is more diversity and multiplicity. But even at the degree of body [there are variations], for the sphere's body is more strongly united [with form] and more simple than the elements' bodies.

---

[70] I.e., the intellectual knowledge of species and genera via the sense-knowledge of particulars.

[71] Wisdom is called here an attribute of substance/essence, although, strictly speaking, there is no distinction between attribute and substance/essence in First Substance. As usual, *'ezem* is translated 'substance' or 'essence,' depending upon context.

And the higher of the elements is more strongly united [with form] and more simple than the lower. This serves as proof that universal matter and universal form are adjacent to unity, by being the immediate products of origination.[72] But in nature matter receives the form of unity as a distinct and separate thing, because the one is subject and the other predicate.

68   It follows from what was previously stated that First Substance (blessed be He) exists in a certain way[73] that distinguishes it [essentially] from all other things. It follows that a substance precedes from it in a certain way, namely, matter and form. This procession occurs of necessity, though the sages called matter 'possibility' because in it is the possibility to receive form, i.e., to be covered in its light. This necessity is subordinate to will, for will is superior to form.[74]

69   Form comes from above and matter receives it below, i.e., matter is a substratum in the sense that it exists below form, and form is supported by it. The proof is that the giver of form is above all things, from which follows that the receiver of form is below it. Moreover [First Substance] is the truly Existent, thereby implying that existence flows from It. Hence, the closer an existent is to the source of existence, its light will be stronger and its existence more permanent. Sense testifies to this, for substance is more worthy of [being attributed with] existence than is accident; and quantity is more worthy of [being attributed with] existence than is quality.

70   Matter receives form from First Substance through the intermediary of will, which is the giver of the form that resides and dwells in it. The proof that will is something other than form is the latter's need of a mover, estimator, and divider, as well as other matters that serve as a proof for will.

71   I have already compared for you creation to the flow of water from its source, and the reflection of the form in a mirror. You may also liken creation to the word which man pronounces. For when a man pronounces a word, its form and its meaning is impressed upon the ear and the intellect of the hearer. According to this simile it is said that the Creator (blessed and exalted be He) pronounced a word, and its meaning is impressed upon the essence of matter, which preserves it, i.e., created form is impressed and imprinted upon matter. Sound corresponds to universal matter, for sound is a universal matter that supports all particular sounds that support

---

[72] Hence they are virtually indistinguishable in this form.   [73] Lit.: 'attribute.'
[74] The procession of existence from First Substance is necessary by virtue of the divine will.

tones, movements, and stops. The external form is the form of speech that is heard, which is divided into particular forms that are supported by each particular matter – by particular matters I mean tones. The internal form is the meaning which the word signifies. Each of these things needs an agent for its being and existence.

72   From all the above it has been demonstrated that nothing besides matter and form exist in created things. It has been demonstrated that movement is a force that is transmitted from will, and will is a divine force that permeates everything, as light permeates air, soul permeates body and intellect permeates soul.

73   You should always strive to understand the essence of universal matter and universal form in abstraction from each other, as well as the diversity that accrues to form, and how it is transmitted and permeates absolute matter, and how it proceeds to all substances according to their rank. Discriminate matter from form, form from will, will from movement. Make a true distinction between each one of them in your intellect. When you cognize this correctly, your soul will be refined, and your intellect will be purified and will permeate the world of intellect. Then your gaze will encompass the universal matter and form, and matter with all its forms will be to you as a book resting in your hands. You will look at all its descriptions, and you will contemplate its figures in your mind. Then you will be hopeful of knowing what follows it. The aim of all this is to know the world of Divinity, which is the maximum totality. Whatever is below this is insignificant in comparison. There are two ways to achieve this noble knowledge. The first is through the knowledge of the will insofar as it [flows into all matter and form. The second is through the knowledge of the will insofar as it][75] encompasses matter and form, which is the most exalted power, and which is not invested with anything material or formal. The way to ascend to the knowledge of the power that is separate from anything material or formal is by conjoining with the power that wears matter and form, and by ascending by means of this power, level after level, one reaches its principle and its root. The select fruit of this effort is the salvation from death and the attachment to the source of life.

[75] Based on the Latin text.

3

Moses Maimonides, from *The Guide of the Perplexed*

[Part I Chapter 73]

A call upon the reader's attention

Know, you who studies this Treatise: if you are of those who know the soul and its powers and have acquired true knowledge of everything as it really is, you already know that imagination exists in most living beings. As for the perfect animal, I mean the one endowed with a heart, the existence of imagination in it is clear. Accordingly, man is not distinguished by having imagination; and the act of imagination is not the act of the intellect but rather its contrary. For the intellect divides composite things and differentiates their parts and makes abstractions of them, represents them to itself in their true reality and with their causes, and apprehends from one thing very many notions, which differ for the intellect just as two human individuals differ in regard to their existence for the imagination. It is by means of the intellect that the universal is differentiated from the individual, and no demonstration is true except by means of universals. It is also through the intellect that essential predicates are discerned from accidental ones. None of these acts belongs to the imagination. For the imagination apprehends only that which is individual and composite as a whole, as it is apprehended by the senses; or compounds things that in their existence are separate, combining one with another: the whole being a body or a force of the body. Thus someone using his imagination imagines a human individual having a horse's head and wings and so on. This is what is called a thing invented and false, for nothing existent corresponds to it at all. In its apprehension, imagination is in no way able to hold itself aloof from matter, even if it turns a form into the extreme of abstraction. For this reason there can be no critical examination in the imagination.

Hear what the mathematical sciences have taught us and how capital are the premises we have obtained from them. Know that there are things that a man, if he considers them with his imagination, is unable to represent to himself in any respect, but finds that it is as impossible to imagine them as it is impossible for two contraries to agree; and that afterwards the existence of the thing that is impossible to imagine is established by demonstration as true, and existence manifests it as real. Thus if you imagine a big sphere of any size you like, even if it be the size of the encompassing heaven; imagine further a diameter passing through the center of the sphere; and thereupon imagine the two human individuals standing upon the two extremities of the diameter so that their feet are put in a straight line with respect to the diameter, so that their feet and the diameter form one and the same straight line – then one of two possibilities must be true: either the diameter is parallel to the horizon or it is not. Now if it is parallel, both individuals should fall. If it is not parallel, one of them – namely the lower one – should fall, while the other is firmly placed. It is in that way that imagination would apprehend the matter. Now it has been demonstrated that the earth is spherical in form and that portions of the inhabited part of it lie at both extremities of its diameter. Thus the head of every individual from among the inhabitants of the two extremities is near heaven while his feet are near the feet of another individual who is opposite him. It is thus impossible in every way that either of them would fall. This cannot even be represented to oneself; for one of them is not placed above and the other below, but each of them is both above and below in relation to the other. Similarly it has been made clear in the second book of the "Conic Sections"[1] that two lines, between which there is a certain distance at the outset, may go forth in such a way that the farther they go, this distance diminishes and they come nearer to one another, but without it ever being possible for them to meet even if they are drawn forth to infinity and even though they come

---

[1] Appolonius, *Conic Sections* 2, theorem 13. On this passage see Gad Freudenthal, "Maimonides' *Guide of the Perplexed* and the transmission of the mathematical tract *On Two Asymptotic Lines* in the Arabic, Latin, and Hebrew medieval traditions," *Vivarium* 26 (1988): 113–40.

nearer to one another the farther they go. This cannot be imagined and can in no way enter within the net of the imagination. Of these two lines, one is straight and the other curved, as has been made clear there in the above-mentioned work.

Accordingly it has been demonstrated that something that the imagination cannot imagine or apprehend and that is impossible from its point of view, can exist. It has similarly been demonstrated that something the imagination considers as necessary is impossible – namely, that God, may He be exalted, should be a body or a force in a body. For according to the imagination, there is nothing existent except a body or a thing in a body.

Accordingly it is clear that there is something else by means of which that which is necessary, that which is admissible, and that which is impossible, can be discerned, something that is not the imagination. How excellent is this speculation and how great its utility for him who wishes to awaken from this dormancy, I mean the state of following the imagination! Do not think that the Mutakallimūn[2] are not aware of anything concerning this point. On the contrary, they are aware of it to a certain extent; they know it and call that which may be imagined while being at the same time impossible – as for instance God's being a body – a fantasy and a vain imagining. And often they clearly state that fantasies are false. For this reason they have recourse to the nine premises we have mentioned,[3] so as to be able to establish with their help the truth of this tenth premise – which asserts the admissibility of those imaginings that they wanted to be declared admissible – in order to maintain the similarity of the atoms to one another and the equality of the accidents with respect to "accidentality," as we have made clear.[4]

Consider, you who are engaged in speculation, and perceive that a method of profound speculation has arisen. For with regard to particular mental representations, one individual claims that they are intellectual representations, whereas another affirms that they are imaginative representations. We wish consequently to find something that would enable us to distinguish the things cognized intellectually from those imagined. For if the philosopher says, as he does: That which exists is my witness and

---

[2] The Muslim dialectical theologians. On them see the Introduction.

[3] 1. Atoms exist. 2. A vacuum exists. 3. Time is composed of instants. 4. Substance cannot exist without accidents. 5. Accidents inhere in atoms. 6. Accidents do not endure for two instants of time. 7. Habits and privations are both accidents requiring an efficient cause. 8. Only substances and accidents exist, and natural forms are accidents. 9. Accidents do not inhere in other accidents.

[4] E.g., accidents like 'living' or 'rational' are no less accidental than 'white' or 'musical.'

by means of it we discern the necessary, the possible, and the impossible; the adherent of the Law says to him: The dispute between us is with regard to this point. For I claim that what exists – which was made in virtue of will and was not a necessary consequence – could have been made in a different way, unless intellectual representation decides, as you think it decides, that something different from what exists at present is not admissible. This is the chapter of admissibility. And about that I have something to say, which you will hear in various passages of this Treatise. It is not something one hastens to reject in its entirety with nonchalance.

[Part II Chapter 13]

There are three opinions of human beings, namely, of all those who believe that there is an existent Deity, with regard to the eternity of the world or its production in time.

The first opinion, which is the opinion of all who believe in the Law of Moses our Master, peace be on him, is that the world as a whole – I mean to say, every existent other than God, may He be exalted – was brought into existence by God after having been purely and absolutely nonexistent, and that God, may He be exalted, had existed alone, and nothing else – neither an angel nor a sphere nor what subsists within the sphere. Afterwards, through His will and His volition, He brought into existence out of nothing all the beings as they are, time itself being one of the created things. For time is consequent upon motion, and motion is an accident in what is moved. Furthermore, what is moved – that is, that upon the motion of which time is consequent – is itself created in time and came to be after not having been. Accordingly one's saying: God "was" before He created the world – where the word 'was' is indicative of time – and similarly all the thoughts that are carried along in the mind regarding the infinite duration of His existence before the creation of the world, are all of them due to a supposition regarding time or to an imagining of time and not due to the true reality of time. For time is indubitably an accident. According to us it is one of the created accidents, as are blackness and whiteness. And though it does not belong to the species of quality, it is nevertheless, generally stated, an accident necessarily following upon motion, as is made clear to whoever has understood the discourse of Aristotle on the elucidation of time and on the true reality of its existence.

We shall expound here a notion that, though it does not belong to the purpose that we pursue, is useful with regard to it. This notion is as

follows. What caused the nature of time to be hidden from the majority of
the men of knowledge so that that notion perplexed them – like Galen and
others – and made them wonder whether or not time had a true reality
in that which exists, is the fact that time is an accident subsisting in an
accident. For the accidents that have a primary existence in bodies, as
for instance colors and tastes, can be understood at the outset and it is
possible to have a mental representation of their notions. But the nature
of the accidents whose substrata are other accidents, as for instance the
glint of a color and the curve and circularity of a line, is most hidden –
more particularly if, in addition, the accident that serves as a substratum
has no permanent state, but passes from one state to another. As a result of
this the matter becomes even more obscure. In time both characteristics
are conjoined. For it is an accident concomitant with motion, the latter
being an accident in that which is moved. Moreover, motion has not the
status of blackness and whiteness, which constitute a permanent state.
For the true reality and substance of motion consist in its not remaining
in the same state even for the duration of the twinkling of an eye. This
accordingly is what has rendered it necessary for the nature of time to be
hidden. The purpose however is that, according to us, time is a created
and generated thing as are the other accidents and the substances serving
as substrata to these accidents. Hence God's bringing the world into existence does not have a temporal beginning, for time is one of the created
things. Consider this matter thoroughly. For thus you will not be attached
necessarily to objections from which it is impossible to escape for anyone
who is not aware of it. For if you affirm as true the existence of time
prior to the world, you are necessarily bound to believe in the eternity [of
the world]. For time is an accident which necessarily must have a substratum. Accordingly it follows necessarily that there existed some thing
prior to the existence of this world existing now. But this notion must be
avoided.

   This is one of the opinions. It is undoubtedly a foundation of the Law
of Moses our Master, peace be on him, and it is second to the foundation
that is the belief in the unity [of God]. Nothing other than this should
come to your mind. It was Abraham our Father, peace be on him, who
began to proclaim in public this opinion to which speculation had led him.
For this reason, he made his proclamation, "in the Name of the Lord,
God of the world" [Gen 21:33]; he had also explicitly stated this opinion
in saying, "Maker of heaven and earth" [Gen. 14:22].

The second opinion is that of all the philosophers of whom we have heard reports and whose discourses we have seen. They say that it is absurd that God would bring a thing into existence out of nothing. Furthermore, according to them, it is likewise not possible that a thing should pass away into nothing; I mean to say that it is not possible that a certain being, endowed with matter and form, should be generated out of the absolute nonexistence of that matter, or that it should pass away into the absolute nonexistence of that matter. To predicate of God that He is able to do this is, according to them, like predicating of Him that He is able to bring together two contraries in one instant of time, or that He is able to create something that is like Himself, may He be exalted, or to make Himself corporeal, or to create a square whose diagonal is equal to its side, and similar impossibilities. It may be understood from their discourse that they say that, just as His not bringing impossible things into existence does not imply a lack of power on His part – since what is impossible has a firmly established nature that is not produced by an agent and that consequently cannot be changed – it likewise is not due to lack of power on His part that He is not able to bring into existence a thing out of nothing, for this belongs to the class of all the impossible things. Hence they believe that there exists a certain matter that is eternal as the Deity is eternal, and that He does not exist without it, nor does it exist without Him. They do not believe that it has the same rank in what exists as He, may He be exalted, but that He is the cause of its existence; and that it has the same relation toward Him as, for instance, clay has towards a potter or iron towards a smith; and that He creates in it whatever He wishes. Thus He sometimes forms out of it a heaven and an earth, and sometimes He forms out of it something else. The people holding this opinion believe that the heaven too is subject to generation and passing-away, but that it is not generated out of nothing and does not pass away into nothing. For it is generated and passes away just as the individuals that are animals are generated from existent matter and pass away into existent matter. The generation and passing-away of the heaven is thus similar to that of all the other existents that are below it.

The people belonging to this sect are in their turn divided into several sects. But it is useless to mention their various sects and opinions in this Treatise. However, the universal principle held by this sect is identical with what I have told you. This is also the belief of Plato. For you will find that Aristotle in the "Physics" relates of him that he, I mean Plato, believed that the heaven is subject to generation and passing-away.[5] You likewise will also find his doctrine plainly set forth in his book *Timaeus*. But he does not believe what we believe, as is thought by him who does not examine opinions and is not precise in speculation; he [the interpreter] imagines that our opinion and his [Plato's] opinion are identical. But this is not so. For as for us, we believe that the heaven was generated out of nothing after a state of absolute nonexistence, whereas he believes that it has come into existence and has been generated from some other thing. This then is the second opinion.

The third opinion is that of Aristotle, his followers, and the commentators of his books. He asserts what also is asserted by the people belonging to the sect that has just been mentioned, namely, that something endowed with matter can by no means be brought into existence out of that which has no matter. He goes beyond this by saying that the heaven is in no way subject to generation and passing-away. His opinion on this point may be summed up as follows. He thinks that this being as a whole, such as it is, has never ceased to be and will never do so; that the permanent thing not subject to generation and passing-away, namely, the heaven, likewise does not cease to be; that time and motion are perpetual and everlasting and not subject to generation and passing-away; and also that the thing subject to generation and passing-away, namely, that which is beneath the sphere of the moon, does not cease to be. I mean to say that its first matter is not subject in its essence to generation and passing-away, but that various forms succeed each other in it in such a way that it divests itself of one form and assumes another. He thinks furthermore that this whole higher and lower order cannot be corrupted and abolished, that no innovation can take place in it that is not according to its nature, and that no occurrence that deviates from what is analogous to it can happen in it in any way. He asserts – though he does not do so textually, but this is what his opinion comes to – that, in his opinion, it would be an impossibility that God's will should change or a new volition arise in Him; and that all that exists has been brought into existence, in the state in which it is at present, by God through His volition; but that it was not produced after having been in a state of nonexistence. He thinks that just as it is impossible that the Deity should become nonexistent or that His essence should

---

5 This may be a reference to *Physics* 251b17ff., as Pines notes, but there the discussion is the createdness of time. Of course, Maimonides' references to Aristotle are, at best, to the Arabic versions of his works.

undergo a change, it is impossible that a volition should undergo a change in Him or a new will arise in Him. Accordingly it follows necessarily that this being as a whole has never ceased to be as it is at present and that will be as it is in the future eternity.

This is a summary and the truth of these opinions. They are the opinions of those according to whom the existence of the Deity for this world has been demonstrated. Those who have no knowledge of the existence of the Deity, may He be held sublime and honored, but think that things are subject to generation and passing-away through conjunction and separation due to chance and that there is no one who governs and orders being, are Epicurus, his following, and those like him, as is related by Alexander [of Aphrodisias]. It is useless for us to mention these sects. For the existence of the Deity has already been demonstrated, and there can be no utility in our mentioning the opinions of groups of people who built their doctrine upon a foundation the reverse of which has been demonstrated as true. Similarly it is useless for us to wish to prove as true the assertion of the people holding the second opinion, I mean that according to which the heaven is subject to generation and passing-away. For they believe in eternity; and there is, in our opinion, no difference between those who believe that heaven must of necessity be generated from a thing and pass away into a thing and the belief of Aristotle who believed that it is not subject to generation and corruption. For the purpose of every follower of the Law of Moses and Abraham our Father or of those who go the way of these two is to believe that there is nothing eternal that exists simultaneously with God; to believe also that the bringing into existence of a being out of nonexistence is for the Deity not an impossibility, but rather an obligation, as is deemed likewise by some[6] of the men of speculation.

After we have expounded those opinions, I shall begin to explain and summarize the proofs of Aristotle in favor of his opinion and the motive that incited him to adopt it.

[Part II, Chapter 14]

I do not need to repeat in every chapter that I compiled this Treatise for your benefit only because of my knowledge of your achievements. I do not need to set forth in every passage the text of the discourse of the philosophers, but only their intentions. I shall not write at length, but

[6] Or, one.

only draw your attention to the methods that they aim at, as I did for you regarding the opinions of the Mutakallimūn. I shall pay no attention to anyone who besides Aristotle has engaged in speculative discourse, for it is his opinions that ought to be considered. And if there are good grounds for refuting him or raising doubt with regard to these opinions as to some point on which we make a refutation or raise doubts, these grounds will be even firmer and stronger with respect to all the others who disagreed with the fundamental principles of the Law.

I say then that Aristotle asserts that motion is not subject to generation and passing-away – he means motion in the absolute sense. For he says that if a motion is produced in time, it should be considered that every-thing that is produced in time is preceded by a certain motion, namely, that consisting in its passage to actuality and its being produced after it had been nonexistent. Consequently a motion exists, namely, the motion by means of which the latter motion was brought into being. Conse-quently the first motion must of necessity be eternal or else the series will go on to infinity. Likewise in conformity with this principle, he asserts furthermore that time is not subject to generation and passing-away. For time is consequent upon, and attached to, motion, and there is no motion except in time; and again time cannot be intellectually con-ceived except through motion, as has been demonstrated. This is a method of his by means of which the eternity of the world is necessarily inferred.

A second method of his: He asserts that the first matter, which is common to the four elements, is not subject to generation and passing-away. For if the first matter were subject to generation, it would have to have a matter out of which it would be generated. It would follow necessarily that the generated matter would have to be endowed with form, for the latter is the true reality of generation. But we have assumed that the matter in question was matter that is not endowed with form. Now such matter necessarily must not be generated from some thing. It is consequently eternal and not liable to be destroyed. These considerations too render obligatory the eternity of this world.

A third method of his: He asserts that the matter of the heaven as a whole has no contraries, for circular motion has no contrary, as has been made clear; and there are contraries only in rectilinear motion, as has been demonstrated. He asserts further that in everything that passes away, the cause of its passing-away consists in there being contraries in it. Accordingly, as there are no contraries in the sphere, it is not subject to passing-away.

Now what is not subject to passing-away is likewise not subject to generation. He thus stated several propositions in an absolute manner and explained them. These propositions are:

Everything that is subject to generation is subject to passing-away.
Everything that is subject to passing-away is subject to generation.
Everything that has not been generated will not pass away.
Everything that will not pass away has not been generated.

This too is a method that renders obligatory the eternity of the world, which he wishes to establish.

A fourth method: He asserts that with respect to everything that is produced in time, the possibility of its being produced precedes in time the production of the thing itself. Similarly with respect to everything that changes, the possibility of its changing precedes in time the change itself. From this premise he inferred that circular motion is perpetual, without beginning and end. His later followers in their turn made it clear by means of this premise that the world was eternal. They said: Before the world came into being, its production in time must have been either possible or necessary or impossible. Now if it was necessary, the world could not have been nonexistent. If its production in time was impossible, it could not be true that it ever would exist. And if it was possible, what was the substratum for this possibility? For there indubitably must be an existent thing that is the substratum of this possibility and in virtue of which it is said of the thing that it is possible. This is a very powerful method for establishing the eternity of the world. However, an intelligent man from among the later Mutakallimūn thought that he had solved this difficulty. He said: Possibility resides in the agent and not in the thing that is the object of action. This, however, is no reply, for there are two possibilities. For with respect to everything produced in time, the possibility of its being produced precedes in time the thing itself. And similarly in the agent that produced it, there is the possibility to produce that which it has produced before it has done so. These are indubitably two possibilities: a possibility in the matter to become that particular thing, and a possibility in the agent to produce that particular thing. These are the most important of

97

the methods followed by Aristotle in establishing the eternity of the world by starting from the world itself.

There also are methods set forth by those who came after him, methods that they derived from his philosophy and by which they established the eternity of the world by starting from the Deity, may His name be sublime.

One of them is as follows. They say that if God, may His name be sublime, has produced the world in time after its having been nonexistent, God must have been an agent in potency before He had created the world; and after He had created it, He became an agent who has acted. God had therefore passed over from potentiality to actuality. Consequently there had been in Him, may He be exalted, a certain possibility and there indubitably must have been in His case something that caused Him to pass over from potentiality into actuality. This also is a great difficulty. Every intelligent man ought to reflect concerning its solution and the disclosing of its secret.

Another method. They say: An agent acts at one time and does not act at another only because of the impediments or incentives that may supervene upon him or in him. For the impediments may render necessary the non-accomplishment of a certain action that the agent wishes to accomplish, and on the other hand the incentives may render necessary a certain wish that the agent did not have before. Now as the Creator, may His name be sublime, has no incentives necessitating the alteration of a will, nor hindrances or impediments that supervene and cease to exist, there is no reason in respect of which He should act at one time and not act at another; but on the contrary His action exists, just as His permanence does, as something actual.

Another method. They say: His acts, may He be exalted, are most perfect; there is nothing in them that is a defect; there is nothing in them that is without an object or is supererogatory. This is the notion always reiterated by Aristotle,[7] who says that nature is wise and does not do anything without an object and that it does everything in the most perfect possible way. They say accordingly: It follows from this that the existent in question is the most perfect existent that is and that it does not serve an end beyond it. Consequently it is necessary that it should perpetually

---

[7] Cf. *Nichomachean Ethics* 1253a9, *On the Parts of Animals* 695b18.

exist, for His wisdom is perpetual, as is His essence; or rather His essence is His wisdom, which has required the existence of this existent.

All the arguments of the believers in the eternity of the world that you may encounter are ramifications of these methods and stem from one of them.

They also say, in order to prove that the opposed doctrines are disgraceful: How could the Deity, may He be honored and sublime, be idle and not do a thing in any respect whatever or cause a happening to take place in the course of the perdurable pre-eternity, so that whereas He did not do a thing throughout the duration of His existence – which is eternal and unending – He inaugurated that which exists when yesterday came? For if you were to say, for instance, that God created many worlds before this one – their number being that of the mustard seeds required to fill the globe of the ultimate sphere – and that each of these worlds has remained in existence a number of years equal to that of the mustard seeds required to fill it, this, in respect to its status compared to His infinite existence, may He be exalted, would have been as if you were to say that God created the world yesterday. For as soon as we affirm the inauguration of that which exists after nonexistence, there is no difference between one's positing that this happened hundreds of thousands of years ago or at a very recent time. Accordingly this is also a way by means of which those who believe in the eternity of the world prove the incongruity of the opposed doctrines.

They also argue through drawing an inference from what was universally admitted in the past among all nations. For this necessitates that this belief is natural and not conventional and that for this reason there was a general consensus regarding it. Thus Aristotle[8] says: All men explicitly affirm the perpetuity and permanence of the heavens. And when they became aware that they were not subject to coming-about and passing-away, they asserted that they were the dwelling-place of God, may He be exalted, and of the spiritual beings – he means to say, of the angels. They attributed the heavens to Him in order to indicate their perpetuity. He also sets forth other points of this kind concerning this subject in order to buttress the opinion, which according to him speculation has shown to be true, by means of universally admitted beliefs.

---

[8] Both Munk and Pines refer the reader to *De Caelo* 270b5ff., but Aristotle's point there is different, at least according to our text, and also according to the Arabic text of Badawi.

[Part II Chapter 15]

My purpose in this chapter is to make it clear that Aristotle possesses no demonstration that the world is eternal, as he understands this. Moreover he is not mistaken with regard to this. I mean to say that he himself knows that he possesses no demonstration with regard to this point, and that the arguments and the proofs that he sets forth are merely such as occur to the mind and to which the soul inclines. Alexander [of Aphrodisias] thinks that they involve a lesser number of doubts. However, Aristotle cannot be supposed to have believed that these statements were demonstrations, for it was Aristotle who taught mankind the methods, the rules, and the conditions of demonstration.

What led me to speak of this is the fact that the latter-day followers of Aristotle believe that Aristotle has demonstrated the eternity of the world. Most of the people who think they philosophize follow Aristotle as an authority in this question and think that everything that he has mentioned constitutes a cogent demonstration about which there can be no doubt. They regard it as disgraceful to disagree with him or to suppose that some concealed point or some false imagining in one of the issues has remained hidden from him. For this reason I thought fit to challenge their opinion on this issue with regard to their opinion and to explain to them that Aristotle himself did not claim to have a demonstration in this question. Thus he says in the *Physics*: "All the physicists preceding us believe that motion is not subject to generation and passing-away, except Plato, who believes that motion is subject to generation and passing-away, and the heaven too according to him is subject to generation and passing-away."[9] This is literally what he says. Now it is certain that if there had been cogent demonstrations with regard to this question, Aristotle would not have needed to buttress his opinion by means of the fact that the physicists who preceded him had the same belief as he had. Nor would he have needed to make all the assertions he makes in that passage concerning the vilification of those who disagree with him and the worthlessness of their opinion. For when something has been demonstrated, the consensus of all knowledgeable men does not increase its correctness nor strengthen one's certainty about it. Nor could its correctness be diminished and certainty regarding it be weakened even if all the people on earth disagreed with it.

[9] *Physics* 251b15ff. The quotation is not exact (Pines).

You will find likewise that Aristotle in *The Heaven and the World*, when embarking upon the explanation that the heavens are not subject to generation and passing-away, states:[10]

"Now after this we wish also to investigate the heavens. We shall accordingly say: Do you regard them as generated from some thing, or not; are they liable to pass away or can they not at all pass away?" After assuming this question to have been posed, he desired to mention the arguments of those who assert the heavens to be generated, and accordingly continues literally as follows. He says: "If we do this our words will be more acceptable for, and more worthy of approval by, those who proceed correctly in speculation, and more particularly if they have first heard the arguments of those who disagree with us. For if, without mentioning the arguments of those who disagree with us, we only mention our opinion and our arguments, these would appear too weak to be accepted by the listeners. It behooves him who wishes to judge according to the truth not to be hostile to those who disagree with him, but to be friendly to, and equitable toward, them – meting out the same measure in granting that their arguments were correct as he would with regard to his own arguments."

This is literally the discourse of the man.

Consequently, O community of people who are engaged in speculation, after this introduction, can any blame remain attached to that man, and can anyone think after reading these words that he had found a demonstration with regard to this question? For can anyone, much less Aristotle, imagine that the readiness to accept a thing that is demonstrated would be feebler if the arguments of those who disagree with it were not heard first? Moreover, there is the fact that he stated that this doctrine [of the eternity of the world] was an opinion and that his proofs in favor of it were mere arguments.

Can Aristotle have been ignorant of the difference between mere arguments and demonstrations, or between demonstrations and opinions which, when considered, may be accepted to a greater or lesser extent, and things of demonstration? Furthermore, does one need in demonstration that rhetorical statement, which he has made by way of introduction, that one should be equitable towards the adversary in order to strengthen one's opinion? No; rather his whole purpose is to make it clear that his

---

[10] Cf. *De Caelo* 279b4ff. (The citations are very close to the Arabic version edited by Badawi [Cairo, 1961], pp. 196–7.)

opinion is more correct than the opinions of those who disagree with him – that is, those who claim that philosophic speculation leads to the belief that the heavens are subject to generation and passing-away, but that they have never been nonexistent, or that they have been generated but will not pass away, and whatever other of these opinions he mentions. Now this is indubitably correct. For his opinion is closer to being correct than the opinions of those who disagree with him in so far as inferences are made from the nature of what exists. However, we do not think so, as I shall make clear. But passions get the better of all sects, even of the philosophers. Consequently the latter wish to establish as a fact that Aristotle produced a demonstration with regard to this question. Perhaps, according to their opinion, Aristotle produced a demonstration with regard to this question without being aware of having done so, so that people noticed it only subsequently. As for me, I have no doubt that none of the opinions mentioned by Aristotle with regard to these subjects – I mean such opinions as that concerning the eternity of the world and that concerning the cause of the difference of the motions of the spheres and the ordered arrangement of the intelligences – are demonstrated. And Aristotle never at any time had the fantasy that what he said in this connection constituted a demonstration. On the contrary, he thought, as he says, that the gates of the ways to inferential reasoning on these matters are closed before us and that we have at our disposition no principle pertaining to them from which to start to draw inferences. You know the text of his words, which reads as follows:[11] "As for the matters concerning which we have no argument or that are too great in our opinion, it is difficult for us to say: 'Why is this so?' For instance, when we say: 'Is the world eternal or not?' " This is literally what he says. However, you know Abū Naṣr's [al-Fārābī] interpretation of this example,[12] his clarification of it, as well as the fact that he considered disgraceful the notion that Aristotle could have doubted of the eternity of the world. He had an extreme contempt for Galen because of the latter's saying that this was an obscure question with regard to which no demonstration is known. As Abū Naṣr holds, it is clear and manifest, being proved by demonstration, that the heavens are eternal whereas that which is within them is subject to generation and passing-away.

---

[11] *Topics* 104b15ff.

[12] This is possibly from al-Fārābī's commentary (*sharḥ*) on the *Topics*, mentioned by an-Nadīm in the *Fihrist*; however, it is not extant.

To sum up: Nothing in the methods that we have set forth in this chapter is capable either of establishing an opinion as correct or of proving it false or of arousing doubts with regard to it. And we have advanced the things we have only because we know that the majority of those who consider themselves as perspicacious, even though they have no understanding of anything in the sciences, decide simply that the world is eternal through acceptance of the authority of men celebrated for their science who affirm its eternity, whereas they reject the discourse of all the prophets, because their discourse does not use the method of scientific instruction, but that of imparting reports coming from God. Only a few whose understanding is acute have been guided aright through this second method. As for what we desire in regard to the subject of the creation of the world according to the opinion of our Law, I shall speak of it in chapters that will follow.

[Part II Chapter 16]

This is a chapter in which I shall explain to you what I believe with regard to this question. After that I shall give proofs for what we desire to maintain. I say then with regard to all that is affirmed by those Mutakallimūn who think that they have demonstrated the newness of the world, that I approve of nothing in those proofs and that I do not deceive myself by describing as demonstrations methods that produce errors. If a man claims that he sets out to demonstrate a certain point by means of sophistical arguments, he does not, in my opinion, strengthen assent to the point he intends to prove, but rather weakens it and opens the way for attacks against it. For when it becomes clear that those proofs are not valid, the soul weakens in its assent to what is being proved. It is preferable that a point for which there is no demonstration remain a problem or that one of the two contradictory propositions simply be accepted. I have already set forth for your benefit the methods of the Mutakallimūn in establishing the newness of the world, and I have drawn your attention to the points with regard to which they may be attacked. Similarly all that Aristotle and his followers have set forth in the way of proof of the eternity of the world does not constitute in my opinion a cogent demonstration, but rather arguments subject to grave doubts, as you shall hear. What I myself desire to make clear is that it is not impossible that the world was created in time, according to the opinion of our Law – an opinion that I have already explained – and that all those philosophic proofs from which it seems that the matter is different from what we have stated, all those arguments have a certain point through which they may be invalidated and the inference drawn from them against us shown to be incorrect. Now inasmuch as this is true in my opinion and inasmuch as this question – I mean to say that the eternity of the world or its creation in time – becomes an open question, it should in my opinion be accepted without proof because of prophecy which explains things to which it is not in the power of speculation to accede. For as we shall make clear, prophecy is not set at nought even in the opinion of those who believe in the eternity of the world.

After I have made it clear that what we maintain is possible, I shall begin to make it prevail likewise, by means of speculative proof, over any other affirmations; I refer to my making prevail the assertion of creation in time over the assertion of eternity. I shall make it clear that just as a certain disgrace attaches to us because of the belief in the creation in time, an even greater disgrace attaches to the belief in eternity. I shall now start to bring into being a method that shall render void the proofs of all those who prove by inference the eternity of the world.

[Part II Chapter 17]

In the case of everything produced in time, which is generated after not having existed – even in those cases in which the thing's matter was already in existence, and in the course of the thing's production it had merely put off one form and had taken on another – the nature of that particular thing after it has been produced in time, has attained its final state, and achieved stability, is different from its nature when it is being generated and is beginning to pass from potentiality to actuality. It is also different from the nature that the thing had before it had moved so as to pass from potentiality to actuality. For example, the nature of the feminine seed, which is the blood in the blood vessels, is different from the nature of this seed as it exists in the state of pregnancy after it has encountered the masculine sperm and has begun to move toward the transition from potentiality to actuality. And even at the latter period, its nature is different from the nature of an animal that, after having been born, achieves perfection.

No inference can be drawn in any respect from the nature of a thing after it has been generated, has attained its final state, and has achieved stability in its most perfect state, to the state of that thing while it moved towards being generated. Nor can an inference be drawn from the state of the thing when it moves towards being generated to its state before it begins to move thus. Whenever you err in this and draw an inference from the nature of a thing that has achieved actuality to its nature when it was only in potency, grave doubts are aroused in you. Moreover, things that must exist become impossible in your opinion, and on the other hand things that are impossible become necessary in your opinion. Consider the following example we have constructed. A man of a most perfect natural disposition is born and his mother dies after she suckled him for several months. And the man, alone in an isolated island, takes upon himself the entire upbringing of him who is born until he grew up, became intelligent, and acquired knowledge. Now this child had never seen a woman or a female of one of the species of the other animals. Accordingly he puts a question, saying to a man who is with him: How did we come to exist, and in what way were we generated? Thereupon the man to whom the question is put replies: Every individual among us was generated in the belly of an individual belonging like us to our species, an individual who is female and has such and such a form. Every individual human being, when small in body, was within the belly; it was moved and fed there, and grew up little by little – since it was alive – until it reached such and such limit to its size. Thereupon an opening was opened up for it in the lower part of the body, from which it issued and came forth. Thereupon it does not cease growing until it becomes such as you see that we are. Now the orphaned child must of necessity put the question: Did every individual among us – when it was little, contained within a belly, but alive and moving and growing – did it eat, drink, breathe through the mouth and nose, produce excrements? He is answered: No. Thereupon he indubitably will hasten to set this down as a lie and will produce a demonstration that all these true statements are impossible, drawing inferences from perfect beings that have achieved stability. He will say: If any individual among us were deprived of breath for the fraction of an hour, he would die and his movements would cease. How then can one conceive that an individual among us could be for months within a thick vessel surrounding him, which is within a body, and yet be alive and in motion? If one of us were to swallow a sparrow, that sparrow would die immediately upon entering the stomach, and all the more the underbelly. Every individual among us would undoubtedly perish within a few days if he did not eat food with his mouth and drink water; how then can an individual remain alive for months without eating and drinking? Every individual among us, if he had taken food and had not given off excrements, would die in very great pain within a few days; how then could the individual in question remain for months without giving off excrements? If the belly of one of us were perforated, he would die after some days; how then can it be supposed that the navel of the fetus in question was open? How is it that he does not open his eyes, put out his palms, stretch his feet, while all the parts of his body are whole and have no defect as you thought? Similarly all the analogies will be carried on in order to show that it is in no respect possible that man should be generated in that manner.

Consider this example and reflect upon it, you who are engaged in speculation, and you shall find that this is exactly our position with regard to Aristotle. For we, the community of the followers of Moses our Master and Abraham our Father, may peace be on them, believe that the world was generated in such and such manner and came to be in a certain state from another state and was created in a certain state, which came after another state. Aristotle, on the other hand, begins to contradict us and to bring forward against us proofs based on the nature of what exists, a nature that has attained stability, is perfect, and has achieved actuality. As for us, we declare against him that this nature, after it has achieved stability and perfection, does not resemble in anything the state it was in while in the state of being generated, and that it was brought into existence from absolute nonexistence. Now what argument from among all that he advances holds good against us? For these arguments necessarily concern only those who claim that the stable nature of that which exists, gives an indication of its having been created in time. I have already made it known to you that I do not claim this.

Now I shall go back and set forth for your benefit the principles of his methods and shall show you that nothing in them of necessity concerns us in any respect, since we contend that God brought the world as a whole into existence after nonexistence and formed it until it has achieved perfection as you see it. He said that the first matter is subject to neither generation nor passing-away, and he began to draw inferences in favor of this thesis from the things subject to generation and passing-away and to make clear that it was impossible that the first matter was generated. And this is correct. For we do not maintain that the first matter is generated as man is generated from the seed or that it passes away as man passes away into dust. But we maintain that God has brought it into existence from nothing and that, after being brought into existence, it was as it is now – I mean everything is generated from it, and everything generated from it passes away into it; it does not exist devoid of form; generation and corruption terminate in it; it is not subject to generation as are the things generated from it, nor to passing-away as are the things that pass away into it, but is created from nothing. And its Creator may, if He wishes to do so, render it entirely and absolutely nonexistent.

We likewise say the same thing of motion. For he [Aristotle] has inferred from the nature of motion that motion is not subject to generation and passing-away. And this is correct. For we maintain that after motion has come into existence with the nature characteristic of it when it has become stable, one cannot imagine that it should come into being as a whole and perish as a whole, as partial motions come into being and perish. This analogy holds good with regard to everything that is attached to the nature of motion. Similarly the assertion that circular motion has no beginning is correct. For after the spherical body endowed with circular motion has been brought into being, one cannot conceive that its motion should have a beginning. We shall make a similar assertion with regard to the possibility that must of necessity precede everything that is generated. For this is only necessary in regard to this being that is stabilized – in this being everything that is generated, is generated from some being. But in the case of a thing created from nothing, neither the senses nor the intellect point to something that must be preceded by its possibility. We make a similar assertion with regard to the thesis that there are no contraries in heaven. That thesis is correct. However, we have not claimed that the heavens have been generated as the horse and palm tree are. Nor have we claimed that, because they are composite they must necessarily pass away, as is the case with plants and animals because of the contraries that subsist in them.

The essential point is, as we have mentioned, that a being's state or perfection and completion furnishes no indication of the state of that being preceding its perfection. It involves no disgracefulness for us if someone says that the heavens were generated before the earth or the earth before the heavens, or that the heavens have existed without stars, or that a particular species of animals has existed without another species being in existence. For all this applies to the state of this universe when it was being generated. Similarly in the case of animals when they are being generated, the heart exists before the testicles – a circumstance that may be ocularly perceived – and the veins before the bones; and this is so in spite of the fact that after the animal has achieved perfection, no part of its body can exist in it if any part of all the others, without which the individual cannot possibly endure, does not exist.

All these assertions are needed if the text of Scripture is taken in its external sense, even though it must not be so taken, as shall be explained[13] when we shall speak of it at length. You ought to memorize this notion. For it is a great wall that I have built around the Law, a wall that surrounds it and wards off the stones of all those who project these missiles against it.

However, should Aristotle, I mean to say he who adopts his opinion, argue against us by saying: If this existent provides no indication for us, how do you know that it is generated and that there has existed another nature that has generated it – we should say: This is not obligatory for us in view of what we wish to maintain. For at present we do not wish to establish as true that the world is created in time. But what we wish to establish is the possibility of its being created in time. Now this contention cannot be proved to be impossible by inferences drawn from the nature of what exists, which we do not set at nought. When the possibility of this contention has been established, as we have made clear, we shall go back and we shall make prevail the opinion asserting creation in time.

In this question no way remains open to him except to show the impossibility for the world having been created in time, not by starting from the nature of being, but by starting from the judgments of the intellect with regard to the Deity: these being the three methods that I have mentioned to you before.[14] By means of these methods they wish to prove the eternity of the world, taking the Deity as their starting point. I shall accordingly show you, in a following chapter, how doubts can be cast on these methods so that no proof whatever can be established as correct by means of them.

[Part II Chapter 18]

The first method they mention is the one through which, in their opinion, we are obliged to admit that the Deity passed from potentiality to actuality inasmuch as He acted at a certain time and did not act at another time.

The way to destroy this doubt is most clear. For this conclusion necessarily follows only with regard to everything composed of matter, which is endowed with possibility, and of form. When such a body acts in virtue of

---

[13] Cf. *Guide* II, 30. [14] See above, pp. 98–9.

its form after not having acted, there is indubitably in it something that was in potency and afterwards made the transition into actuality. Accordingly it undoubtedly must have undergone the action of something causing it to make this transition. For this premise has been demonstrated only with regard to things endowed with matter. On the other hand, that which is not a body and is not endowed with matter, has in its essence no possibility in any respect whatever. Thus all that it has is always in actuality. Accordingly with regard to it, their contention does not necessarily follow; and it is not impossible with regard to it that it acts at a certain time and does not act at another time. For in a being separate from matter, this does not imply change or a passage from potentiality to actuality.

A proof of this is provided by the Agent Intellect[15] as it is conceived by Aristotle and his followers. For the Agent Intellect, on the one hand, is separate from matter; and, on the other, it acts at a certain time and does not act at another time, as Abū Naṣr has explained in his treatise *On the Intellect*.[16] For there he has set down a statement that runs literally as follows. He says: It is clear that the Agent Intellect does not always act; rather it acts at a certain time and does not act at another time. This is literally what he says, and it is clearly true. But even if this is so, it cannot be said that the Agent Intellect undergoes change or that it was acting potentially and became actual, because it did at a certain time what it did not do before. For there is no relation between bodies and that which is not body, and no resemblance in any respect either at the time of their acting or at the time of their abstention from acting. In fact the acts of forms endowed with matter and the acts of a separate being are both called 'act' only by equivocation. Hence it does not follow that if a separate being does not accomplish at a certain time the act that it accomplishes later on, it has passed from potentiality to actuality, as we find it to follow in the case of forms endowed with matter.

Perhaps, however, someone may think that this speech contains something misleading. For if the Agent Intellect necessarily acts at a certain time and does not act at another time, this does not result from a certain cause subsisting in its essence, but from the disposition of the portions of matter. For its action is perpetual with regard to all things properly disposed. Hence if there is an obstacle to this action, this results from a

---

[15] The last of the series of incorporeal intellects, the Agent Intellect is instrumental in the generation and corruption of sublunar existing things, as well as the process of human intellection.

[16] Cf. al-Fārābī, *Risāla fi'l-ʿAql*, ed. M. Bouyges (Beirut, 1938), p. 32.

material disposition and not from the Intellect in itself. He who thinks thus should know that our purpose is not to give information as to the cause for which God, may He be exalted, has acted at a certain time and has not acted at another time. We did not pursue this example to a conclusion; we did not say that just as the Agent Intellect acts at a certain time and does not act at another time, though it be separate from matter, so God, may He be exalted, can do the same. We have not said this nor drawn this conclusion. If we had done this, it would indeed have been misleading.[17] But the conclusion that we have drawn – and this conclusion is correct – is that though the Agent Intellect, which is not a body or a force in a body, acts at one time but does not perform "the same action" at another time – whatever the cause of this may be – it is not said of it that it has passed from potentiality to actuality; nor is it said that there subsists possibility in its essence or that it needs something causing it to make the transition from potentiality to actuality. Thus we are relieved from this great doubt that has been raised against us by him who affirms the eternity of the world. For as for us, we believe that He, may He be exalted, is neither a body nor a force in a body; and hence it does not follow that He changes if He acts after not having acted.

The second method is the one in which eternity is shown to be necessary because there do not subsist for Him, may He be exalted, any incentives, supervening accidents, and impediments. It is difficult to resolve this doubt, and the solution is subtle. Hear it.

Know that every agent endowed with will, who performs his acts for the sake of something, must of necessity act at a certain time and not act at another time because of impediments or supervening accidents. To take an example: a man, for instance, may wish to have a house but does not build it because of impediments – if the building materials are not at hand or if, although they are at hand, they have not been prepared for receiving the form because of the absence of tools. Sometimes, too, both the materials and the tools are at hand, but the man does not build because he does not wish to build since he can dispense with a shelter. If, however, accidents like heat or cold supervene, he is compelled to seek a shelter, whereupon he will wish to build. It has thus become clear that supervening accidents may change the will and that impediments may

[17] It would have been misleading because what inhibits the action of the Agent Intellect, so that it appears to act at one time and not at another, is a material disposition in a body. But clearly that explanation will not work for God's acting to create the world out of nothing

oppose the will in such a way that it is not executed. All this, however, occurs only when acts are in the service of something that is external to the essence of the will. If, however, the act has no purpose whatever except to be consequent upon will, that will has no need of incentives. And the one who wills is not obliged, even if there are no impediments, to act always. For there is no external end for the sake of which he acts and that would render it necessary to act whenever there are no impediments preventing the attainment of the end. For in the case envisaged, the act is consequent upon the will alone.

Somebody might object: All this is correct, but does not the supposition that one wishes at one time and does not wish at another time imply in itself a change? We shall reply to him: No, for the true reality and the quiddity of will means: to will and not to will. If the will in question belongs to a material being, so that some external end is sought thereby, then the will is subject to change because of impediments and supervening accidents. However, in the case of a being that is separate from matter, its will, which does not exist in any respect for the sake of some other thing, is not subject to change. The fact that it may wish one thing now and another thing tomorrow does not constitute a change in its essence and does not call for another cause; just as the fact that it acts at one time and does not act at another does not constitute a change, as we have explained. It shall be explained later on that it is only by equivocation that our will and that of a being separate from matter are both designated as 'will,' for there is no likeness between the two wills. Thus this objection has likewise been invalidated and it has been made clear that no incongruity necessarily follows for us in consequence of this method. As you know this was what we desired to achieve.

The third method: It is the one in which they argue the eternity of the world to be necessary because everything, with regard to which Wisdom decides that it should come forth, comes forth at the very moment of the decision. For His wisdom is eternal as is His essence, and consequently that which necessarily proceeds from it is likewise eternal. This is a very feeble way of going on to an obligatory conclusion. For in the same way as we do not know what was His wisdom in making it necessary that the spheres should be nine – neither more nor less – and the number of the stars equal to what it is – neither more nor less – and that they should be neither bigger nor smaller than they are, we do not know what was His wisdom in bringing into existence the universe at a recent period after it had not existed. The universe is consequent upon His perpetual and immutable wisdom. But we are completely ignorant of the rule of that wisdom and of the decision made by it. For, in our opinion, volition too is consequent upon wisdom; all these being one and the same thing – I mean His essence and His wisdom – for we do not believe in attributes. You shall hear much about this notion, when we shall speak of providence. By looking at the matter in this way, this disgracefulness is thus abolished.

As for Aristotle's remark that the nations were agreed in past time that the angels dwell in heaven and that the Deity is in heaven – something similar occurs in the external meaning of the scriptural texts – this does not serve as an indication of the eternity of the heavens, as he wishes to consider it. But this has been said because it serves as an indication that the heaven proves to us the existence of the separate intellects, who are the spiritual beings and the angels, and the heaven proves to us the existence of the Deity, who is its mover and its governor, as we shall explain. We shall make it clear that there is no proof indicating to us the existence of the Maker, according to our opinion, like the indication deriving from the heaven. The latter also proves, as we have mentioned, according to the opinion of the philosophers, the existence of the Mover of the heaven and His not being either a body or a force subsisting in a body.

After having explained to you that our contention is possible and not – as is thought by him who affirms the eternity of the world – an impossibility, I shall return in the following chapters to explain that our opinion can be shown, by means of speculation, to outweigh the other in the scales and to make manifest the disgraceful consequences necessarily deriving from his opinion.

[Part II Chapter 19]

It is clear to you from the doctrine of Aristotle, as well as from that of everyone who affirms the eternity of the world, that in his view that which exists has proceeded from the Creator in virtue of a necessity; that He, may He be exalted, is a cause and this world an effect and it was necessary that this should be so. Just as one does not ask with regard to Him, may He be exalted, why He exists or how He exists thus – I mean to say as One and incorporeal – so it may not be asked with regard to the world as a whole why it exists or how it exists thus. For all this, both the cause and the effect, exist thus necessarily, and it is not possible for them in any respect not to exist or to change the way they exist. Hence it follows necessarily from this opinion that of necessity everything must remain permanently as it is according to its nature, and that nothing can change as far as its nature is concerned. For, according to this opinion, it is impossible that a thing from among the existents should change as far as its nature is concerned. Accordingly no thing has come into being through the purpose of One who purposes, and who chose freely and willed that all things should be as they are. For if they had come into being in virtue of the purpose of One possessing purpose, they would not have existed thus before they were purposed.

Now as for us, the matter is clear in our opinion: namely, that all things exist in virtue of a purpose and not of necessity, and that He who purposed them may change them and conceive another purpose, though not absolutely any purpose whatever. For the nature of impossibility is stable and cannot be abolished, as we shall make clear.

My purpose in this chapter is to explain to you, by means of arguments that come close to being a demonstration, that what exists indicates to us of necessity that it exists in virtue of the purpose of One who purposed; and to do this without having to take upon myself what the Mutakallimūn have undertaken – to abolish the nature of that which exists and to adopt atomism, the opinion according to which accidents are perpetually being created, and all their principles, which I have explained to you and which they only wished to use as an introduction in order to establish the method of particularization. Do not think that they have also said what I shall say. On the other hand, there is no doubt that they wished what I wish. They have also mentioned the same things that I shall mention and observed in them particularization. But in their opinion there is no difference between plants particularized through being red rather than white, or through being sweet rather than bitter, or between the heavens being particularized through having the shape they have instead of having been made square or triangular. They have established particularization by means of their premises, which you already know. I, on the other hand, shall establish particularization regarding the things with respect to which it ought to be established by means of philosophic premises derived from the nature of that which exists.

I shall explain this method after first setting forth this premise: In every case in which things differing in any way from one another possess a common matter, there must of necessity be a cause other than, and different from, the common matter – a cause that rendered it necessary that some of the things have a certain attribute, others have a different one. Or there may be several causes according to the number of the things differing from one another. This premise is unanimously accepted both by those who believe in the eternity of the world and by those who believe in its having come into being in time. After having set forth this premise, I shall begin to explain what I wanted to explain by means of questions and answers concerning Aristotle's opinion.

We put a question to Aristotle, saying to him: You have demonstrated to us that the matter of everything that is beneath the sphere of the moon is one and common to everything. What then is the cause of the differences between the individuals of every species?

Then he gives us an answer to this, saying: The cause of the differences lies in changes in the mixture of the compounds that are composed of this matter. For this common matter has in the first place received four forms, each of which determines two qualities. In virtue of these four qualities, matter was transformed into elements for that which is composed of it. For these elements were first mixed through the action of the motion of the sphere and then they combined. Consequently, the differences in the compounds representing a mixture of the elements came about through the differing measures of the warm, the cold, the humid, and the dry. For in virtue of these various combinations, various dispositions to receive various forms come about in the compounds. Again through these forms, the compounds become disposed to receive other forms. And this continues constantly in this manner. Again the matter of the specific form, which is one, has great latitude with regard to quantity and quality, and the individuals of the species differ in a way corresponding to this latitude, as has been elucidated in the natural science. All this is correct and clear to whoever treats his own soul equitably and does not deceive it.

Thereupon we again put a question to Aristotle, saying to him: Since the mixture of the elements is the cause of the various matters being predisposed to receive the various forms, what is it that prepared this first matter so that a part of it receives the form of fire and part of it the form of earth and that which is intermediate between these two parts is prepared to receive the forms of water and of air, while at the same time the matter of the universe is one and common to all things? Why is the matter of earth more fitted for the form of earth and the matter of fire for the form of fire?

Thereupon Aristotle gave an answer to this, saying: This has been made necessary by the differences between the various places, for these differences have made it necessary for this one matter to have various dispositions. For the part that is near the encompassing sphere, was endowed by the latter with an impress of subtlety and swiftness of motion and nearness to the nature of the sphere. Consequently it received, in virtue of this disposition, the form of fire. And the more distant matter is from the encompassing sphere in the direction of the center of the earth, the thicker and denser and less luminous it becomes, so that it becomes earth. The same cause obtains with regard to water and air. Thus this is necessary; for it is absurd that the matter in question should not be in a place, or that the encompassing sphere should be the center of the earth, and the center of the earth the encompassing sphere. This has been made necessary by the particularization of matter by means of various forms; I mean by this the disposition to receive various forms.

Thereupon we put a question to him, saying: Is the matter of the encompassing sphere – I mean to say the heavens – the same as the matter of the elements?

He said: No. That is another matter and those are other forms. And the term 'body,' applied to the bodies that are with us and to the heavenly bodies, is equivocal, as has been explained by latter-day thinkers. All this has been demonstrated.

From here on listen, you who are engaged in the study of this my Treatise, to what I shall say. You already know Aristotle's demonstration that the difference of forms may be inferred from the difference of acts. Consequently, inasmuch as the motions of the four elements are rectilinear and the motion of the sphere is circular, it is known that the matter of these elements is not the matter of the sphere. And this is correct according to natural speculation. And as you have also found that the elements whose motions are rectilinear differ from one another with regard to direction – some of them moving upwards and the others downwards – and as it has likewise been found that in considering those that move in the same direction, one is quicker and the other is slower, it is known that the elements differ with regard to their forms. And thereby it is known that there are four elements. If one has recourse to this very kind of inference, it also follows necessarily that the matter of all the heavenly spheres is one, as all of them have circular motion, and that the form of every sphere is different from that of every other sphere, as one moves from the East

to the West and another from the West to the East and as they also differ
in their rapidity or slowness.

Accordingly the following question should be put to him, and it should
be said to him: Inasmuch as the matter in question is common to all the
heavenly spheres and, on the other hand, since every substratum in them
has been particularized so as to receive a certain form other than the forms
received by the others, who is it that has particularized these substrata
and has predisposed them to receive various forms? Is there beyond the
sphere something else to which this particularization can be attributed
except God, may He be cherished and exalted?

Here I shall call your attention to the depth of Aristotle's penetration
and to his extraordinary apprehension, and to the extent to which this
objection undoubtedly pressed hard upon him so that he wished to escape
from it by recourse to means in which the nature of that which exists did
not help him. Even though he does not mention this objection, it appears
from what he says that he wished to bring order for our benefit into the
being of the spheres, as he has brought order for us into the existence
of that which is beneath the sphere. He wished to do this in order that
the whole should exist in virtue of natural necessity and not in virtue
of the purpose of one who purposes according to his will whatever it
be and the particularization of one who particularizes in whatever way he
likes. Now this task has not been accomplished by him, nor will it ever
be accomplished. For he wished to give a cause for the fact that the sphere
moves from the East and not from the West; and he wished to give a cause
for the fact that some of them are swift of motion and others slow and
that this is necessary because of the order of their position with regard to
the highest sphere. He also wished to give a cause for the fact that every
planet from among the seven has a number of spheres, while this great
number of fixed stars is to be found in one sphere. He wished to assign
causes for all this so that these things would be ordered for us in a natural
order that is due to necessity.

However, he has accomplished none of these undertakings. As a matter
of fact, all that he has explained to us regarding what is beneath the sphere
of the moon follows an order conforming to that which exists, an order
whose causes are clear. One can say of it that it derives of necessity from
the motion and the powers of the sphere. On the other hand, one can say of
all that he has stated with regard to matters pertaining to the sphere, that
he has assigned no clear cause with regard to this, and that the matter,

as he sets it out, does not follow an order for which necessity can be claimed. For we see that in the case of some spheres, the one that moves more swiftly is above the less swift; that in the case of others, the one that moves more slowly is above the swifter; and that, again in another case, the motions of the spheres are of equal velocity though one be above the other. There are also other very grave matters if regarded from the point of view that these things are as they are in virtue of necessity. I shall deal with these points in a special chapter of this Treatise.[18]

To sum up: It was undoubtedly when Aristotle realized the feebleness of what he said in setting forth and expounding the ground and the causes of these things, that he prefaced his starting upon these investigations with a statement that runs literally as follows: Now we desire to make a sufficient inquiry into two questions. For it is obligatory for us to inquire into them and to speak concerning them according to the capacity of our intellects, our knowledge, and our opinion. However, no one ought to attribute this undertaking to overboldness and temerity on our part, but rather should our desire and ardor for philosophy be admired. When, therefore, we seek out noble and important questions and are able to propound for them – though it be only to some small extent – a well-founded solution, it behooves the hearer to feel great joy and jubilation.[19] This is literally what he says. It has thus become clear to you that he was indubitably aware of the feebleness of those assertions; and all the more so since the science of mathematics had not been perfected in his time and since the motions of the sphere were not known in his time to the extent to which we know them today.

It appears to me that his assertion in the *Metaphysics*[20] that a separate intellect should be supposed for every sphere is also made with a view to the notion in question: namely, in order that there should be something that would particularize every sphere by means of some motion with which it would be endowed. We shall explain later on that he gains nothing by this. With regard to his saying in the text that I have set out for you, "according to the capacity of our intellects, our knowledge, and our opinion": I shall explain to you the meaning of this, a meaning that I have not seen set forth

[18] Cf. below, pp. 132–7.

[19] Cf. *De Caelo* 291b24ff. The citation is quite close to the Arabic version, ed. Badawi, pp. 274–5 (cf. n.1 on p. 274, where Badawi cites a marginal variant. The variant is also found in the passage cited here by Maimonides).

[20] Cf. *Metaphysics* 1074a15.

by any of the commentators. When saying "our opinion," he has in mind the point of view of necessity that is represented by the affirmation of the eternity of the world. When saying "our knowledge," he has in mind the clear and generally accepted point that each of those things certainly has a cause and ground, and that it is not a thing that happens by chance. When saying "our intellects," he has in mind our incapacity to assign causes for things of such perfection and accomplishment. But he deemed that to a small extent these might be assigned, and he did this. For his statement regarding the rapidity of the universal motion and the slowness of the sphere of the fixed stars because of its opposite direction has recourse to a strange and bizarre cause. Similarly he says that as the distance of a sphere from the eighth sphere is greater, its motion is more rapid. However, this is not consistently so, as I have made clear to you. There is something even more striking: namely, that there are spheres beneath the eighth that move from the East to the West. These consequently must be more rapid than what is beneath them and likewise moves from the East to the West, even though the rapidity of the motion of the latter spheres moving from the East is near to that of the motion of the ninth sphere. However, as I have let you know, the science of astronomy was not in his time what it is today.

Know that on the basis of our opinion, that is, the opinion of the community of those who affirm the production of the world in time, all this becomes easy and is consistent with our principles. For we say that there is a being that has particularized, just as it willed, every sphere in regard to its motion and rapidity; but we do not know in what respect there is wisdom in making these things exist in this fashion. Now if Aristotle had been able – as he thought – to give us the cause for the differences between the motions of the spheres, so that these differences would correspond to the relative position of the spheres in relation to each other, this would have been extraordinary. In that case the cause of particularization would have been constituted by the differences between the motions of the spheres, just as the cause of the differences between the elements lies in their various positions between the encompassing sphere and the center of the earth. However, things are not ordered thus, as I have explained to you.

A fact that makes even more clear than what has been said about the existence of particularization in the sphere, and with regard to which no one would be able to find a cause particularizing it other than the purpose of one who purposes, is the existence of the stars. For the fact that a sphere is always in motion and a star is always fixed proves that the matter of the stars is not the matter of the spheres. In fact Abū Naṣr in his glosses on the *Physics*[21] has made a statement of which the literal text is as follows. He said: There is a difference between a sphere and the stars, for a sphere is transparent whereas the stars are not transparent. The cause for this lies in the fact that there is a difference between the two matters and the two forms. But this difference is small. This is literally the text of his statement. I, however, do not say "small," but say that they are very different. For I do not infer this from the fact of transparency but from the motions. Accordingly it has become clear to me that there are three kinds of matter and three kinds of forms: the bodies that are always by themselves at rest – these are the bodies of the stars; the bodies that are always in motion – these are the bodies of the spheres; the bodies that are sometimes in motion and sometimes at rest – these are the elements. Would that I knew what made the two kinds of matter between which there is either an extreme difference (this is what it appears to be to me), or a small difference (as is stated by Abū Naṣr), and who has provided the kinds of matter in question with the dispositions necessary for this union.

To sum up: It would be a strange thing that there should be two different bodies, one of which, being fixed in, but not mixed with, the other, should be localized in the latter in a particular place and attached to this second body; and that this should come about without its having been produced through the purpose of one who purposed it. And it is even stranger that there should exist the numerous stars that are in the eighth sphere, all of which are globes, some of them small and some big, one star being here and another at a cubit's distance according to what seems to the eye, or ten stars being crowded and assembled together while there may be a very great stretch in which nothing is to be found. What is the cause that has particularized one stretch in such a way that ten stars should be found in it and has particularized another stretch in such a way that no star should be found in it? Again the body of the whole sphere is one simple body in which there are no differences. What accordingly can be the cause for the fact that a certain part of the sphere should be more fitted to receive the particular star found in it than another part? All this and everything that

---

[21] No longer extant.

is of this sort would be very unlikely or rather would come near to being impossible if it should be believed that all this proceeded obligatorily and of necessity from the Deity, as is the opinion of Aristotle.

If, however, it is believed that all this came about in virtue of the purpose of who purposed to make this thus, that opinion would not be accompanied by a feeling of astonishment and would not be at all unlikely. And there would remain no other point to be investigated except if you were to say: What is the cause for this having been purposed? What is known may be epitomized as follows: All this has been produced for an object that we do not know and is not an aimless and fortuitous act. In fact you know that the veins and nerves of any individual dog or ass have not happened fortuitously, nor are their measures fortuitous. Neither is it by chance that one vein is thick and another thin, that one nerve has many ramifications and another is not thus ramified, that one descends straight down and another is bent. All this is as it is with a view to useful effects whose necessity is known. How then can one who uses his intellect imagine that the positions, measures, and numbers of the stars and the motions of their various spheres are without an object or are fortuitous? There is no doubt that all of these things are necessary according to the purpose of one who purposes.

On the other hand, the supposition that all these things have been ordered in virtue of necessity and not in virtue of a purpose is very remote indeed from being conceivable. To my mind there is no proof of purpose stronger than the one founded upon the differences between the motions of the spheres and upon the fact that the stars are fixed in the spheres. For this reason you will find that all the prophets used the stars and the spheres as proofs that the Deity exists necessarily. Thus in the traditional story of Abraham, there occurs the tale, which is generally known, about his contemplation of the stars. Again Isaiah, calling attention to the conclusions to be drawn from the stars, says: "Lift up your eyes on high, and see: who hath created these?" and so on [Isa. 40:26]. Jeremiah says similarly: "He made the heavens" [Cf. Jer. 32:17, 10:12, and 51:15]. Abraham says: "The Lord, the God of the heavens" [Gen. 24:7]. And the chief of the prophets says: "Who rides upon the heaven" [Deut. 33:26], an expression we have explained.[22] This is the correct proof, which is not exposed to doubt.

[22] *Guide* I, 70.

The explanation thereof is as follows: With regard to all the differences in the things beneath the sphere and even though the matter subsisting in these things is one, as we have explained, you can make out that they were particularized through the powers of the sphere and through the various positions of matter with regard to the sphere, just as Aristotle has taught us. But who is the one who particularized the differences that are found in the spheres and the stars unless it be God, may He be exalted? If, however, someone says that the separate intellects did it, he gains nothing by saying this. The explanation of this is as follows: The intellects are not bodies, which they would have to be in order to have a local position in relation to the sphere. Why then should one particular sphere move in its motion induced by desire toward its separate intellect in an eastern direction, and another in a western? Do you consider that one particular intellect is to be found in an eastern direction and another in a western? Then there is the fact that one sphere is relatively slower, while another is more rapid; and this, as you know, does not correspond to the relations obtaining between the distances of the various spheres from each other. Thus, of necessity, one cannot avoid saying that the nature and substance of that particular sphere require that its motion be in a certain direction and with a certain velocity and that a necessary concomitant of its desire for a certain notion should manifest itself in this manner. And this is what Aristotle says and explicitly states.

We have accordingly come back to the point we were dealing with at first. Accordingly we shall say: If the matter of all the spheres is one and the same, in virtue of what thing has any sphere been so particularized as to receive a nature other than the nature of any other sphere? How then is there to be found in that sphere a certain desire, different from the desire of that other sphere, that obliges one sphere to move in this direction and the other to move in another direction? There must of necessity be something that particularizes them. This examination has thus conducted us to the investigation of two problems, one of which may be stated as follows: Is it of necessity obligatory or not, considering the existence of these differences, that these should be due to the purpose of one who purposed and not due to necessity? The second problem may be stated as follows: Supposing that all this is due to the purpose of one who purposed and who particularized the spheres in this way, is it obligatory that this should have been produced after its having been nonexistent, or is it not obligatory so that He who particularizes has never ceased doing this? This second opinion has also been affirmed by some[23] of those who believe in the eternity of the world. In the following chapters I shall begin to treat of these two problems, and I shall explain what is necessary to explain concerning them.

[Part II Chapter 20]

Aristotle demonstrates regarding all natural things that they do not come about by chance – his demonstration being, as he has stated it: the fortuitous things do not occur either always or in the majority of cases;[24] the natural things, however, occur either always or in the majority of cases. Thus the heavens and all that is in them remain always in certain states that do not change, as we have explained, either in their essences or through change of place. As for the natural things that are beneath the sphere of the moon, some of them occur always and others in the majority of cases. Instances of what occurs always are the heating action of fire and the falling-down of a stone, while instances of what occurs in the majority of cases are the shapes and acts of the individuals of every species. All this is clear. Now if the particular things of the world are not due to chance, how can the whole of it be due to chance? This is , a demonstration proving that these beings are not due to chance. Here is the text of the statement of Aristotle in his refutation of those of his predecessors who believed that this world has happened to come about by chance and spontaneously, without a cause. He says: "Other people have thought that the cause of these heavens and all these worlds is to be sought in their spontaneity. They say that the revolution and the motion that has differentiated and constituted all things according to this order were due ' to their spontaneity. Now this is a point that arouses strong astonishment; I mean the fact that they say concerning animals and plants that they do not come about and are not produced by chance, but have a cause, which is either nature or intellect or some other similar thing – for not any haphazard thing is generated from every seed or sperm, but from this particular seed there comes into being an olive tree and from that sperm a human being – and that at the same time, they say of the heavens and of the bodies that alone are divine among all the visible bodies, that they have come into being spontaneously and that they have no cause at all such as is possessed by the animals and the plants."[25] This is the text of

[23] Or, one.   [24] Cf. *Physics* 196b10ff.   [25] Cf. *Physics* 196a25ff (Pines).

his statement. Then he starts to explain in a more lengthy passage the falsity of these imaginings.

Accordingly it is clear to you that Aristotle believes and demonstrates that none of these beings exist through chance. Now what contradicts their having come into being through chance is their having come into being essentially – I mean their having a cause that renders it necessary for them to come into being in this particular fashion. It is because of this cause that they exist in the way they do. This is what has been demonstrated, and this is what Aristotle believes. But it is not clear to me that Aristotle believes that, because these beings have not come into being spontaneously, it follows necessarily that they have come into being in virtue of the purpose of one who purposed and the will of one who willed. For to me a combination between existing in virtue of necessity and being produced in time in virtue of a purpose and a will – a combination uniting these two – comes near to a combination of two contraries. For the meaning of necessity, as Aristotle considers it, is that everything among the beings, which is not an artifact, cannot but have a cause necessitating that particular thing – a cause that has brought it into being as it is – and that this cause has a second cause and this second cause similarly a third one, until finally a first cause is reached from which everything is necessarily derived. This is so because of the impossibility of an infinite series of causes.

However, he does not believe withal that the necessity in virtue of which the existence of the world is derived from the Creator – I mean to say from the First Cause – is like the necessity in virtue of which shadow is derived from a body or heat from fire or light from the sun, as those say of him who do not understand what he said. Rather he believes that this necessity is somewhat like the necessity of the derivation of an intellectum from an intellect, for the intellect is the agent of the intellectum in respect of its being an intellectum. For the First Cause – though it is, according to him, an intellect of the highest and most perfect rank of being, so that he says that it wills what is necessarily derived from it and rejoices and takes pleasure in it – cannot will anything contrary to this. Now this is not called purpose, and the notion of purpose is not included in it. For a man may will to have two eyes and two hands, and rejoice in having them and take pleasure in it and cannot will anything contrary to this. However, that individual does not have two eyes and two hands because of a purpose on his part and because of his having particularized this shape and these actions. For the notions of purpose and of particularization only apply to a nonexistent thing for which it is possible to exist just as it was purposed and particularized and for which it also is possible not to exist in this fashion. I do not know whether the discourse and speech of Aristotle that these things must necessarily have a cause was understood by certain latter-day men to refer to purpose and particularization, or whether they disagree with him on this and choose the opinion affirming purpose and particularization, deeming that it does not contradict the eternity of the world.

After what we have explained, I shall begin to treat of the opinion of these latter-day men.

[Part II Chapter 21]

Know that among the latter-day philosophers who affirm the eternity of the world there are some[26] who maintain that God, may He be exalted, is the Agent of the world, who chose that it should exist, purposed it, and particularized it so that it should be as it actually is. They think, however, that it is impossible that this should have happened at one particular time rather than at another; according to them the world has always been and will always be like this. They say: What compels us to conceive of an agent as unable to effect a thing, unless the agent precedes the act in time, is the fact that this necessarily happens to us when we effect something. This is so because in every agent of whom this may be predicated, there is a certain privation; accordingly he is at first an agent in potency and, when he acts, he passes into actuality. But the Deity, may He be exalted, in whom there is no privation and nothing at all in potency, does not precede His act, for He has always been an agent in actuality. And just as there is a difference – and what a difference – between His essence and ours, so there is a difference between the relation linking His act and Himself and the relation linking our act and ourselves. They draw the same analogy with regard to particularization and will. For there is no difference between your saying, when treating of this matter: an agent, one who wills, one who purposes, one who chooses freely, or one who particularizes. And they say it is also impossible that His act or His will should change, as we have explained.[27]

It has already become clear to you, who are engaged in the study of this my Treatise, that these people have altered the term 'necessity,' but have

---

[26] Or, one.   [27] Cf. *Guide* II, 13.

let its meaning remain. Perhaps they intended to choose a more beautiful expression or to get rid of one that is shocking. For the meaning of the assertion, as maintained by Aristotle, that this being proceeds necessarily from its cause and is perpetual in virtue of the latter's perpetuity – that cause being the Deity – is identical with the meaning of their assertion that the world derives from the act of the Deity or exists in virtue of His purpose, will, free choice, and particularization, but that it has always been and will always be as it is – just as the sunrise is indubitably the agent of the day, though neither of them precedes the other in point of time. But this is not the meaning of purpose, as we propose to conceive it. For we wish to signify by the term that it – I mean the world – does not necessarily proceed from Him, may He be exalted, as an effect necessarily proceeds from its cause without being able to be separated from it or to change unless its cause or one of its modes also changes. Now if you understand the meaning of the term in this way, it is already known that it is absurd to say that the world necessarily proceeds from the being of the Deity as an effect proceeds from its cause, and it is further known that the world has come about through an act of the Deity or through His particularization.

Accordingly the matter is reduced to this, and the discussion finally leads us to an inquiry concerning the diversity existing in the heavens, with regard to which it has been demonstrated that it must necessarily have a cause. The inquiry concerns the question whether this cause is the ground of this diversity, the latter having necessarily proceeded from the existence of this cause, or whether this cause is the agent that has brought about this diversity and has particularized it in the way in which we, the followers of Moses our Master, believe. We shall speak of this after we have first set forth a preface by which we shall explain to you the meaning of the necessity maintained by Aristotle, so that you should conceive it. Thereupon I shall begin to explain to you, with the help of speculation and philosophic proofs devoid of falsification, my preference in favor of the opinion according to which the world has been produced in time.

When he[28] says that the first intellect necessarily proceeds from God, the second from the first, and the third from the second, and also when he holds that the spheres necessarily proceed from the intellects, and when he sets forth the famous order that you know from various passages in his

[28] I.e., the Aristotelian philosopher.

writings – that order of which we have already expounded a part here – it is clear that he does not wish to signify thereby that first a certain thing was, and then, later, the thing necessarily proceeding from the first thing was produced in time. For he does not say that any of these was produced in time. By the term 'necessity,' he merely means to signify causality; it is as if he said the first intellect is the cause of the existence of the second intellect, the second of the third, and so on till the last of them. The same applies to the discourse concerning the spheres and the first matter; according to him, none of these things precedes in time, or exists without, any of these other things. It is, to take an example, as if someone said that roughness, smoothness, hardness, softness, thickness, and absorbency, necessarily derive from the first qualities. For no one doubts that these qualities – I mean heat, cold, humidity, and dryness – produce roughness, smoothness, hardness, softness, thickness, abssphereency, and other similar qualities. Accordingly they necessarily derive from the four first qualities, even though it is impossible that a body should exist endowed with the four first qualities and devoid of the secondary ones.

It is in an exactly analogous way that Aristotle says, concerning that which exists in general, that in it this particular thing necessarily proceeds from that, and so forth till the series ends with the First Cause, as he himself says, or the first intellect or however you may wish to call it. All of us aim at one and the same principle. But he holds, as I have recounted to you, that everything that is other than it necessarily proceeds from it. We affirm that all these things have been made by Him in virtue of a purpose and a will directed toward this particular being, which did not exist and now became an existent in virtue of His will, may He be exalted. Now I shall begin to set forth in the following chapters my proofs and my preference in favor of the world's having been produced in time according to our opinion.

[Part II Chapter 22]

A proposition universally agreed upon, accepted by Aristotle and by all those who have philosophized, reads as follows: It is impossible that anything but a single simple thing should proceed from a simple thing. If the thing is composite, there may proceed from it several things according to the number of simple things of which the compound is composed. Thus, for instance, what proceeds from fire, in which two qualities – heat and dryness – have combined is the action of heating by means of its heat and that of drying by means of its dryness. Similarly in the case of a thing composed of matter and form, certain things proceed from it in respect to its matter and certain other things in respect to its form, if it is of multiple composition. In accordance with this proposition, Aristotle says that what first proceeded from God was constituted by a single simple intellect only.

A second proposition: Any thing at random does not proceed from any other thing at random, but there subsists necessarily a certain conformity between the cause and its effect. Even in the case of accidents, one accident at random does not proceed from any other accident at random, as would be the case if, for instance, a quantity would proceed from a quality, or a quality from a quantity. Similarly form does not proceed from matter nor matter from form.

A third proposition: Every agent, acting in virtue of purpose and will and not in virtue of its nature, accomplishes many different acts.

A fourth proposition: A whole composed of various juxtaposed substances may more appropriately be termed a composition than a whole composed of various substances that have combined with one another. For instance, a bone, flesh, a vein, a nerve, are simpler than the whole of a hand or that of a foot composed of nerves, flesh, veins, and bones. This is too clear to require additional discourse.

After having set forth these premises, I say: With regard to Aristotle's statement that the first intellect is the cause of the second, the second of the third, and so on – even if there were thousands of steps, the last intellect would indubitably still be simple. How can then something composite have come to exist since, according to Aristotle, composition exists in the beings in virtue of necessity? We shall concede to him all that he says concerning a composition of various notions coming about in the intellects, as their intellecta are multiple, when the intellects get farther away from the First Cause. But even if we grant him this guess and conjecture, how can the intellects be a cause for the procession of the spheres from them? And what relation can there be between matter and that which, being separate, has no matter at all? And supposing that we concede that the cause of every sphere is, in the fashion stated, an intellect – inasmuch as there subsists composition in the intellect, which intellectually cognizes itself and what is other than itself, so that it is as it were composed of two things, from one of which another and lower intellect proceeds, whereas a sphere proceeds from the other – he should still be asked: How does a sphere proceed from the one simple thing from which it proceeds? A sphere is composed of two kinds of matter and two forms: the matter and the form of the sphere itself and the matter and the form of the star fixed in the sphere. Now if this comes about in virtue of a procession, we cannot but require for this compound a composite cause, the procession of the body of the sphere being occasioned by one of its parts and that of the body of the star by the other. This would be so if the matter of the stars were all of it one and the same. However, the substance of the bright stars may be a certain substance and that of the dim ones may be another substance. It is also known that every body is composed of its matter and its form.

Accordingly it has become clear to you that these things do not conform to the conception of necessity that he sets forth. Similarly the diversity of the motions of the spheres does not agree with the order of their arrangement one beneath the other, in such a way that necessity could be claimed in this field. We have already mentioned this.[29] There is, furthermore, another point that ruins everything that has been established with regard to natural things if the state of the heavens is considered. For if the matter of all the spheres is one and the same, why is it not necessary for the form of one particular sphere to be transferred to the matter of another, in accord with what happens beneath the sphere of the moon because of the aptitude of matter? And why is one particular form permanently in one particular matter although the matter of all is common? Unless – by God! – someone asserts that the matter of every sphere is different from that of the others. In that case the form of the motion of the spheres would not be indicative of their matter. This would be the ruin of all principles. Furthermore, if the matter of all the stars is one and the same, what differentiates them as individuals – is it their forms or their accidents? In either case it would be necessary that the forms or accidents in question should be transferred one after the other to each of the stars, so that they receive what they deserve.[30] Hereby it has become clear to you that when we say the matter of the spheres or the matter of the stars, these expressions contain none of the meaning of this matter here,[31] this being a case of the equivocal use of terms; and that

---

[29] Cf. II, 19.
[30] Lit.: 'in order that the merit (*al-'istiḥāl*) not be negated.' Following Munk, Pines translates this, "in order that the aptitude of matter not be set at naught."
[31] I.e., sublunar matter.

every being from among the bodies of the spheres has an existence that is proper to it and that it does not have in common with anything other than itself. How then could it happen that the spheres have in common their circular motion and the stars their fixity?

If, however, we believe that all this has been produced through the purpose of one who purposed, made, and particularized it – as His wisdom, which cannot be grasped, required – none of these questions affects us, whereas they do affect him who claims that all this has come about through necessity and not through the will of one who wills. This is an opinion that does not agree with the order of that which exists, an opinion in favor of which no cause and no new persuasive proof have been brought forward. Withal very disgraceful conclusions would follow upon it. Namely, it would follow that the Deity, whom everyone who is intelligent recognizes to be perfect in every kind of perfection, could, as far as all the beings are concerned, produce nothing new in any of them; if He wished to lengthen a fly's wing or to shorten a worm's foot, He would not be able to do it. But Aristotle will say that He would not wish it and that it is impossible for Him to will something different from what is; that it would not add to His perfection but would perhaps be a deficiency from a certain point of view. I shall sum up for your benefit, and though I know that many men imbued with a partisan spirit shall tax me because of this statement either with having but little comprehension of their argument or with deliberately deviating from it, yet shall I not, because of that, refrain from saying what I in my inadequacy have apprehended and understood. Accordingly this summing-up will be as follows:

Everything that Aristotle has said about all that exists from beneath the sphere of the moon to the center of the earth is indubitably correct, and no one will deviate from it unless he does not understand it or unless he has preconceived opinions that he wishes to defend or that lead him to a denial of a thing that is manifest. On the other hand, everything that Aristotle expounds with regard to the sphere of the moon and that which is above it is, except for certain things, something analogous to guessing and conjecturing. All the more does this apply to what he says about the order of the intellects and to some of the opinions regarding the divine that he believes; for the latter contain grave incongruities and perversities that manifestly and clearly appear as such to all the nations that propagate evil, and that he cannot demonstrate.

Do not criticize me for having set out the doubts that attach to his opinion. You may say: "Can doubts disprove an opinion or establish its contrary as true?" Surely this is not so. However, we shall treat this philosopher as his followers have enjoined us to treat him. For Alexander has explained that, in every case in which no demonstration is possible, the two contrary opinions with regard to the matter in question should be posited as hypotheses, and it should be seen what doubts attach to each of them: the one to which fewer doubts attach should be believed. Alexander says that things are thus with respect to all the opinions regarding the divine that Aristotle sets forth and regarding which no demonstration is possible. For everyone who has come after Aristotle says that what Aristotle stated about them arouses fewer doubts than whatever else might be said about them. We have acted in this way when it was to our mind established as true that, regarding the question whether the heavens are generated or eternal, neither of the two contrary opinions could be demonstrated. For we have explained the doubts attaching to each of the opinions and have shown to you that the opinion favoring the eternity of the world is the one that raises more doubts and is more harmful for the belief that ought to be held with regard to the Deity. And this, in addition to the fact that the world's being produced in time is the opinion of Abraham our Father and our prophet Moses, may peace be on both of them.

As we have mentioned that opinions should be examined by means of the doubts they arouse, I see fit to explain to you something with regard to that.

[Part II Chapter 23]

Know that when one compares the doubts attaching to a certain opinion with those attaching to the contrary opinion and has to decide which of them arouses fewer doubts, one should not take into account the number of the doubts but rather consider how great is their incongruity and what is their disagreement with what exists. Sometimes a single doubt is more powerful than a thousand other doubts. Furthermore this comparison can be correctly made only by someone for whom the two contraries are equal. But whoever prefers one of the two opinions because of his upbringing or for some advantage, is blind to the truth. While one who entertains an unfounded predilection cannot make himself oppose a matter susceptible of demonstration, in matters like those under discussion such an opposition is often possible. Sometimes, if you wish it, you can rid yourself of an unfounded predilection, free yourself of what is habitual, rely solely on speculation, and prefer the opinion that you ought to prefer. However, to do this you must fulfill several conditions.

The first of them is that you should know how good your mind is and that your inborn disposition is sound. This becomes clear to you through training in all the mathematical sciences and through a grasp of the rules of logic. The second condition is to have knowledge of the natural sciences and to apprehend their truth so that you should know your doubts in their true reality. The third condition concerns your morals. For whenever a man finds himself inclining – and to our mind it makes no difference if this happens because of his natural disposition or because of an acquired characteristic – towards lusts and pleasures or preferring anger and fury, giving the upper hand to his irascible faculty and letting go its reins, he shall be at fault and stumble wherever he goes. For he shall seek opinions that will help him in whatever he is inclined to by his nature. I have drawn your attention to this in order that you should not be deceived. For someone may some day lead you into vain imaginings through setting forth a doubt concerning the Creation of the world in time, and you may be very quick to let yourself be deceived. For in this opinion is contained the destruction of the foundation of the Law and a presumptuous assertion with regard to the Deity. Be therefore always suspicious in your mind as to this point and accept the authority of the two prophets [i.e, Abraham and Moses] who are the pillars of the well-being of the human species with regard to its beliefs and its associations. Do not turn away from the opinion according to which the world is new, except because of a demonstration. Now such a demonstration does not exist in nature.

Furthermore, the student of this Treatise should not engage in criticism because I use this rhetorical mode of speech in order to support the affirmation of the newness of the world. For Aristotle, the prince of the philosophers, in his main writings has likewise used rhetorical speeches in support of his opinion that the world is eternal. In such cases it may truly be said: "Shall not our perfect Torah be [worth as much] as their frivolous talk?"[32] If he refers to the ravings of the Sabians to support his opinion, how can we avoid referring to the words of Moses and Abraham, and to everything that follows from them, in support of our opinion?

[32] *Baba Batra*, 116a; *Megillat Taʿanit*, ch. 5.

I have promised you a chapter in which I shall expound to you the grave doubts that would affect whoever thinks that man has acquired knowledge of the arrangement of the motions of the sphere, and of their being natural things going on according to the law of necessity, things whose order and arrangement are clear. I shall now explain this to you.

[Part II Chapter 24]

You know of astronomical matters what you have read under my guidance and understood from the contents of the *Almagest*.[33] But there was not enough time to begin another speculative study with you. What you know already is that, as far as the action of ordering the motions and making the course of the stars conform to what is seen is concerned, everything depends on two principles – either that of the epicycles or that of the eccentric spheres or on both of them. Now I shall draw your attention to the fact that both those principles are entirely outside the bounds of reasoning and opposed to all that has been made clear in natural science.

In the first place, if one affirms as true the existence of an epicycle revolving round a certain sphere, positing at the same time that that revolution is not around the center of the sphere carrying the epicycles – and this has been supposed with regard to the moon and to the five planets – it follows necessarily that there is rolling, that is, that the epicycle rolls and changes its place completely. Now this is the impossibility that was to be avoided, namely, the assumption that there should be something in the heavens that changes its place. For this reason Abū Bakr Ibn al-Sā'igh [Ibn Bājja] states, in his extant discourse on astronomy, that the existence of epicycles is impossible. He points out the necessary inference already mentioned. In addition to this impossibility necessarily following from the assumption of the existence of epicycles, he sets forth other impossibilities that also follow from that assumption. I shall explain them to you now.

The revolution of the epicycles is not around the center of the world. Now it is a fundamental principle of this world that there are three motions: a motion from the midmost point of the world, a motion toward that point, and a motion around that point. But if an epicycle existed, its motion would not be from that point, nor toward it, nor around it.

---

[33] The great astronomical work by Ptolemy (c. 85- c. 165) was very influential in its Arabic translation.

Furthermore, it is one of the preliminary assumptions of Aristotle in natural science that there must necessarily be some immobile thing around which circular motion takes place. Hence it is necessary that the earth should be immobile. Now if epicycles exist, theirs would be a circular motion that would not revolve round an immobile thing. I have heard that Abū Bakr has stated that he had invented an astronomical system in which no epicycles figured, but only eccentric circles. However, I have not heard this from his pupils. And even if this were truly accomplished by him, he would not gain much thereby. For eccentricity also necessitates going outside the limits posed by the principles established by Aristotle, those principles to which nothing can be added. I was the one who drew attention to this point. In the case of eccentricity, we likewise find that the circular motion of the spheres does not take place around the midmost point of the world, but around an imaginary point that is other than the center of the world. Accordingly, that motion is likewise not a motion taking place around an immobile thing.

If, however, someone having no knowledge of astronomy thinks that eccentricity with respect to these imaginary points may be considered – when these points are situated inside the sphere of the moon, as they appear to be at the outset – as equivalent to motion round the midmost point of the world, we would agree to concede this to him if that motion took place round a point in the zone of fire or of air, though in that case that motion would not be around an immobile thing. We will, however, make it clear to him that the measures of eccentricity have been demonstrated in the *Almagest* according to what is assumed there. And the latter-day scientists have given a correct demonstration, regarding which there is no doubt, of how great the measure of these eccentricities is compared with half the diameter of the earth, just as they have set forth all the other distances and dimensions. It has consequently become clear that the eccentric point around which the sun revolves must of necessity be outside the concavity of the sphere of the moon and beneath the convexity of the sphere of Mercury. Similarly the point around which Mars revolves, I mean to say the center of its eccentric sphere, is outside the concavity of the sphere of Mercury and beneath the convexity of the sphere of Venus. Again the center of the eccentric sphere of Jupiter is at the same distance – I mean between the sphere of Mercury and Venus. As for Saturn, the center of its eccentric sphere is between the spheres of Mars and Jupiter. See now how all these things are remote from natural speculation. All this will become clear to you if you consider the distances and dimensions known to you of every sphere and star, measuring them according to half the diameter of the earth, so that everything is calculated according to one and the same proportion and the eccentricity of every sphere is not evaluated in relation to the sphere itself.

Even more incongruous and dubious is the fact that in all cases in which one of two spheres is inside the other and adheres to it on every side, while the centers of the two are different,[34] the smaller sphere can move inside the bigger one without the latter being in motion, whereas the bigger sphere cannot move upon any axis whatever without the smaller one being in motion. For whenever the bigger sphere moves, it necessarily, by means of its movement, sets the smaller one in motion, except in the case in which its motion is an axis passing through the two centers. From this demonstrative premise and from the demonstrated fact that vacuum does not exist and from the assumptions regarding eccentricity, it follows necessarily that when the higher sphere is in motion it must move the sphere beneath it with the same motion and around its own center. Now we do not find that this is so. We find rather that neither of the two spheres, the containing and the contained, is set in motion by the movement of the other nor does it move around the other's center or poles, but that each of them has its own particular motion. Hence necessity obliges the belief that between every two spheres there are bodies other than those of the spheres. Now if this be so, how many obscure points remain? Where will you suppose the centers of those bodies existing between every two spheres to be? And those bodies should likewise have their own particular motion. Thābit[35] has explained this in a treatise of his and has demonstrated what we have said, namely, that there must be the body of a sphere between every two spheres. All this I did not explain to you when you read under my guidance, for fear of confusing you with regard to that which it was my purpose to make you understand.

As for the inclination and deviation that are spoken of regarding the latitude of Venus and Mercury, I have explained to you by word of mouth and I have shown you that it is impossible to conceive their existence in those bodies. For the rest Ptolemy has said explicitly, as you have seen,

---

[34] I.e., the centers of the eccentric spheres (orbs) are different.
[35] Thābit Ibn Qurra (d. c. 900), astronomer, philosopher, and translator.

that one was unable to do this, stating literally: "No one should think that these principles and those similar to them may only be put into effect with difficulty, if his reason for doing this be that he regards that which we have set forth as he would regard things obtained by artifice and the subtlety of art and which may only be realized with difficulty. For human matters should not be compared to those that are divine."[36] This is, as you know, the text of his statement. I have indicated to you the passages from which the true reality of everything I have mentioned to you becomes manifest, except for what I have told you regarding the examination of where the points lie that are the centers of the eccentric circles. For I have never come across anybody who has paid attention to this. However this shall become clear to you through the knowledge of the measure of the diameter of every sphere and what the distance is between the two centers as compared with half the diameter of the earth, according to what has been demonstrated by al-Qabīsī in the "Epistle Concerning the Distances." If you examine those distances, the truth of the point to which I have drawn your attention will become clear to you.

Consider now how great these difficulties are. If what Aristotle has stated with regard to natural science is true, there are no epicycles or eccentric circles and everything revolves round the center of the earth. But in that case how can the various motions of the stars come about? Is it in any way possible that motion should be on the one hand circular, uniform, and perfect, and that on the other hand the things that are observable should be observed in consequence of it, unless this be accounted for by making use of one of the two principles or of both of them? This consideration is all the stronger because of the fact that if one accepts everything stated by Ptolemy concerning the epicycle of the moon and its deviation towards a point outside the center of the world and also outside the center of the eccentric circle, it will be found that what is calculated on the hypothesis of the two principles is not at fault by even a minute. The truth of this is attested by the correctness of the calculations – always made on the basis of these principles – concerning the eclipses and the exact determination of their times as well as of the moment when it begins to be dark and of the length of time of the darkness. Furthermore, how can one conceive the

---

[36] Cf. *Almagest* III, 2, trans. G. J. Toomer (Princeton, NJ: Princeton University Press, 1998), p. 600.

retrogradation of a star, together with its other motions, without assuming the existence of an epicycle? On the other hand, how can one imagine a rolling motion in the heavens or a motion around a center that is not immobile? This is the true perplexity.

However, I have already explained to you by word of mouth that all this does not affect the astronomer. For his purpose is not to tell us in which way the spheres truly are, but to posit an astronomical system in which it would be possible for the motions to be circular and uniform and to correspond to what is apprehended through sight, regardless of whether or not things are thus in fact. You know already that, in speaking of natural science, Abū Bakr Ibn al-Ṣā'igh expresses a doubt whether Aristotle knew about the eccentricity of the sun and passed over it in silence – treating of what necessarily follows from the sun's inclination, inasmuch as the effect of eccentricity is not distinguishable from that of inclination – or whether he was not aware of eccentricity.

Now the truth is that he was not aware of it and had never heard about it, for in his time mathematics had not been brought to perfection. If, however, he had heard about it, he would have violently rejected it; and if it were to his mind established as true, he would have become most perplexed about all his assumptions on the subject. I shall repeat here what I have said before. All that Aristotle states about that which is beneath the sphere of the moon is in accordance with reasoning; these are things that have a known cause, that follow one upon the other, and concerning which it is clear and manifest at what points wisdom and natural providence are effective. However, regarding all that is in the heavens, man grasps nothing but a small measure of what is mathematical; and you know what is in it. I shall accordingly say in the manner of poetical preciousness: "The heavens are the heavens of the Lord, but the earth has He given to the sons of man" [Ps. 115:16]. I mean thereby that the Deity alone fully knows the true reality, the nature, the substance, the form, the motions, and the causes of the heavens. But He has enabled man to have knowledge of what is beneath the heavens, for that is his world and his dwelling-place in which he has been placed and of which he himself is a part. This is the truth. For it is impossible for us to accede to the points starting from which conclusions may be drawn about the heavens; for the latter are too far away from us and too high in place and in rank. And even the general conclusion that may be drawn from them, namely, that they prove the existence of their Mover, is a matter the knowledge of which cannot be reached by human intellects.[37] And to fatigue the minds with notions that cannot be grasped by them and for the grasp of which they have no instrument, is a defect in one's inborn disposition or some sort of temptation. Let us then stop at a point that is within our capacity, and let us give over the things that cannot be grasped by reasoning to him who was reached by the mighty divine overflow so that it could be fittingly said of him: "With him do I speak mouth to mouth" [Num. 12:8].

That is the end of what I have to say about this question. It is possible that someone else may find a demonstration by means of which the true reality of what is obscure for me will become clear to him. The extreme predilection that I have for investigating the truth is evidenced by the fact that I have explicitly stated and reported my perplexity regarding these matters, as well as by the fact that I have not heard nor do I know a demonstration as to anything concerning them.

[Part II Chapter 25]

Know that our shunning the affirmation of the eternity of the world is not due to a text figuring in the Torah according to which the world has been produced in time. For the texts indicating that the world has been produced in time are not more numerous than those indicating that the Deity is a body. Nor are the gates of figurative interpretation shut in our faces or impossible of access to us regarding the subject of the creation of the world in time. For we could interpret them as figurative, as we have done when denying His corporeality. Perhaps this would even be much easier to do: we should be very well able to give a figurative interpretation of those texts and to affirm as true the eternity of the world, just as we have given a figurative interpretation of those other texts and have denied that He, may He be exalted, is a body.

Two causes are responsible for our not doing this or believing it. One of them is as follows. That the Deity is not a body has been demonstrated; from this it follows necessarily that everything that in its external meaning disagrees with this demonstration must be interpreted figuratively, for it is known that such texts are of necessity fit for figurative interpretation. However, the eternity of the world has not been demonstrated. Consequently in this case the texts ought not to be rejected and figuratively

---

[37] The translation of this line has recently been debated. See H. Davidson, "Further on a Problematic Passage in *Guide of the Perplexed* 2.24," *Maimonidean Studies* 4 (2000): 1–14.

interpreted in order to make prevail an opinion whose contrary can be made to prevail by means of various sorts of arguments. This is one cause.

The second cause is as follows. Our belief that the Deity is not a body destroys for us none of the foundations of the Law and does not give the lie to the claims of any prophet. The only objection to it is constituted by the fact that the ignorant think that this belief is contrary to the text; yet it is not contrary to it, as we have explained, but is intended by the text. On the other hand, the belief in eternity the way Aristotle sees it – that is, the belief according to which the world exists in virtue of necessity, that no nature changes at all, and that the customary course of events cannot be modified with regard to anything – destroys the Law in its principle, necessarily gives the lie to every miracle, and reduces to inanity all the hopes and threats that the Law has held out, unless – by God! – one interprets the miracles figuratively also, as was done by the Islamic internalists; this, however, would result in some sort of crazy imaginings.

If, however, one believed in eternity according to the second opinion we have explained[38] – which is the opinion of Plato – according to which the heavens too are subject to generation and corruption, this opinion would not destroy the foundations of the Law and would be followed not by the lie being given to miracles, but by their becoming admissible. It would also be possible to interpret figuratively the texts in accordance with this opinion. And many obscure passages can be found in the texts of the Torah and others with which this opinion could be connected or rather by means of which it could be proved. However, no necessity could impel us to do this unless this opinion were demonstrated. In view of the fact that it has not been demonstrated, we shall not favor this opinion, nor shall we at all heed that other opinion, but rather shall take the texts according to their external sense and shall say: The Law has given us knowledge of a matter the grasp of which is not within our power, and the miracle attests to the correctness of our claims.

Know that with a belief in the creation of the world in time, all the miracles become possible and the Law becomes possible, and all questions that may be asked on this subject, vanish. Thus it might be said: Why did God give prophetic revelation to this one and not to that? Why did God give this Law to this particular nation, and why did He not legislate to the others? Why did He legislate at this particular time, and why did He not

[38] II, 13.

legislate before it or after? Why did He impose these commandments and these prohibitions? Why did He privilege the prophet with the miracles mentioned in relation to him and not with some others? What was God's aim in giving this Law? Why did He not, if such was His purpose, put the accomplishment of the commandments and the nontransgression of the prohibitions into our nature? If this were said, the answer to all these questions would be that it would be said: He wanted it this way; or His wisdom required it this way. And just as He brought the world into existence, having the form it has, when He wanted to, without our knowing His will with regard to this or in what respect there was wisdom in His particularizing the forms of the world and the time of its creation – in the same way we do not know His will or the exigency of His wisdom that caused all the matters, about which questions have been posed above, to be particularized.

If, however, someone says that the world is as it is in virtue of necessity, it would be a necessary obligation to ask all those questions; and there would be no way out of them except through a recourse to unseemly answers which would include denying and annulling all the external meanings of the Law with regard to which no intelligent man has any doubt that they are to be taken in their external meanings. It is then because of this that this opinion is shunned and that the lives of virtuous men have been and will be spent in investigating this question. For if creation in time were demonstrated – if only as Plato understands creation – all the overhasty claims made to us on this point by the philosophers would become void. In the same way, if the philosophers would succeed in demonstrating eternity as Aristotle understands it, the Law as a whole would become void, and a shift to other opinions would take place. I have thus explained to you that everything is bound up with this problem. Know this.

4

Isaac Albalag, from *The Emendation of the "Opinions"*

[On the knowability of future possibles]

49   The translator [Isaac Albalag] said: The possible is divided into
many types that follow from the division of its causes into types. Therefore,
one must examine if all the types are possible in the same sense in order to
determine whether the foreknowledge of them all may be posited equally
or not.

Let us begin by asserting that some of the causes of the possible are
efficient and others are material, and both must join together for the real-
ization of the possible effect. Furthermore, some of these efficient causes
are natural; some are volitional; and others are accidental. Of the natural causes some causes maintain a knowable order – that is, their activity
appears at known, ordered intervals and ceases in the same manner. Other
[natural causes] maintain an order [that is unknown]. Of those causes that
maintain an order, some can be prevented from acting by a volitional,
unordered natural, or accidental hindrance, or can be prevented from
receiving [a form] by a material hindrance, so that their effect does not
appear at its customary time.

Others cannot be [so prevented]. This is certainly the case regarding a possible effect which, prior to its actualization, is necessitated to
occur, such as the eclipse of the sun or the reappearance of the moon.
For its cause does not require the assistance of a volitional or accidental cause, and a volitional, accidental or unordered natural hindrance
cannot prevent it. [In contrast,] there is the possible whose existence
and non-existence is[1] dependent on one or many volitional or accidental

---

[1] Reading *asher* for *ve-ein*, following Budapest, Kaufmann 287.

causes that help or hinder it. For example, consider an event such as Reuben's accidentally wounding his eye at a certain time by lifting his finger upward. Neither the time nor the occurrence of the event can be predicted. For the time and the occurrence of [its] causes and effects do not maintain an order, and the occurrence of the effects does not follow necessarily from the occurrence of the causes. The occurrence of the final effect certainly does not result necessarily from the occurrence of the first cause. For the wounding of the eye does not result necessarily from the raising of the finger, nor is the finger's encounter with the eye a necessary event when the finger is raised. True, the wounding of the eye follows necessarily from the finger encountering it, and that encounter follows necessarily from the finger's being led in a direct line towards the eye. Nevertheless, the finger's following *that* line rather than any other line upward can only have been brought about by an accidental cause.

Moreover, it is common knowledge that the volitional cause hinges solely upon the power of the chooser. And even if his choice has a necessitating cause, this cause may perhaps proceed from an accidental cause or an imaginative cause that has no external existence, as when Reuben stumbles on a stone that has fallen from the roof as a result of the movement of a mouse who thinks that there is bread before him or a cat behind him. For certainly the appearance of this image to the mouse does not have a cause that acts in a necessary manner; what I mean is that there is nothing in the nature of the cause that necessitates this image in the mouse, or in the nature of the image that it necessarily occurs in this way. Therefore, knowledge of the first necessitating[2] causes is not sufficient to ascertain the nature of the effects, and not everything possible has causes that ascend to it[3] one after another as essential causes and effects do.

In short, I maintain that for any possible thing, if all its proximate and remote causes succeed each other essentially and maintain order in their actions, and no hindrance can prevent any of them, then it is to be judged the same as a necessary thing with respect to the knower. However, regarding other possibles, one cannot know with certain knowledge[4] the fact or the time of their occurrence before it occurs.

---

[2] Reading *meḥayyevot* for *meḥuyyavot*, following *bet* and *tet* in Vajda's edition.
[3] Reading *lo* for *lahen*.   [4] Heb.: *daᶜat bari'*.

You think, perhaps, that I deny God's knowledge of possible things before they come about. Heaven forbid! I merely reject that God knows them in the way that al-Ghazālī claims. For there can be no doubt that this knowledge is of the same kind as human knowledge of possible things, there only being a difference of degree. This is clear from his words and from the comparison he makes with astrology.

It is suitable to teach al-Ghazālī's view to the multitude, but it is unsuitable to affirm it among those who seek to know the view upon which eternal life depends.[5] And when you examine al-Ghazālī's statements carefully, you will find that they entail the annulment of man's choice and the conclusion that his actions are compelled, as well as the annulment of the nature of the possible altogether. These opinions not only constitute repudiations of philosophy but also heresy with respect to the Torah. Other ancients have already endeavored to refute these opinions, some according to faith, others according to philosophy, so that they have left me nothing further to say.

---

5 Albalag's remark is based on the Talmudic saying, "There are things which are suitable to preach but not suitable to practice"; cf. *Hagigah* 14b, *Tosefta Hagigah* 3.

5

Moses of Narbonne (Narboni), *The Treatise on Choice*

The *Treatise on Choice* by Moses of Narbonne,
which he composed about three months before his death.[1]

I looked about and saw that a scholar, one of the distinguished of his generation (and whom I encountered towards the end of his life), composed the *Letter on the Decree*.[2] He maintained therein that the possible does not exist, that everything is necessitated, and that everything is predestined by Divine decree. In a word, he said that the early authorities recognized this proposition as true, but that they concealed it so as not to annul the nature of endeavor. He also claimed that although everything is necessitated, [this does not imply that] intermediate causes are to be annulled; rather it is necessary to endeavor to achieve the desired result. For the result, though predestined, comes about[3] through endeavor and application. He explained that he was led to affirm both propositions because when the sage proclaimed "If the Decree is true, endeavor is futile"[4] he meant endeavor on behalf of the contrary result rather than on what has been predestined. This is the gist of his remarks in the letter he composed on the topic. Although he went on at length embellishing his thesis and eliminating its implausibility, this is the substance of his comments.

Now I say that the first principle is absurd, because it is not the case that everything is predestined. But if it were true, then his premises

---

[1] On the dating of the treatise see Introduction.
[2] The reference is to a treatise by Abner of Burgos that is no longer extant, perhaps an abbreviated version of *A Jealousy Offering*, his treatise on predestination.
[3] Reading *yagiʿuhu* for *yagiduhu*.
[4] See *Mivḥar ha-Peninim* (*The Choice Diadem*), attributed to Solomon ibn Gabirol, §43.

would contradict one another. For if things are predestined, then his statement that nonetheless one should not refrain from endeavor, for through endeavor one achieves the predestined desired result, is absurd. Moreover, his interpretation of "If the Decree is true, endeavor is futile," namely, that the endeavor to achieve the contrary result[5] rather than the predestined one is futile, also contradicts his second premise. I shall briefly explain all this.

First I say: All his statements claiming that the possible does not exist and that everything is predestined were already refuted by Aristotle in *On Interpretation*, the *Physics*, and Book Six of the *Metaphysics*.[6] For Aristotle showed there that some things are of the nature of the possible, and of these some exist accidentally and by chance; that inasmuch as there are existents that occur for the most part, it follows that there will be some that occur rarely; and that not everything that is generated from something bears a necessary relation to it. He explained and confirmed these points at length, but the gist is that we are acquainted with many things of which we are the cause. If we wish to do them, we do them; if we wish not to actualize them, they will not come into existence. Now if everything is necessitated, then the person who makes an endeavor for something will be equal to the one who makes an endeavor to annul it, and all future things will be necessary. This opposes all that is sensibly perceived and intellectually cognized.

Second, his point about the need to endeavor on behalf of the sought-after outcome, because, though predestined, it is achieved through this endeavor, conflicts with his [first] premise. For since it is predestined, then what we mentioned in the name of Aristotle must be the case, namely, that the endeavor towards a thing will be the same as the endeavor towards its opposite. Even if it is conceded that a person has to endeavor, I say that since the outcome is predestined, and that which is predestined, requires endeavor, he is compelled to make that endeavor. This secret need not be concealed from a person in order that he not refrain from making an endeavor, for he is powerless to refrain. But this is precisely the question at hand: inasmuch as something is predestined, whatever leads to it is necessitated, and whatever leads to its annulment is absurd.

---

[5] Reading *ha-maqbil* for *ha-magbil*.   [6] *De Interpretatione* IX, *Physics* II, 4–5, *Metaphysics* VI, 2–3.

Third, his interpretation of "If the decree is true, endeavor is futile" as referring to endeavor on behalf of the alternative result contradicts what he previously posited in the second premise, namely, that even though a thing is predestined one should not refrain from making an endeavor to achieve it. For if making an endeavor on behalf of the opposite of the predestined outcome is futile, since that which is predestined is unpreventable, then failing to endeavor to achieve it will not prevent it either.

The following example will illustrate this principle: It is futile for a man who is predestined to become immensely rich to strive not to become so, because it is impossible for him not to become rich. Now if endeavor on behalf of not becoming rich cannot prevent riches, then certainly indolence and abstention from any endeavor to become rich "will not keep the goodness from whom it belongs" – he must become wealthy. This is a first principle. For if the outcome will not be prevented by endeavoring to achieve the opposite, then the same applies certainly to not endeavoring to achieve either the outcome or its opposite. Thus, his remarks are self-contradictory.

We need to realize that although the positions of the heavenly bodies bestow the mixtures, they [merely] prepare, move, and aid one of the alternative [states-of-affairs], but they do not compel us in our actions. For then man would not possess choice, which is one of the essential differences that distinguishes[7] living things under certain conditions. Now though the causes stretch back to the movement of the sphere, this does not imply[8] predestination. For while the existence of the cause follows from the existence of the effect, the existence of the effect does not follow from the existence of the cause, save in form and end.[9]

Thus, accidental causes are originated that destroy a thing before its natural destruction, and accidental causes prevent the generation of a thing that has the power to come into existence. Now Aristotle has already explained in the *Metaphysics* that there are non-generating and non-destroying causes[10] that by accident make things miss their mark. For the existence of subsequent things does not follow from the existence of antecedents as the existence of antecedent causes follows from what is

---

[7] *Va-yishᶜaru*, 'gauges.'   [8] Reading *mehayyev* for *mehuyyav*.   [9] Cf. *Metaphysics* 1070a.

[10] *ᶜIlot bilti mehavot ve-lo mafsidot*. In *Metaphysics* VI Aristotle claims that there are origins and causes that are generable and destructible without going through a process of being generated or destroyed. However Ibn Rushd, reflecting the Arabic translation, understands the latter verbs as *transitive*, i.e., there are generable and destructible causes *that are non-generating and non-destroying*. Narboni follows suit.

subsequently originated.[11] Similarly, if it were necessary that every cause generates and destroys,[12] then whatever may be generated will be generated of necessity, thus eliminating the nature of the possible, which is at variance with sense-experience and truth itself. Moreover, because generable things require prior entities that indubitably bring them into existence, the former are judged to be generated indubitably through their natures and essences; just as whatever is generated is judged to be destroyed indubitably later, e.g., the death of a living thing, and the destruction and disintegration of composite part, because it is composed of contraries and must return to its [fundamental] element. Still, a destructible thing will not be destroyed without illness or violence: it will be destroyed either if there is illness or violence. But one of the alternatives relates to it naturally, namely, illness, which is something necessary, and the other accidentally, namely, violence. So although destruction exists in itself,[13] it may become mixed with something of the accidental, thereby originating a destruction that is possible and non-compulsory; likewise generation in general is not contained in what is generated as an antecedent entity, but it is possible not to be generated.[14]

For example: everything that is generated and destroyed possesses causes that do not go on indefinitely but reach[15] first causes. Now something must possess one of the opposites[16] that is the first cause of one of the [future] contingent opposites, as in the following example: So-and-so will die if he is struck or becomes ill. He will not die if he is not struck or does not become ill. Also, if he obeys the king, follows his craving, goes to war, eats tasty and harmful food, and becomes ill, he will die. If he does not obey the king, follow his craving, go to war, eat harmful food, and become ill, he will not die. Without a doubt the matter must end

---

[11] Reading *meziut* for *bi-meziut*, the point being that although an effect implies the existence of a cause, the converse does not hold.

[12] Omitting *be-miqreh*.   [13] Or "exists in its substance," and hence it is necessary.

[14] Narboni's point is that there is an important dissimilarity between generation and destruction. Destruction is necessary in natural things because the "seeds of destruction," the contrary elements, are contained within every composite entity. Generation is not necessary because the causes of generation are not contained within the generated entity. However, generation is comparable to *accidental* destruction, for in both processes natural causes become mixed with accidental causes, and hence the specific result is non-necessary.

[15] Reading *megiʿot* for *meniʿot*.

[16] Reading *me-ha-hafakhim* for *mithapkhim*. It is difficult to find any consistent distinction between *hefekh* ("opposite") and *maqbil* ("alternative"). One is tempted to understand the former as the conjunct in a contradiction (*p* and *-p*) and the latter as a disjunct in an alternation (*p* or *q*). But sometimes they should be taken synonymously.

with him possessing [as cause] one of these alternatives, e.g., "obeying the king" or "following his craving." Now if the existence of subsequent things followed of necessity from the existence of antecedents, then when he possessed one of the two alternative efficient causes it would follow of necessity that he would possess one of the two contingent alternatives.[17] There would be no room for accidental and rare causes that prevent a possible death or hasten a natural one.[18] But this is entirely false. The same thing applies to the generation of something generable, for several causes may prevent the generation of a man from the warm[19] blood that is potentially in the progenitor; the subsequent thing does not follow of necessity from the antecedent.

In sum, this causal origin, which is the actually existing agent of the two alternatives, and the "now" at which [future] possibly existing things terminate, is not the causal origin of their existence of necessity. Nor are the alternatives agents[20] of necessity (as is the case with what[21] is necessarily generated from the positions of the heavenly bodies, e.g., heat, cold, light, and darkness) with the result that all things are necessary. Rather, possibly existing things terminate in an original cause whose existence is for the most part, and whose agency is for the most part, such as "obeying the king" and "following one's craving." Hence, there is a causal origin here called 'chance.'[22] And chance may arise in what is potential, or it may not arise, as our sense and intellect indicate.

In general, even if all movements go back ultimately to the first movement this does not indicate that everything is decreed. For since there is a subsequently originated thing it follows that there is an antecedent, and this proceeds back to the prime mover. But what is subsequent does not follow of necessity from the antecedent, for this originated thing does not follow of necessity from the first thing moved. For non-necessarily-existing causes may be found among the intermediate causes, and hence what is originated from them will be non-necessary. A cause may

---

[17] I.e., if he obeys the king then he will die violently of necessity, or if he follows his craving then he will die naturally of necessity.

[18] This example bears a family resemblance to Aristotle's example at *Metaphysics* VI, 3, 1027b1-10, but due to the commentorial tradition it has changed considerably. Narboni's general point is that if the effect is entailed by the distant cause, then as soon as one of the initial causes obtains, then the outcome of its chain is necessitated.

[19] Lit.: 'cooked.'   [20] Or, "efficient causes."

[21] Reading *ka-ᶜinyan bameh* for *ba-ᶜinyan kemah.*

[22] I.e., from the fact that some causal origins operate frequently, but not always, it may be inferred that some act infrequently, and these are called 'chance.'

intervene[23] among them that obstructs an agent that belongs to the causes that are intermediate between the first cause and this originated thing. Or perhaps an accidental cause intervened that is the cause of the origination of this thing, and the essential causes that obstruct its origination missed their mark. For not all causes are necessary nor is their activity necessary. Chance figures among them, for ill and for good, the latter being called good fortune.

God's knowledge also does not compel the possible, for God's knowing everything and man's possessing ability is a contradiction. Rather God knows Himself, which in a certain respect is all existing things. Therefore, when He thinks Himself He thinks all existing things in a more excellent manner. The existing things follow from Him[24] as the intelligible follows from the intellect, but not so the voluntary activities. For just as it is within the stone's power to descend with the removal of what compels it to remain in its unnatural place, it is likewise within the power of man, who possesses choice, to will or not to will, to act or not to act. God's knowledge compels [the existence of] this possibility, orders it within man, and arranges him as possessing choice and as unconstrained.

All of [the scholar's] doubts have now been resolved. Understand this, for it is a sufficient basic principle.

In general, because God is the most perfect existent and the most separate and most excellent form, He is intellect *per se* and independent of any other. What is caused by Him is dependent upon Him, for its essence[25] consists in what it apprehends of Him. The essence[26] of the First, however, consists in what His essence apprehends, so that His essence is revealed to His essence, and He is His essence. What He himself thinks is not the sublunar order of existents, for this very order relates to these existents as[27] the conception which the artisan possesses relates to his artifacts,[28] and it is obvious, however, that His essence is the cause of existents and not vice-versa. Nor is [His order] homonymous [with the sublunar order], for in that case it would not be the cause of existents. Hence, one stands to the other in a relationship of priority and posteriority, as is the case with the word 'heat,' which is said of fire and of hot things, and, in short, of all the causes of existents in this world, where the perfect [existent] is

---

[23] Reading *tikanes* for *tikanem*.   [24] Reading *mi-menu* for *mi-min* and *ke-ḥiyyub* for *ke-ḥayyat*.

[25] Reading *mahuto* for *mahuti*, i.e., the essence of that which is caused by God.

[26] *'Azmut*, "substantial reality."   [27] Reading *kemo* for *bameh*.

[28] Reading *ma'asav* for *ma'asuyav*.

the cause of the deficient one of that description. Were He to apprehend the existents in the manner in which they exist, then they would be prior in nature to Him, just as the intelligible is prior to the intellect; in that case the cause would become the effect.[29] God, however, perfects intellect, and is not perfected. He is active and not passive. It follows of necessity that He thinks the existents in a more excellent manner, such that they are consequent upon His knowledge, and that His knowledge of Himself is the same as His knowledge of what is other than Himself, such that, in His case, the intellect is the intelligible in all respects, and not incidentally, as in our case. [The Divine intellect] does not, in its thinking the existents, rely on actually existing things, in which case it would be perfected through them, and would be diminished by what it thinks of their nature. But existents are actualized by virtue of its thinking, just as the form of the cupboard in the soul of the carpenter is the cause of the form belonging to the cupboard. It is as if[30] you were to imagine that the artisan's own conception of the spiritual form, without being appropriated from outside the artisan, suffices to bring the form of the cupboard into being without any tools and labor besides the conception, due to its power and force.[31] This [conception] is related to [Divine intellection], but the latter is prior, and they are not identical. For what the maker thinks of his product is also a cause insofar as he is an artisan.[32] On the other hand, the writ that is the Divine handwriting portrays the existents in the most excellent manner. Written by the finger of God, the letters fly upwards, their images becoming fortified within the existents, just as the intelligible acts as the cause of the sensible. The portrait is consequent upon, and inseperable from, the artist, notwithstanding the latter's essential priority. May the Planner be exalted, whose plan is the cause of their plan and whose conception is the cause of their existence!

---

[29] In human knowledge the sublunar order of reality is the cause of the acquisition of knowledge (intelligibles are acquired by the intellect), which is not the case with Divine knowledge.

[30] Reading *ke-'ilu* for *'ilu*.

[31] The text is far from clear here. The parallel text from Narboni's Commentary on *Guide of the Perplexed* III, 21 reads *ke-'ilu damita she-ziyyur ha-'uman le-zurah ha-'aronit hu ha-sibah be-hamza'at ha-zurah mi-beli kelim* ('as if you imagined that the artisan's conception of the form of the cupboard is the cause of bringing the form into existence without tools,' etc.). The phrase translated as 'without its being appropriated from the outside' seems like an interpolation, because that point is not made until two sentences later, when God's intellect is distinguished from that of the artisan.

[32] Or, "is a cause of his being an artisan." The point appears to be that the knowledge the artisan possesses of his craft, through which he makes new artifacts, derives ultimately from the external order. This is different, of course, from God's causal knowledge.

It follows of necessity that God thinks the existents through His intellect and by virtue of His essence, not by virtue of their essence. Hence his knowledge cannot be described as applying to universals or to particulars. Universals are intelligibles that are derived[33] from existents through the repetition of individuals and what comes subsequently from them. But existents are derived from this [i.e., God's] knowledge. Once His knowledge cannot be described as applying to particulars, it cannot be described as applying to possible particulars. This is obvious to anyone with a rudimentary education in the art of logic. For just as the objects known are not the cause of His knowledge, for He is the agent and plan of the existents, and is not passive; and His knowledge does not become multiple by virtue of the [objects'] multiplicity, but everything is united within Him, the finite equal to[34] the infinite – so, too, changes do not bring about any change within His knowledge, nor do new objects of knowledge bring about any origination therein. His knowledge does not determine[35] one of the possibles, for His knowledge cannot be described as applying to possible particulars since it is not derived from them; rather, they are derived from it. Nevertheless, the possible that is originated will not escape His notice inasmuch as it is an existent, and the existent comes from God's actuating knowledge. Hence, it is said that even a pumpkin seed does not escape the notice of God. So how can He be ignorant of what exists potentially, although there are degrees of knowledge? Thus, everything is manifest and revealed before God.

Now the various existents differ in their reception of the plan and goodness according to what their natures allow them to receive of it, and according to the matter – the cause of evils – that is mixed with it. It is not that evil is mixed with the First Cause, since He is the perfect good; nor that the plan belonging to the First Cause is deficient in the emanation of the good; nor that the existents are capable by nature not to receive evil. Rather the natures [of the existents] cannot possibly receive the good that is the perfect order and equilibrium. The impossible has a stable nature; although goodness flows from Him, may He be exalted, by virtue of His inner plan, and the fact that He is always thinking Himself, [parts of] the world do not receive that goodness equally, but in proportion to being near or distant from Him. In sum, everything that obtains does so

---

[33] Reading *nimshakhim* for *'u-meshanim*.   [34] Reading *va-yashveh* for *ve-yeshut*.
[35] Reading *tikhra͑* (or, *takhri͑a*) for *tigra͑*.

from His knowledge, and every good proceeds from Him; the possible is known to him without being compelled. In this way Rabbi Akiba's dictum – "Everything is observed yet authority is granted"[36] – should be understood.

This is what I have seen fit to explain on this topic briefly, and I have done so without prejudice and without becoming habituated in customary beliefs. If we have the leisure, we shall respond to everything that he claimed there that flies in the face of true reality, and we shall offer a fuller explanation. But this amount is sufficient for our purposes and stands on its own.

Now we regarded this man, called Abner, as quite sagacious "when His light flickered over his head" [Job 29:3]. So I do not believe that he erred in this [letter] but rather he deceived [others]. For when he saw that times were hard, and that his correligionists, far from supporting him, were opposed to him due to their indifference, their lack of wisdom, and their hostility and hatred towards the wise, he turned to the "arrogant and to the companions of deceit" [Ps. 40:5] in the guise of instruments that would press him on to the imagined felicity, as an instrument to achieve eternity. He was not one of the pious scholars, perfect in wisdom, who are content with a "weekly bushel of carobs,"[37] for one should only turn to the objects of the senses as necessary, and the necessary here is quite sufficient. Rather he was one of the sages who provided for the preservation of the [material] substratum, since it is a part of the composite, and is the dwelling place for the formal essence.[38] Once he had committed evil even in the eyes of Wisdom (for a sage should not oppose the law in which he has been raised because it is the beginning of his kingdom and the starting point of his felicity; this is certainly true in the case of the true and sacred Divine law, lest the sage retreat behind the Lord's back in order to leave the country, and the "individual become a sectarian") he argued as a defender of the universal Decree that everything is determined. He did this to signify that although he was rinsed by the perfidious waters, his heart remained steadfast and unmoistened by the gentile spring, and that an unfavorable constellation and the Decree compelled him [in his actions]; since everything is necessitated, its contradictory is impossible, for the impossible has a stable nature, and is not the activity of an agent. Now he

---

[36] *Mishnah Avot* III, 15. [37] Cf. *Berakhot* 17b.
[38] The sentence should doubtlessly be taken ironically.

realized that to abolish all actions opposes what is known and perceived. So he embellished his phrases and removed their strangeness, claiming that one should not nullify human deeds. And he explained the other principle in order to be compatible with this one. But this is sophistical, since it contradicts what we have said.

In sum, I say that he was led to wander[39] into a "land of desolation" [Lev. 16:22] and to posit the Decree by what he mandated for himself, rather than by speculative truth. For the Decree is at variance with what is thought. God knows that He gave of his wisdom to flesh and blood, and to those who fear him, and that He set before them the blessing and its alternative, and life and goodness and their alternatives. He did not compel us by saying, "Choose life," for these things come essentially from Him, may He be blessed, and by His light, the lamp of truths, until the perfect truth, which is the First light, may He be blessed and exalted, Amen.

The *Treatise on Choice* and concerning the *Letter on the Decree* is now complete, "for I do not desire harsh decrees, says the Lord."

He, who would
The Good.
Shall rejoice
In choice.
Composed in Souria, Wednesday, 12 Tebet, 1361.

---

[39] Omitting *lo*.

6

Levi Gersonides, from *The Wars of the Lord*[1]

The third treatise, concerning God's knowledge (blessed be He)[2] of [sublunar] things, is divided into six chapters:

Chapter 1, in which we mention the views of our predecessors concerning this question.

Chapter 2, in which we mention the arguments that establish each view according to what we have found in the statements of their proponents, or their import.

Chapter 3, in which we investigate whether the arguments that Maimonides brings [to rebut the philosophers] are sufficient or not.

Chapter 4, in which is completed the discourse concerning God's knowledge of things, and is shown that there is nothing in our predecessor's arguments that rejects what has become evident to us regarding this knowledge.

Chapter 5, in which is shown fully that what we have understood of this knowledge is most apt in every respect.[3]

Chapter 6, in which is shown that the view to which speculation has led us is that of the Torah.

---

[1] The Hebrew term translated here as "Lord" will be translated as "God" for the remainder of the selection.

[2] The honorific phrase "(blessed be He)," which accompanies the mention of God, will henceforth be omitted in the translation of this section.

[3] Ẓad is translated here as 'respect' or 'aspect' depending upon context.

Chapter One

We ought to investigate whether or not God knows particular possible sublunar things and, if He does know them, in what way He knows them. Since the philosophers and the Torah sages are divided on this question, we should investigate first their views. Whatever we find to be correct we shall adopt. Whatever we do not find to be correct we shall, when refuting it, explain in what respect it is true.

We say that we find two views in the writings of our predecessors whose discussions are worth examining: [1] the view of the Philosopher[4] and his followers, and [2] the view of the great Torah sages.

[1] The Philosopher believed that God does not know these particular matters. His followers were divided between two opinions. The first group held that, according to the Philosopher, God has no knowledge of things in the sublunar world, either universals or particulars. For if He were to know either universals or particulars then His cognitions[5] would be multiple, hence His essence[6] would be multiple. Indeed, His essence would be divided into a more perfect part and a less perfect part, as is the case with definable things. For in a definition, one part perfects the other. The second group held that, according to the Philosopher, God knows what things in the sublunar world possess from the aspect of their universal nature, namely, their essential properties,[7] and not what they possess insofar as they are particular, namely, their possible properties. This does not imply multiplicity in His essence, since He only knows Himself, and through knowing Himself He knows what all existing things possess from the aspect of their universal nature.[8] For He is the law, order, and equity[9] of existing things. Particulars lack order from the aspect of their being unknown by God; they possess order and equity from the aspect of their being known by God. In Treatise Five of this book we shall show that this is the view of the Philosopher.

However, the great sages of our Torah, such as the superior philosopher Maimonides (blessed be he)[10] and others of our Torah who agree

---

[4] I.e., Aristotle. [5] *Yedi'otav*, lit. 'knowledges' or 'knowings.'

[6] c*Atzmuto*, translated 'essence,' 'essentiality,' 'substantiality,' depending upon context.

[7] Lit.: 'things.'

[8] E.g., God knows Reuben and Simeon as subjects bearing essential properties (e.g., *rational*) but not non-essential properties (e.g., *hot-tempered*).

[9] *Yosher*, 'equilibrium,' 'rightness,' 'justice.'

[10] The honorific phrase will henceforth be omitted in the translation of this section.

with him, hold that God does know all possible particular things from the aspect in which they are particular. Indeed, they believe that in one cognition He knows all these things, which are infinite. This is the view of Maimonides, for he says in Chapter Two of Part III of his noble treatise, *The Guide of the Perplexed*: "Similarly we say that the various things that come about are known to Him before they exist, and that He does not cease knowing them. Hence, no new knowledge comes about for Him at all. For example, let His knowledge be that a particular person is now nonexistent, will exist at some later date, and will continue to exist for some time and then will be nonexistent. Now when this person actually does exist according to the previous knowledge, nothing new has been added to His knowledge, and nothing comes about that was not known to Him. But something comes about that was previously known would come about in the way that it actually did. It follows from this belief that knowledge can have at its object[11] the nonexistent and encompass the infinite. Indeed, we accept this belief. We say that it is not impossible for knowledge to have as its object the nonexistent whose coming into existence was known to God prior to its occurrence, and which can be brought into existence by God." This shows that Maimonides holds that God knows possible particular things from the aspect in which they are particular.

Chapter Two

After having mentioned these views on this question, we should examine which is the true one. Hence we should first examine the arguments that establish each view, and those that refute them.

At the outset we say that the Philosopher's position that God does not know particulars appears to be established by many considerations: First, a particular thing is not apprehended except by means of a hylic faculty, for example, by sense or imagination, and so forth. But it is obvious from the notion of God that He has no hylic faculty. It follows thereby that God does not apprehend these particulars. The following syllogism can be constructed: "God possesses no hylic faculty" and "Whoever apprehends a particular possesses a hylic faculty," which yield, "God does not apprehend a particular."

---

[11] Lit.: 'is attached to' or 'hangs upon.'

Second, particular things are temporal, i.e., their existence is at a designated time. But someone who is not described as in motion or at rest cannot apprehend temporal notions. Now God is not described as in motion or at rest. It follows thereby that He does not apprehend particular things. The following syllogism can be constructed: "God is not described as in motion or at rest" and "Whoever is not described as in motion or at rest cannot apprehend temporal phenomena"; hence "God cannot apprehend temporal notions." If we add to this conclusion a self-evident premise, namely, "Particulars are temporal notions," it follows thereby that "God does not apprehend particulars."

Third, if it is assumed that God knows these things, then one might think that it follows that the superior is perfected by the inferior, for knowledge perfects the knower. But this is utterly absurd, and whatever implies an absurdity is itself absurd. It is accordingly evident that God does not apprehend these things. This argument seems to imply that God knows only Himself, i.e., that He knows neither universals nor particulars.

Fourth, if God did apprehend such things, and since the intellect becomes substantial by virtue of its knowledge, then one might think that it follows thereby that God is not one but many, because of the many apprehensions by virtue of which He becomes substantial. This, however, is completely absurd, and what implies an absurdity is itself absurd. It is accordingly evident that God does not know particulars; indeed, this argument may lead one to think that God knows only Himself.

Fifth, there are infinitely many particular things. But knowledge is something that is inclusive and encompassing. Now a cognition cannot include or encompass what is infinite. This argument implies that knowledge does not pertain to particulars in their entirety insofar as they are particulars, neither by God nor by anyone else.

Sixth, if it is assumed that God knows things that come about, the following dilemma is unavoidable: either [1] He possesses this knowledge before they occur, or [2] He possesses this knowledge only simultaneously with their occurrence, but not beforehand. Now if we were to assume that [1] He possesses this knowledge before they occur, then His knowledge would have as its object what is nonexistent. But this is absurd, for knowledge necessarily pertains to what is existent. Moreover, the foreknowledge he possesses of things that come about implies the following dilemma: either [a] He knows such things according to their possible nature, in which case the contradictory disjunct of what He knows to occur will remain possible. Or [b] He knows perfectly which disjunct will come about, in which case its contradictory is no longer possible. Now if we assume that [a] He knows such things according to their possible nature, it follows that the knowledge He possesses of such things before they come about will change when they come about. For before they actually come into existence it is possible for them to occur or not to occur. But after they exist, then that possibility is removed. Now since the intellect becomes substantial by virtue of what it knows, it thereby follows that God is in constant flux – but this is utterly absurd. If [b] God knows perfectly which disjunct of the contradiction will come about, it follows that there is nothing here that may or may not be realized. This implies further that all things are necessitated, which is completely absurd and disgraceful. Hence we have shown that it is absurd that God possesses knowledge of things that come about before they occur. Yet if we assume that [2] God possesses this knowledge only simultaneously with their occurrence, then he will constantly possess new knowledge. And since the intellect becomes substantial by virtue of what it knows, it thereby follows that God's substance is in constant flux – but this is utterly absurd.

Seventh, if God knows particular things, then the following disjunction is unavoidable: Either [1] God guides and orders them according to a good, perfect, and complete arrangement; or [2] He is unable to order them and has no power over them; or [3] He has the power to order them well, but He abandons and forgets them either because they are despicable, lowly, and inferior in His eyes or because of envy. Now the latter two of these three alternatives are obviously false. It is evident that God can do whatever He wishes, and that He does not desist in providing perfection to each existing thing as much as possible. This is marvelously displayed in the wisdom evident in the creation of animals and in the great power God has in creating things that are as good and as perfect as possible, so that it is impossible for them to be any more perfect than they are. Hence, the only remaining alternative is that God orders these particulars in a good, perfect, and complete way if He knows them. But this is contrary to what we in fact perceive of these particulars. They frequently contain injustice and disorder, so that many evils befall the righteous and the sinner benefits from many goods. Indeed, the philosophers consider this to be the strongest argument that God does not know these particular things. It seems that it was this argument that led the Philosopher to say that God does not know particulars. This is evident from what he says in his *Metaphysics*.[12] In short, these are the arguments that we have extracted from the Philosopher's discussions, and their import, that maintain that God does not know particulars.

We also find an eighth argument that appears to establish the claim that God does not know particular things. We have seen the argument advanced by some later thinkers, who take it to imply that a continuous quantity can be divided into that which is indivisible. We have decided to mention it here, because one may think that it demonstrates that God has no knowledge of particulars. For if God did know all these things, it would seem to follow that the impossible becomes possible. It has been shown that a continuous quantity is divisible into what is divisible. But if it is assumed that God has complete knowledge of that into which this quantity, insofar as it is a quantity, can be divided, there will be in this quantity parts that are known by God that are indivisible. For if they were divisible, God would not know completely that into which this quantity can be divided. But it is absurd to say that a continuous quantity as such contains indivisible parts. Some of the later thinkers have considered this argument and inferred from it that a continuous quantity is divisible into what is indivisible. What brought them to this conclusion was that they initially received from tradition that God knows everything and is ignorant of nothing; hence, they inferred from this that a continuous quantity is divisible into what is indivisible.

These are then the arguments that establish the view that God does not know any of these particular things; in themselves they refute the view of those who assert that God does know particulars.

By contrast, the view of the sages of our Torah that God does know particular notions also is established by some considerations:

First, since all who speculate[13] concede that God is the most perfect being, it is improper to attribute to Him the deficiency of ignorance, i.e., that He does not know some thing; for ignorance is the greatest deficiency. Someone who chooses to attribute to Him ignorance of particulars rather than to ascribe to Him the inability to arrange these particulars in an

---

[12] Cf. Aristotle, *Metaphysics* 1094b32. Gersonides' references to Aristotle are almost always to Ibn Rushd's Paraphrases (Middle Commentaries), which were available to him in Hebrew translation. Since these are not readily available to the reader (some are still unpublished), our references are to the text of Aristotle.

[13] *ᶜIyun*, 'speculation' in the sense or rational insight and reflection, and not just forming a surmise or hypothesis.

orderly manner flees from one evil and falls into something worse. For it is apparent from the nature of the recipient that it cannot receive a greater amount of perfection. This is not a deficiency with respect to God.

Second, it is not proper that we consider an agent to be ignorant of what he effects. Rather, his knowledge of what he effects is more perfect than that possessed by someone else. For he knows, in one cognition, everything that will come about from what he has produced, and by virtue of the property he has placed within it. Someone else, however, acquires his knowledge of [this property] from the completed artifact. When he observes some new feature coming about by virtue of the nature with which [the artifact] has been endowed, this will give rise to new knowledge of that new feature. And so when [other] things come about, they will cause him to acquire new knowledge successively. Indeed, perhaps he will never complete his knowledge of things derived from the product if they are exceedingly numerous. Thus, since God is the agent of all that exists, He has a complete knowledge of what comes about, a knowledge that is incommensurable with our knowledge. For He knows in one cognition everything that will come about and by virtue of the nature with which He has endowed [everything that exists]. In contrast, we know these things only as they occur. Hence, it is not proper to reason analogously between our knowledge and His knowledge, saying that if God were to have these cognitions, He would have many cognitions, and hence His essence would be subject to plurality. For God knows through one knowledge what we know through many. For our knowledge does not encompass the many things that come about in the world by virtue of the nature with which God has endowed the world.

These two arguments are given by Maimonides in the third part of his noble treatise, *The Guide of the Perplexed*, to establish the claim that God knows all these particular notions. It is clear that the second argument, in addition to establishing that God knows all the things that occur, disproves some of the arguments of the philosophers that refute God's knowledge of particulars. Still, some of the philosophers rebutted the first argument on behalf of divine knowledge of all particulars by saying that it is not a deficiency for God not to know particular things. For not every privation is a deficiency. It is a deficiency only for something which is customarily described as possessing that thing, not for something which is not so described. For example, motion is a perfection for those who possess souls. But to say of God that He is immobile is a perfection rather than a deficiency. Similarly, they say that God's not knowing these particular things is a perfection rather than a deficiency, for His knowledge is of the worthiest of objects, and of these inferior matters. This is why the Philosopher says in Treatise XII of the *Metaphysics* that he who does not see many things is superior to one who does.[14]

Maimonides rebutted all the aforementioned arguments, and others like them, that were thought to imply that God does not know particular things, when he said that it is not appropriate to make analogies between our knowledge and divine knowledge. For just as His level of existence is superior to ours, so, too, His knowledge is superior to ours. And this is a necessary consequence, since His knowledge is identical with His essence, as the philosophers have explained. Accordingly, Maimonides often chastises the philosophers for making analogies between our knowledge and divine knowledge, and then inferring from these [analogies] that God does not know particulars. They themselves have shown us in a certain manner that the term 'knowledge' is said of God and us only homonymously. And it is evident that a demonstration cannot proceed from one thing to another if the two are homonymous. Through this argument, Maimonides became convinced that the arguments of the philosophers do not render impossible the position that God knows all these particular things. And when it has been shown that it is not impossible, it is clearly proper then to assume that He knows them, in order to remove from Him the deficiency of ignorance.

Maimonides advanced the idea that five characteristics[15] distinguish God's knowledge from ours, i.e., if, in Maimonides' view, any of these characteristics is found in God's knowledge then that characteristic cannot be found in our knowledge. I shall explain this to you by mentioning the five characteristics.

First, [in the case of God] a knowledge that is numerically one corresponds and is equivalent to many objects that differ in species. You should know that this is inconceivable with respect to our knowledge, as long as the many objects known are not unified, i.e., in a unity in which one thing completes and perfects the other. But it is important to realize that this kind of knowledge cannot be attributed to man as long as the many things known are not unified, i.e., in a unified system where one particular is the perfection of the other. For this is the only way in which

---

[14] See note 12 above.   [15] Lit.: 'things.'

many things become numerically one. For example, when we say of *man* that he is a *rational, sentient, nutritive, body*, [the definition] indicates a notion that is numerically one, even though the parts of the definition are many, for one part is the perfection and completion of the other. But it is clear that multiple notions whose parts do not perfect or complete one another cannot become unified in our knowledge.

Such is the case with particular things, which are infinite insofar as they are particular, even assuming that we can have knowledge of them. For they lack an aspect by which they can become unified. They certainly cannot become one in the sense of utmost simplicity, as is the case with God's knowledge, which is one in the sense of utmost simplicity, because He is one in the sense of utmost simplicity. Now it is clear that particular things cannot possibly stand in the relation of form and perfection to one another. For they proceed to infinity, which is clearly impossible for things that serve as form to one another, as has been shown in the *Metaphysics*.[16] Moreover, they are cyclical, i.e., with respect to the species, although not with respect to the individual, and that which is cyclical cannot possibly serve as the form and perfection for all other things. For if that were assumed to be the case, then the same thing would serve as the form of itself, which is utterly absurd. For example, let '*a*', '*b*', and '*c*' be accidents that come about, and let them proceed in an unending cycle. Let *b* be the perfection of *a*, *c* the perfection of *b*, and let *a* return and be the perfection of *c*. In that case, *a* is the perfection of *a*, and it is shown thereby that *b* is the perfection of *b*, and *c* the perfection of *c*.

Since something like this is inconceivable for us (a non-unifiable plurality becoming one in the sense of utmost simplicity and unity), Maimonides said that in this respect divine knowledge differs from human cognition. He was able to conceive of such a thing as possible [with respect to God] because of his view that the term 'knowledge' is merely homonymous when applied to God and man.

The second characteristic that distinguishes divine knowledge from human knowledge, according to Maimonides, is that God's knowledge has as its object the nonexistent. You should know that Maimonides was obliged to assume this distinction between divine and human knowledge because he had already assumed that God knows all particulars. This implies that God knows those that are nonexistent now, but will exist at

[16] *Metaphysics* 994b16.

some time and then cease to exist at some [later] time. Hence, God possesses actually existent knowledge of an accident that is now nonexistent, and so the object of His knowledge is nonexistent. This sort of thing is inconceivable with respect to our knowledge. For since knowledge and its object are numerically the same thing, then when the object is nonexistent, so is the knowledge of it. Hence, with respect to our knowledge, if the knowledge actually exists, then the object of our knowledge exists.

One ought not object that there are cases in which our knowledge is actual, yet its object nonexistent, such as our knowledge of the many mathematical figures that do not exist extramentally. We have already shown in Treatise One of this book that our knowledge of these figures refers[17] to the intelligible order pertaining to these things in the soul of the Agent Intellect, where this order is always present.[18] Maimonides could not say that God's knowledge of things that come about refers to the intelligible order belonging to them in His soul, which is always present. For if this were so, God would not have knowledge of particulars insofar as they are particulars. Rather, he would know them from the aspect of the intelligible order pertaining to them in His soul; that is the aspect in which they are not particulars. Therefore, Maimonides concluded that God's knowledge is distinguished from our knowledge with respect to this point as well. He was able to conceive of such a thing as possible [with respect to God] because of his view that the term 'knowledge' is merely homonymous when applied to God and man.

You should know that Maimonides' aforementioned second argument in support of the claim that God knows particulars as particulars appears to imply that this divine knowledge refers to the intelligible order of the world that is always in His soul, in accordance with the nature with which He has stamped it. This is why he says that the agent's knowledge of the artifact is more perfect than another's knowledge of it. For things that come about within the artifact derive from His knowledge, for he fashioned it in such a way that such things will come about within it. [By contrast], the knowledge of humans who contemplate the artifact derives from the things that come about.[19] Thus, it might be thought that some of Maimonides' statements contradict others. For it appears from what he mentioned in the second argument that God does not know particular things insofar as they are particulars but rather He knows the

---

[17] *Nismakh*, lit.: 'is attached.'   [18] *Wars* I, 10–11.   [19] *Guide* III, 21.

intelligible order pertaining to them in His soul. In order to resolve this doubt we should say that Maimonides did not wish this argument to explain *how* God knows things, for this is impossible for man to apprehend, as Maimonides has often mentioned. Rather, he wished to explain from this argument *that* God knows things, and that there is a great difference between His knowledge and our knowledge. Hence, we ought not to reason about His knowledge analogously from our knowledge, as did the philosophers. This is quite evident to those who carefully consider Maimonides' discussion on this matter; let it be examined further there.

The third of the five distinguishing characteristics is that God's knowledge encompasses what is infinite from the aspect of its being infinite. Maimonides was obliged to assent to this because he posited that God knows particulars insofar as they are particulars, and this is the aspect in which they are infinite. Now this characteristic is inconceivable with respect to our knowledge. For knowledge qua knowledge entails that the object of knowledge is a thing that is limited and encompassed, while knowledge cannot comprehend and encompass that which is infinite. Hence Maimonides said that this characteristic also distinguishes God's knowledge from human knowledge. He was able to conceive of such a characteristic as possible [with respect to God] because of his view that the term 'knowledge' is merely homonymous when applied to God and to us, as we mentioned previously.

One should not object that our knowledge also encompasses the infinite because definitions and universal statements contain an infinite number of individuals. For upon reflection this statement is incorrect. For individuals are not known from their individual aspect (and this is the aspect in which they are infinite) through definitions and universal propositions. But rather they are known from their unitary aspect, namely, the common nature. This is obvious. And if one objects that human knowledge encompasses the infinite because we know that a continuous quantity is infinitely divisible, and that a number is infinitely augmentable, then we shall reply to him that we possess this knowledge as well from the aspect of these parts being one, and not from the aspect of their being many. For our knowledge of [the divisibility of] parts is not from the aspect of, say, one part being a fingerbreadth, another a half-fingerbreadth, and another a quarter-fingerbreadth, which is the aspect in which they are many. Rather, [we know it] from the aspect in which each part is a continuous quantity, and we know that all continuous quantities are divisible.

Similarly, in the case of numbers: we do not know [that numbers are infinitely augmentable] from the aspect of, say, one number being 20, another 21, and a third 22, which is the aspect in which they are many. Rather [we know them] from the aspect in which every one of them is a number, and we know that every number can be augmented.

The fourth of the five [distinguishing] characteristics is that God's knowledge of things that come about in the future does not necessitate that the object known will be realized; rather its contradictory remains possible. Maimonides was obliged to believe this because he could not nullify the nature of the possible. For both speculation and the Torah necessitate the existence of possible things. Hence, it follows that when we assume that God knows things that will come to pass in the future, the contradictory of the thing to be realized according to God's knowledge may itself be realized, [in which case] what God knew would be realized will not [in fact] be realized. For if what God knew will be realized would undoubtedly be realized, then its contradictory disjunct would not be possible, and the nature of the possible would be negated. This is what Maimonides wanted to avoid. Now this characteristic is inconceivable with respect to our knowledge. For if Maimonides intended that God knows that one of a pair of disjuncts which he knows will be realized may not actually be realized, and that its contradictory disjunct may be realized – and this is how Maimonides' intention should be understood – then we would not call something like this knowledge but rather opinion. This is self-evident. For when we say that we possess knowledge which one of two contradictory disjuncts[20] will be realized, we consider it impossible for that disjunct not to be realized. But if we reckon that it may not be realized then we call something like this 'opinion,' not 'knowledge.' I mean that we would say in that case: "We *think* that this disjunct will be realized," rather than, "We *know* that it will be realized." And if what we thought would be realized is not in fact realized, then we consider this opinion to be an error, rather than knowledge. This is self-evident.

If Maimonides intended that God [i] knows clearly which one of two possibilities will be realized, and [ii] that He does not know that it may not be realized, and [iii] that this [its non-realization] is indeed a possibility – i.e., that it may not be realized but its contradictory disjunct may be

---

[20] E.g., 'Socrates will go to the store' or 'Socrates will not go to the store.' Since Socrates' going to the store in the future is possible, these disjuncts are sometimes called below 'disjuncts' or 'parts' of the possible.

realized – then this would not be considered by us to be knowledge but error – i.e., when the contradictory disjunct of what we judged would be realized is itself realized. This is self-evident.

Hence, it is evident that, according to this principle, what is knowledge with respect to God is the opposite[21] of what is knowledge with respect to us. For error is the opposite of knowledge, and opinion is also the oppositie of knowledge in some manner. For this reason, then, Maimonides considered divine knowledge to differ from human knowledge. This may be the difference between these two sorts of knowledge according to Maimonides' view, because he holds that 'knowledge' is absolutely homonymous when applied to God and to us.

One ought not object that Maimonides intended that God does not determine by His knowledge which one of the alternative possibilities will be realized. For he believed that God knows distinctly and precisely which disjunct will be realized. This is clear from his language when he mentions this difference. Indeed, even if we were to concede this objection, this characteristic would also be inconceivable with respect to our knowledge. For we do not call such a thing knowledge but rather 'perplexity' and 'confusion.' We would say that we are perplexed and unable to reckon which possibility among several will occur. And the strength of the perplexity increases in proportion to the number of disjuncts.

Perplexity and confusion are opposites of knowledge, certainly when perplexity is interpreted in this manner. For something that comes into existence has an almost infinite number of disjuncts in the thousand years, for example, that precede its existence. Assume that each of one of the intermediate accidents may or may not exist, and then assume that, when it exists, it may be in a certain way or not in that way. If you consider things in this manner, then the last accident that comes about, as a result of the rest of the accidents when they have been realized, will have infinite pairs of contradictory disjuncts [preceding it]. Now this sort of thing would be called by us utter confusion and perplexity, i.e., a situation where one is perplexed over whether an infinite number of disjuncts are in a certain way. Perplexity and uncertainty are less frequent when the contradictory disjuncts are fewer in number. Hence, the answer that specifies in more detail one thing from another is a more complete answer, although it may not specify that thing completely. For example, when one says of a

---

[21] *Maqbil.*

boat that it is a *body, wooden, crafted, possessing an interior*, and *uncovered*, each one of these specifications adds to our knowledge, since it removes the perplexity contained in the preceding specification, although none of them specifies a boat completely from something else.[22]

The fifth of these five characteristics is that God's knowledge does not change when the things about which He had foreknowledge come about, even though the object of His knowledge has changed. For the thing [known] was at first possibly existent and afterwards actually existent. Maimonides was obliged to believe this, for God's knowledge is His essence, a point indubitably shown in various places. And since His essence does not change, it follows that His knowledge is unchanging. Now when we examine the matter, we clearly see that this characteristic is inconceivable with respect to our intellect and wisdom. According to Maimonides' aforementioned position, God knows that the thing that will come about is nonexistent at a certain time, then is existent at a certain time, and then is nonexistent at a later time. This is true of all the things in the world that come about. When the thing actually comes about there is no additional knowledge, and nothing comes about that was unknown to God previously. Rather what comes about is what God knew would come in the way that it actually did. Since this is so, it is evident that God knows, according to this position, everything that will come about and everything that has come about. This is also an obligatory conclusion for anyone who wishes to avoid attributing to God ignorance of such things. For ignorance of what has come about is greater, and [hence] a more serious deficiency, than ignorance of what will come about. This is self-evident.

Since this is so, the following dilemma is inevitable: either God knows that one of the disjuncts of the possible,[23] whose coming about He had foreknown, has now come about; or, He knows that the actually occurring disjunct has now come about, although it is not the disjunct whose coming about had been known to him before the coming about of the actually occurring disjunct. If we say that He knows that the disjunct of the possible, whose coming about He had foreknown, has come about, it follows that His knowledge of many of these things would be of the class of what we consider error and not knowledge. This is so because the

---

[22] This is a subtle and perhaps ironic reference to *Guide* I, 59, where Maimonides instructs the reader how to render one's concept of God more specific and accurate.

[23] I.e., one of a pair of contradictory possibilities.

disjunct that he knew would occur might *not* occur, and it may happen with respect to many of these things, that the disjunct that God knew would occur does not in fact occur. Whoever thinks that a thing has occurred which has not in fact occurred is undoubtedly in error. If we say that God knows that the actualized disjunct of the possible has come about, although it is not the disjunct that He had known would occur prior to its actualization, this is certainly an origination of knowledge and a change in God's knowledge. This is what Maimonides tried to avoid when he laid down [the fifth characteristic] as a principle concerning God's knowledge.

One should not say that the disjunct that God foreknew would come to pass is indubitably the disjunct that occurs. For if that were assumed, then all things would be necessitated, and there would be nothing possible in this world. Now this is the falsehood that Maimonides wished to avoid and that led him to conclude that the contradictory of what God knows will occur may indeed occur.

Since this is so, it is clear that such a characteristic is completely inconceivable for us. For this sort of 'knowledge' is either considered 'error' with respect to us, or it contains origination and change, rather than unchange and unorigination, which was laid down as a principle [of God's knowledge.] This characteristic [of God's knowledge] is absolutely inconceivable for our knowledge. For what we call with respect to God 'unchanging knowledge' we call with respect to us 'error' or 'originated and changing knowledge.' Each one of these is the opposite of unchanging knowledge, for error is the opposite of knowledge in our case, and originated and changing knowledge is the opposite of unchanging and unoriginated knowledge in our case. And because this characteristic is inconceivable for our sort of knowledge, Maimonides concluded that God's knowledge differs from ours also in this respect. This was possible for him because [of his view that] the term 'knowledge' is merely homonymous when applied to God and man. And Maimonides held that due to the exalted rank of God's knowledge, we are not able to apprehend what He knows and how He knows it. For our attempt to know the how [of divine knowledge] would be the same as our attempt to become Him, and for our apprehension to become His. Consequently, when we attempt to investigate how God knows things, we arrive at great absurdities, since the nature of this knowledge necessitates that we cannot conceive or comprehend it.

Chapter Three

We should first investigate whether Maimonides' rebuttals of all the possible arguments of the philosophers who disagree with him are sufficient before we investigate whether the arguments that the philosophers advance to establish their view are correct or not, and whether they entail what they are claimed to entail. For if Maimonides' rebuttals of these arguments are sufficient, we shall not have to investigate them in another manner.

We say that our method in this matter is first to investigate (1) whether it is possible that the similarity[24] between God's knowledge and our knowledge reaches the degree of difference claimed by Maimonides, i.e., that God's knowledge is the opposite of our knowledge to such an extent that what we consider 'opinion' or 'error' or 'perplexity' is considered 'knowledge' with respect to God;[25] or (2) whether the similarity is such that this sort of difference is impossible between them.

It appears that Maimonides' view on God's knowledge does not proceed from speculative principles since, as I shall demonstrate, speculation rejects it. Rather it appears that the Torah exerted considerable pressure upon him in this matter. Now we shall investigate whether this view is required by the Torah after we complete our investigation into what speculation requires.

That speculation rejects Maimonides' position on God's knowledge will be shown by what I shall now say. For it appears that God's knowledge is associated with our knowledge by priority and posteriority, i.e., that the term 'knowledge' is said of God by priority, and of another besides Him by posteriority. For He possesses knowledge by virtue of His essence, whereas another's knowledge is caused by [God's] knowledge. In such a case, the term is said of the former by priority and of other things to which the term applies by posteriority. Similarly with respect to such terms as 'exists,' 'one,' 'essence' and other terms that behave in this fashion, i.e., they are said of God by priority and of others beside Him by posteriority. This is so because His existence, oneness, and essence belong to Him by virtue of Himself, and from Him emanate the existence, oneness, and

---

[24] *Shittuf*, lit.: 'sharing' or 'having in common.' According to the first alternative, God's knowledge and our knowledge share only the name 'knowledge'; their meanings are opposite. This is what is often translated here as 'homonymy.'

[25] In that case we would 'associate' merely the name.

essence of every existent. This is evident entirely to one who examines this treatise, and it will be elucidated completely in the Treatise Five of this book.[26] Since this is so, it seems that the only difference between God's knowledge and our knowledge is that God's knowledge is more perfect than our knowledge, for this is the case with terms that are said by priority and by posteriority. Now if what we have posited is true, and since it is evident that a more perfect knowledge is truer with respect to determinateness and clarity, it seems that God's knowledge is truer with respect to determinateness and clarity. Hence it cannot be that what is called 'knowledge' with respect to God is called 'opinion,' 'error,' or 'perplexity' with respect to us.

We can demonstrate through another method that the difference between God's knowledge and ours cannot be the difference that Maimonides mentioned: When we affirm something of God, we proceed from things with which we are familiar, as if one were to say that we affirm of God that he is knowing because of the knowledge found in us. For example, because we apprehend that the knowledge found in our intellect is a perfection for the intellect – without which it could not be an intellect in act – we say that God is a knower, because we have shown that He is undoubtedly an intellect in act. Now it is self-evident that when we affirm a predicate of something because of its existence in something else, it is not said of those two things with complete homonymy. For no analogy can be drawn between merely homonymous things. For example, just as we cannot say that man possesses intellect because body is continuous, so, too, we cannot say this if we apply the same term for 'body' and 'intellect' with complete homonymy. This is self-evident. Since this is so, it is clear that knowledge is not said of God and of us with complete homonymy.

Now since it is [also] clear that it cannot be said of God and of us univocally, clearly all that remains is for it be said of God and of us by priority and posteriority. The other things said of God and of us are to be explained in the same way. Accordingly, we have shown that the only difference between God's knowledge and our knowledge is that God's knowledge is much more perfect, and that this sort of knowledge is truer with respect to determinateness and clarity. The homonymy between God's knowledge and our knowledge is like the homonymy between His

---

[26] *Wars* V, 3, 12.

substance and the substance of the acquired intellect belonging to us,[27] for knowledge and the knower are numerically the same, as we mentioned above. And just as his substance is more perfect than the substance of the acquired intellect belonging to us, such is the case with His knowledge and our knowledge.

We can demonstrate by another method that the difference between God's knowledge and ours cannot be the difference that Maimonides mentioned. When we investigate what things should be affirmed or negated of God, it is evident that we accord the exact same meaning to those predicates in affirmations or negations. For example, when we investigate whether God is a body or not a body, it is evident that the term 'body' possesses the same signification, in a certain manner, in both disjuncts. For if the name 'body' were said with complete homonymy in the negative and affirmative disjuncts, then we would not consider the disjuncts to be contradictory disjuncts. This is self-evident. For example, just as one does not say, "I shall examine whether the wall is a body or not a color," he does not say that if he posits a single term for both body and color. For these disjuncts are not contradictory disjuncts. Since this is so, and since it is clear that when we deny existing things of God, the predicate does not signify [the attribute] in God and in us with complete homonymy, so, too, when we affirm some existing thing of Him that we possess, the principle is the same. For example, we say of God that He is immobile,[28] for if He were mobile, he would be a body, since this is true of that which is mobile qua mobile. Now it is evident that the term 'mobile' in this proposition is not said completely homonymously with the term 'mobile' used in propositions that are said in reference to us. For if that were the case, then we would lack proof showing that God is immobile, since the mobile thing that implies corporeality is the mobile thing to which we refer. But if 'mobile' is said [in reference to God] and to us with complete homonymy, then there is no implication that God is a body. Since this is so, and since it is clear that the predicates that we deny of God are not said in reference to Him and in reference to us with complete homonymy, it is also clear that the predicates that we affirm of God are not said in reference to Him and in reference to us with complete homonymy. For at first we were doubtful about whether these

---

[27] The 'acquired intellect' refers to the unified collection of intelligibles (*muskalot*), i.e., the real definitions and eternal truths acquired by the mind.

[28] *Bilti-mitnoᶜeᶜa*: lit.: 'immobile,' 'unmovable.'

predicates should be affirmed or denied of God, until we completed our investigation, and then we affirmed or denied them of Him.

Indeed, were the things that we affirmed of God said with complete homonymy in reference to Him and us, it would not be more worthy to deny rather than affirm of God any of the terms that are predicated of things in our world. Thus, one could say, for example, that God is a body, and not intend by 'body' something possessing quantity, but something completely homonymous with what we call 'body.' Likewise, one could say that God is unknowing, since the term 'knowledge' does not signify for him in this statement what our term 'knowledge' signifies.

One should not object that we deny corporeality of God because it is a deficiency for us, and that we affirm knowledge because it is a perfection for us. For the *term* 'corporeality' is not a deficiency, but rather its *meaning* is a deficiency; likewise, the term 'knowledge' is not a perfection, but rather its meaning is a perfection. The proof of this is that were we to signify by the term 'corporeality' what the term 'knowledge' signifies, and by the term 'knowledge' what 'corporeality' signifies, then corporeality would be a perfection for us and knowledge a deficiency. Moreover, we do not affirm or deny anything of God unless we have first investigated whether the presence of that thing befits Him or not. We do not investigate whether it is a perfection or imperfection for us. Since this is so, it is clear that speculation rejects the notion that the term 'knowledge' is said of Him and of us with complete homonymy.

There is another method showing that speculation rejects the notion that the term 'knowledge' is said of Him and of us with complete homonymy. Even if we conceded that God's knowledge is completely homonymous with our knowledge, it is impossible that this knowledge contains a combination of opposites, i.e., that it is unchanging and unoriginated, while being changing and originated. Maimonides already accepted the presence of opposites in these things, as we explained concerning the principle that he laid down with respect to God's knowledge. Moreover, because he desired to avoid attributing the term 'ignorance' to God, he said that God knows all things. Yet he kept the notion of [ignorance] with God, as we explained concerning the principle that he posited with respect to God's knowledge, i.e., we call that sort of knowledge 'ignorance' rather than 'knowledge.'

Now the Torah exerted pressure on Maimonides to believe what he believed concerning God's knowledge, as we mentioned, and when he saw that speculation varied greatly from his belief, he said what he said concerning God's knowledge in order to evade all their arguments and to establish what he thought the Torah demands. We shall investigate the latter after we have completed our discussion of the current topic.

Still, one finds a certain plausibility in Maimonides' claim that knowledge is said of God and of us with complete homonymy, since it has already been shown that there is no ratio[29] between God and any of the existing things. Consequently, it is impossible to say anything of Him and of his creatures except with complete homonymy. It is also not proper for God to be described by any attribute, since every attribute implies multiplicity, i.e., the matter of [the composition of] subject and attribute. For this reason as well it is evident that when God is described by any attribute at all, that attribute is said with complete homonymy of Him and of us. For in God it signifies a notion that is identical with the essence of that which is described, a point Maimonides developed a great deal in his noble treatise, *The Guide of the Perplexed*.

Now since this last argument seems to necessitate the position that attributes are said in reference to God and to us with complete homonymy, and the previous arguments that we raised necessitate that these attributes are not said with complete homonymy, would that I knew the resolution of the contradiction!

We say that close reflection reveals that there are attributes in our world that are said of God and something other than God by priority and by posteriority, and yet do not entail multiplicity. This is so because not every utterance that is said of something in an essential manner[30] entails multiplicity. It does so if the first part serves as the real subject for the second part. If it is not the real subject,[31] even though it is the nominal subject,[32] no multiplicity is entailed. For example, when we say of a case of redness that it is the "color red," it does not follow that the redness is composed of "color" and "red." For color is not an existing thing that serves as the subject for red, but rather it is a nominal subject only. This is the case no matter how many specifications you bring, as when you say: "It is a color that is intermediate between black and white, inclining more to black than white," all these [specifications] signify only one simple thing;

[29] *Yaḥas*, 'relation,' 'proportion.'   [30] *Mi-derekh ma hu*, lit: 'of the way of' 'what is it?'
[31] Lit.: 'subject-in-existence.'   [32] Lit.: 'subject-in-statement.'

the multiplication of conditions and specifications explain which simple color this is.

The same principle applies to things that have no [real] subject, i.e., the utterance that is said of them does not signify any multiplicity in them. For example, if we say of the intellect that moves the sphere of the sun that it is "the intellect that apprehends the particular order according to which the movement of that sphere is ordered," this utterance does not signify multiplicity [in the intellect], because the subject there is only nominal and not real. Even though "intellect" is said of other separate intellects besides this one, the point is not that they agree in subject and differ with respect to their specific differences. But rather [the utterance] is said of the particular intellect from among the simple [intellects] that are included by the term 'intellect' in this utterance. For these intellects differ from each other essentially without their agreeing in anything. For if they were to agree, then they would be composite and not simple.[33] They differ in the same way that their conceptions differ.[34] Since this is so, it is evident that when God is described by one or many attributes, these attributes do not imply multiplicity within Him, for He has no subject, and hence these attributes only signify something simple.

Now our claim that attributes are said of God by priority and of the rest of existing things by posteriority is compatible with our acknowledgment that there is no ratio between Him and his creatures. For terms said by priority and posteriority can be found that behave in this manner. For example, the term 'existent' is said of substance by priority and of accidents by posteriority, as has been shown in the *Metaphysics*.[35] Now it is clear that there is no ratio between substance and accidents. You should know that there are attributes by which God must be described, such as your saying that he is a substance. It is not that the term 'substance' is said of him and others univocally, but rather by priority and by posteriority. For that which disposes all things described by a certain attribute to be

[33] The separate intellects are not different individuals of the same species, nor are they different species belonging to the same genus, for that would imply that a separate intellect's essence is composite, defined by a genus ("intellect") and specific difference ("that conceives a certain order"). Rather, each separate intellect is *sui generis*. So the phrase "intellect that conceives a certain order" indicates one simple notion and not a composite one.

[34] Indeed, because of the Aristotelian identification of the cognizing intellect and its object, the separate intellects are identical with their conceptions. They are cognizers cognizing cognitions as it were.

[35] *Metaphysics* 1028a, 13–29.

described by that attribute – because of what they have acquired primarily and essentially from it – is more properly named by that term. Now God is that which disposes all other things to be substances, because he gives them their substantiality. Hence, he is more properly called substance. Moreover, his substantiality is self-existent, whereas all other existents [receive their substantiality] from another. Now what is self-existent is more properly called 'substance' than what exists on account of something else.

It has been shown likewise that God is more properly called 'existent' and 'one' than anything else. In our commentary on the *Metaphysics* we already explained the defect in Ibn Sīnā's arguments that try to refute describing God by these attributes.[36] The Torah also agreed that these two attributes signify his essence more than any other thing, and for this reason singled Him out by the tetragrammaton name, which signifies being and existence, and by the name 'One.' This is made clear in [Moses'] statement: "Hear O Israel, God is our God, God is One" [Deut. 6:4]. It was also made clear from what Moses our Teacher, peace be upon him, asked: "They will ask me "What is his name?" What shall I say to them?" [Exod. 3:13], to which was answered, "I am what I am," which is a term signifying being and existence. Through this it may be shown that it is impossible for God not to be described as 'intellect,' 'living,' 'conceiving,' 'provident,' 'beneficent,' 'powerful,' and 'willing,' and that He is more properly described by these names than others are apart from him. This is evident after [only] a little reflection by the reader of this treatise, together with the foregoing remarks on the subject. It shall be shown further, God willing, in Treatise Five of this book. Still, these various terms intend one thing that is utterly simple, as we already explained. The disparity between the intention of these and similar attributes when said of God and when said of things beside Him, is [the same] as the disparity between the rank of God and the rank of others with respect to essential perfection and nobility, i.e., they are said of God in a more perfect manner from the manner in which they are said of others.

Now that all this has been settled, it is evident that speculation shows that 'knowledge' is said of God and of others beside Him by priority and by posteriority, not with complete homonymy, and that this

---

[36] Gersonides' commentary on the *Metaphysics* (Ibn Rushd's paraphrase thereof) is no longer extant. But he also takes up the criticism of Ibn Sīnā in *Wars* v, 3, 12, where he argues against Ibn Sīnā's view that *oneness* and *existence* are accidents that are predicated of substances.

speculation rejects what Maimonides posited as a principle concerning God's knowledge in order to rebut the arguments of the philosophers.

Chapter Four

We have shown that speculation rejects what Maimonides posited in order to rebut the arguments of the philosophers, and that it is obvious that the dispute with them concerning the rebuttal of their arguments should be from the perspective of speculation, and not merely from that of the Torah. So now we ourselves should investigate whether the arguments employed by the philosophers to imply that God does not know any of the particular possible things are valid or not, and if so, whether or not they imply what the philosophers claimed they imply. But before we undertake to investigate their arguments, we have seen fit to complete our investigation of God's knowledge, in a summary fashion. For in that way, what I shall say about the claims of the philosophers will be clearer and more complete to one who examines our words.

We say that several considerations show that God knows particular things.

First, it is evident that God is the agent of everything that comes about in the sublunar world, substance or accident, and that the Agent Intellect and the heavenly bodies function as His instruments. This is so because all things derive from the effluence that flows upon the Agent Intellect and the celestial bodies from God. Now it is evident that an instrument qua instrument does not move to perform its function without the knowledge of the artisan. Hence, evidently one may hereby infer that God knows all these things.

Second, it is obligatory that God knows His essence according to His rank in existence. Now His essence is such that all existents flow from it hierarchically. Hence it follows that He knows all the existents that flow from Him. For if He did not know them, His knowledge of His essence would be deficient since He would not know what may flow from Him according to its existence within Him. Since this is so, and since it is evident that whatever substances and accidents that come about flow from Him, it is clear that He knows whatever substances and accidents come about. Hence it follows that God knows all these particular things.

Third, it has previously been shown that the Agent Intellect possesses knowledge, in some manner, of the things that come about in the sublunar world. Since this is so, and since God is the agent, the form, and the end of the separate intellects, as has been shown in the *Metaphysics*,[37] it follows that He possesses the knowledge belonging to the other intellects, for their knowledge relates to God's, may He be blessed, as matter to form. This is like the [master artisan] who, through knowing the form of the house, knows the forms of the beams and bricks that are known by the artisans whose crafts are ancillary to the craft of building. [Unlike them,] however, the principal artisan knows these things in a more perfect manner, i.e., insofar as they are part of the house, as was noted previously. Hence it is clear that the knowledge of sublunar things, which was previously shown beyond a shadow of a doubt to belong to the Agent Intellect, belongs to God, may He be blessed, in a more perfect manner. This also shows that God knows these particular things.

Once this has been settled, i.e., that these arguments establish that God knows particular things, and that the aforementioned arguments of the philosophers rule out such knowledge, we can only assert that He knows them in one respect and not in another. Would that I knew [in which respects]!

Now it was shown above that possible things are determined and ordered from one aspect and are possible in another. Hence it is clear that the aspect in which [God] knows them is the aspect in which they are ordered and determined, as we previously showed regarding the Agent Intellect. For this is the aspect in which knowledge pertains to them. The aspect in which He does not know them is the aspect in which they are undetermined, namely, the aspect in which they are possible. For in this aspect it is impossible for knowledge to pertain to them. God does know, however, that [these possibilities] may not come about because of the power of choice that He disposed within man in order to complete what is lacking in the protection of the heavenly bodies, as was explained in the previous treatise.

[God] does not know which of the disjuncts of the possible comes about from the aspect in which it is possible. For if He did, then nothing in the sublunar world would be possible. Now the lack of His knowing which of the disjuncts of the possible comes about insofar as it is possible does not constitute a deficiency for Him. For perfect knowledge of a thing occurs when it is known as it really is. When it is apprehended differently

[37] Aristotle, *Metaphysics* XII, 7.

from what it really is, this is error and not knowledge. Therefore, He knows all these things in the most perfect manner possible, for he knows them from the aspect of their being ordered clearly and determinately, yet he also knows what possibility they possess due to [human] choice, according to their real possible nature. This explains why men who are supposed to suffer evils are commanded by God, through His prophets, to improve their behaviour so that they will be saved from them, as was the case of Zedekiah, [who was commanded] to make peace with the King of Babylonia. This indicates that God knows that a future possible may not necessarily come to pass. He knows [the possible] from the aspect in which it is ordered, together with His knowledge that it is possible that it may not come about, from the aspect in which it is possible.

We shall now explain that the aforementioned arguments establishing God's knowledge of particulars do not establish that God knows more than the amount [we indicated], and that the arguments adduced by the philosophers to refute God's knowledge of particulars do not at all refute the manner of knowledge which we have necessitated of God. That the aforementioned arguments do not imply that God knows more than this measure of knowledge is evident.

The first argument established that God has knowledge of all particulars because the Agent Intellect and the heavenly bodies are His instruments for His activities in the sublunar world. It is evident, however, that this argument implies only that God knows the orders from which these activities flow. A separate substance[38] qua separate substance acts upon anything that is prepared to receive its action without having apprehension of each part qua that specific part. In this manner the Agent Intellect effects all sublunar phenomena, as has been previously explained. It is true, however, that a corporeal agent, insofar as it is corporeal, does not effect anything of its craft without apprehending the particular that is the recipient of the actions. Thus, the productive activities are via the intellect and the imagination, as has been explained in *On the Soul*.[39] This is the case because the [corporeal] agent must approach the recipient, for the recipient will not receive the agent's volitions unless he encounters it; then the agent will shape it as he wishes. Matter receives the volition of an incorporeal agent, however, much more easily, and hence it is not

---

[38] I.e., separate from matter, incorporeal.   [39] Aristotle, *On the Soul* III, 3.

required that the incorporeal agent apprehend the particular that it makes qua this particular.

We can ascertain the ease in which matter receives the form's volition if we ascertain the movements of a man that are measured according to his mental conception. For example, when a man wishes to sing a song that he has conceived in his soul, the conception moves immediately the vocal cords in such wondrous movements that cannot be produced by musical instruments. In this way the mental conception will move a musician's fingers easily without his concentrating on how each movement should be executed. Likewise with speech: a man effortlessly pronounces and says the letters he wants without concentrating upon the proper way of pronouncing each letter at the time it is pronounced. Since this is so, it is evident that it is possible for God to be the agent of these things without knowing them from the aspect in which they are particulars. However, He does know them in a more perfect manner.

The second argument established that God knows these things on account of His knowing His essence. It is also evident that this argument implies only that He knows the intelligible order that pertains to these things whose existence emanates from Him.

The third argument established that God knows particulars because the Agent Intellect knows them. It is also evident that this argument implies only that He knows the intelligible order that pertains to these things because the knowledge that the Agent Intellect possesses of these things is in this manner, as was shown in what proceeded. Now God's knowledge of this order differs from that of the Agent Intellect in being more perfect, as we mentioned previously. A more complete explanation of this will be provided in Treatise Five of this book, with God's help.

Nor does what we have mentioned of Maimonides' arguments establishing that God knows all these things imply that God knows more than the amount [we indicated]. His first argument established that God knows these things in order to avoid attributing ignorance to Him. It is clear that if God knows these things in the way we have explained He will not be ignorant of them at all. Indeed, He knows them completely as they really are. As for the second argument, we noted when discussing it that it implies that God knows the intelligible order of these things from which their existence flows, not more than that amount. Now this is what we have assumed here concerning God's knowledge.

Having shown this point, we shall now show that none of the aforementioned arguments of the philosophers implies that God does not know
these things in the manner we have assumed. The first of the aforementioned arguments of the philosophers (which says that God does not
apprehend particular things because he has no hylic faculty) does not
imply that God does not know the intelligible order pertaining to these
things from the aspect of their being ordered and determined. This argument implies only that He does not know them from the aspect of their
being particular and designated. This is self-evident.

The second argument (which says that God does not know particular
things because they are temporal) does not imply a refutation of what we
assumed concerning God's knowledge of particular things. For we did not
assume that He knows them from the aspect in which they are temporal;
rather we assumed that He knows the intelligible order pertaining to them
from the aspect in which they are ordered. From this aspect they are not
temporal.

As for the third argument (which says that it is impossible for God to
apprehend these things, either as universals or as particulars, for if this
were possible then the superior would be perfected by the inferior, which
is clearly absurd) – we have found upon investigation that the consequent
of this conditional syllogism does not follow from the antecedent. For it
does not follow from our position – that God knows the intelligible order
pertaining to sublunar substances and accidents – that He is perfected by
these things. For God does not acquire this knowledge from these sublunar things; rather, His knowledge of them is based upon the intelligible
order pertaining to them in His soul. Consequently, it is evident that this
knowledge does not cause God to be perfected by something besides Him.
Rather, the intelligible order in the divine soul is that which gives to all
these things their existence. It is clear that this argument, then, is correct.

As for the fourth argument (which says that if God apprehended these
particulars His essence would become multiple, from which it was concluded that God does not know particulars, either the things they share,
i.e., their essential properties, or the things by virtue of which they are
particulars, i.e., their possible properties[40]) – investigation shows that the
consequent of this argument does not follow from the antecedent. For

[40] Lit.: 'things.'

our position does not imply that God's essence becomes multiple. For the orders that pertain to these things become unified, i.e., they have an aspect in which they are one, as we have mentioned on numerous occasions. God knows them from this aspect, and not from the aspect in which they are not unified, i.e., the aspect in which they are particular and designated. For from this aspect they cannot be apprehended except through a hylic faculty. Now this is a deficient apprehension because its manner is accidental and not essential, and, consequently, cannot be attributed to God. As for the claim that if God apprehended these things, His essence would be divided into the more perfect and the more deficient, this is incorrect. The Agent Intellect is one simple thing, as is the acquired intellect, even though there is a sort of multiplicity in their concepts. This will be explained more fully in Treatise Five of this book, God willing.

As for the fifth argument (which says that since particulars are infinite, there cannot be any knowledge comprehending them) – it is evident that it does not imply the refutation of our position on God's knowledge of these things. For the intelligible orders pertaining to these things are not infinite but rather bounded of necessity, and from this aspect [such things] may be known. But this argument does imply that they are not subject to knowledge from the aspect in which they are particular, which is the aspect in which they are infinite.

As for the sixth argument, which says that it is impossible for God to know things that come about, for if that were possible, then either [1] He would know them before their occurrence, or [2] He would know them only simultaneously with their occurrence. If [1] He knew them before their occurrence, then His knowledge would have as its object the nonexistent. Moreover, if this were the case, then the following would be unavoidable: either [a] He knows them according to their possible nature, in which case the contradictory will be possible of what He knows, from among these things, happens to occur, or [b] he knows perfectly which contradictory disjunct will occur, and its contradictory is no longer possible. Now if we assume that [a] He knows such things according to their possible nature, it follows that the knowledge He possesses of such things before they come about will change when they come about. For before they come into existence, it is possible for them to occur or not to occur. But after they have come into existence, then that possibility is removed. Now since the intellect becomes substantial by virtue of what it knows, it thereby follows that God's essence is in constant flux, but this is utterly absurd. If we assume that [b] God knows perfectly which disjunct of the contradiction will come about, it follows the nature of possibility is removed. Yet if it is assumed that [2] God possesses this knowledge only simultaneously with their occurrence, then he will constantly possess originated knowledge, and his essence changes. Now since all this is absurd, we inferred from [the argument] that God does not know these things at all.

We say that it is evident that this argument does not imply the refutation of our position on God's knowledge of these things. For when we posited that God knows these sublunar things in the aspect in which they are ordered, and that He also knows the nature of possibility which they possess due to human choice, none of the absurdities mentioned in the argument follow. Thus, it does not follow that His knowledge has as its object the nonexistent, for we posited His knowledge of these things as referring to the intelligible order in his soul pertaining to them, and not to the particulars that themselves come about. It also does not follow that the nature of the possible is removed when we assume that He knows which of the disjunct possibilities will occur. We assume that He knows that this disjunct ought to come about from the aspect of these things being ordered, and not absolutely. For he gauges that it is possible for this not to be realized from the aspect of choice. And this is the aspect in which these things are possible.

As for the seventh argument (which says that if God knew these particular things, then He should order them in an equitable and perfect order, but that this is the opposite of what our senses perceive of these particular things, namely, that they possess injustice and considerable disorder) – when it has been shown that the order pertaining to these possible things, and the possibility that has been ascribed to them, display the utmost order and equity, this argument will be refuted. We have already shown this completely in our commentary on Job and we shall show it further, with God's help, in the fourth treatise of this book.

As for the eighth objection (which says that if God did know all these things, it would follow that the impossible becomes possible. For it has been shown that when a continuous quantity is divided, the possibility remains within it to be divided [further], insofar as it is a quantity. But if it is assumed that God knows all these things, it follows that He knows all the divisions into which this continuous quantity can be divided. In that case the continuous quantity would possess indivisible parts, i.e., the parts at which God's knowledge of these parts terminates. For if this were not the case, then this sort of divine knowledge would be deficient) – we say that this argument is incorrect. For if we concede that God knows the nature of every individual body insofar as it is divisible, this does not imply that [the body's] division will end. Rather He knows the division according to its [true] nature; I mean that He knows that whatever is divided retains within itself the possibility of being divided [further] insofar as it possesses quantity – not that He knows the end of a division that, by its very nature, has no end. For such knowledge would be considered error, and not knowledge. Moreover, according to our explanation of God's knowledge, we say that He knows that the universal nature of quantity qua quantity is one of perpetual divisibility – not that He knows this of each quantity. For if this were the case, then His knowledge would be deficient since it would not be [of a particular] essentially. Divisibility belongs to each particular only insofar as it is a quantity, and not insofar as it is, for example, wood or copper.[41]

As for the explanation based on this argument that some recent thinkers have advanced (that a quantity is composed of indivisible parts, because of their claim that God knows the capacity of a quantity to divide – for if those parts were themselves divisible, then God's knowledge would not encompass all the parts to which the quantity divides) this is also clearly absurd: Our claim that God knows all these things does not imply that He knows all the divisions that this quantity is capable of dividing into. For the utterance "all the divisions" is clearly absurd, for in that utterance we attribute universality to that which cannot be universalized, since the infinite cannot be universalized. Rather, [the aforementioned claim] implies that He knows that every part to which quantity divides retain the capacity of dividing [further] insofar as it is a quantity. In this manner He knows this capacity according to its nature of limitless division. But He does not know the limit of what naturally possesses no limit, for this would be error, not knowledge!

This doubt is similar to the doubt discussed by the Philosopher in his *On Generation and Corruption*, where he explains the notion that a body is divisible into things that are incapable of [further] division. For if it were assumed that a body is divisible entirely into every part into which it can

---

[41] To know of quantity that it is perpetually divisible is to know something of it essentially; to know of this pen that it is perpetually divisible is to know something of it accidentally, since it is divisible only insofar as it possesses quantity.

be divided, this would be a possible falsehood, yet not an absurdity. But if this is assumed to be the case, then a body will be divided into indivisible things. For if they were divisible, then the body would not be divisible into everything into which it is capable of being divided, as was originally assumed. Since this is so, one would think that this implies that a body is divisible into what is not divisible.[42]

We should not solve the doubt using the method of Ibn Rushd, who understood it to be the Philosopher's solution in this passage. For the solution is incorrect and does not resolve the doubt, as we shall show. For to solve this doubt Ibn Rushd said there:

"That a body divides completely *ad infinitum* is not impossible in all respects but is possible in one respect and impossible in another. The respect in which we consider it to be possible is that of potential division and not the actual division of all its points together. For if that were true, then a body could be broken down into indivisible things. But it does not follow from a body's potentially complete division at every one of its points *ad infinitum* that it is actually divisible thus. This is so because when every point in a body is equally divisible, it does not follow that all of them can be divided concurrently, and that the body itself can be divided at all of these points concurrently, even if it is divisible equally at each of these points, just as it does not follow from the statement 'A man can grasp all the sciences' that he can grasp them all together. For what is true of a thing when separate, may not be true of it when composite, as has been explained in *On Sophistical Refutations*.[43] That sort of fallacy occurs here.

"However, a body would be capable of division concurrently at [all] its points if one point were in contact with another. But it has been shown in the sixth treatise of the *Physics* that one point is not consecutive with another.[44] Hence, when we divide a magnitude at a point, the division cannot happen at a point consecutive to it. It would have been possible previously for the division to have happened at another point, just as it was possible for the division to have happened at the [actual] point. But once the division happened at the first point, the possibility of the division occurring at the point consecutive to it was nullified. Thus, let us take a point at any place we wish where the magnitude can be divided. After we

---

[42] *On Generation and Corruption*, 316a15–317a2.
[43] Aristotle, *On Sophistical Refutations* 166a, 23–33.   [44] Aristotle, *Physics* 231b, 8–9.

have divided the magnitude at that point, it is impossible to divide it at any second point at a place we wish, for it is impossible to divide it at a point consecutive to the first point."[45]

It is clear that this solution is incorrect. For from the aspect of the nature of quantity there is nothing to prevent the division from taking place at every one of the points, i.e., nothing to prevent the division happening at one point because it has already happened at a consecutive point. If this cannot [in fact] take place in a body, the [impossibility] stems from the aspect of that body being physical, for from that aspect the division terminates at a fixed measure, less than which cannot be received by the form for that body, as has been shown in the *Physics*. [Moreover,] it is clear that this solution does not resolve the doubt. For whatever lies *between* any two of the infinite points that, according to this position, are potentially in the body cannot be itself divisible. Thus, the body will be composed of indivisible things, and these things would be in the body potentially. The doubt cannot be resolved by our saying that it is not possible to arrive at these things through actual division, which is what Ibn Rushd's solution says.

We, however, solve the doubt as follow: when we characterize 'the possible' as "that which, when assumed, no absurdity results," [it is understood that] what has been assumed to exist is indeed possible. If what has been assumed to exist is not possible, then an absurdity results. Now we can show that, in the aforementioned statement [from *On Generation and Corruption*], something has already been assumed to exist that is not possible. For if we assume that continuous quantity, when divided, divides into what is divisible, as was demonstrated elsewhere, this already implies that it is impossible for it to be divided into what is indivisible. Thus when we assume a body to be *actually* divided at every place where it *can* be divided, we have assumed what cannot possibly exist. For [a body] cannot be divided except into that which is divisible. Now this error occurred because they assumed the possibility of complete and concurrent [division] of that whose [division] *per se* cannot be completed or encompassed.

This solution also enables us to solve the aforementioned doubt posed by recent thinkers with respect to the division of continuous quality

45 Cf. Ibn Rushd, *On Aristotle's De Generatione et Corruptione: Middle Commentary and Epitome*, trans., with notes and introd., S. Kurland (Cambridge, MA: Medieval Academy of America 1958), p. 10.

because of God's knowledge. For our assumption that God knows completely the division of continuous quantity does not imply that, with respect to God's knowledge, such division terminates at indivisible things. Rather it implies that He knows this division as it is in its nature, namely, that whenever continuous quantity is divided, it is divided into divisible things, and not that He knows the division's terminus *which it does not possess in its nature*. The same doubt that was raised concerning the division of continuous quantity can be raised concerning number: one can claim that a number exists that cannot be augmented and this number is known by God. For a number is augmented to what can be augmented [further], and so if we assumed that God knew completely all these augmentations, or if we assumed the actualization of what is potential in numbers, then there would be a number that suffers no increase, which is absurd. Now it is proper to call something knowledge only if it is according to the nature of the thing known, and not something other than the nature of the thing known. For the latter is more properly called ignorance and error than knowledge.

We should not neglect to mention that Ibn Rushd erred in his explanation of the Philosopher's solution in another respect from the one cited above. For his assumption that each and every one of an infinite number of points existing concurrently and potentially within a body can be divided is clearly absurd. For if in a finite body there were a potentially infinite number of points, then since these are not consecutive, as was shown in the the sixth treatise of the *Physics*, then there would be some amount between each pair of points. And since the points were assumed to be infinite, then the amounts between each pair of points would also be infinite in number. Since it is evident that when any amount is multiplied infinitely, the resultant amount will be infinite, it follows that an finite body is infinite, which is utterly absurd.

Since this is so, it is evident that a continuous quantity does not have an infinite number of points, either potentially or actually. The indefiniteness that is characteristic of the division of continuous quantity pertains to *the operation of division*, and not to *the number of parts*. For the number of the divisible parts is always finite, although this number can always be augmented. For example, when we regard an [amount] to be divided into two parts, each one of the parts can be divided into two parts, in which case the total parts will be four, and then each one of them can be divided into two parts, in which case the total parts will be eight. The number of parts will always increase to whatever it increases, although the parts will always be finite in number. The indefiniteness of division should be regarded like the indefiniteness of numerical augmentation: just as number is not augmented, neither potentially nor actually, to what is infinite in number, so, too, in the case of the division of continuous quantity. That number is not augmented to what is infinite potentially can be shown from two propositions: the first is that every number is finite, since very number is either even or odd, and both of those are finite; the second is that through augmentation number has the potential to be something greater than it was, but lacks the potential to be something that is not number. Since this is so, it is clear that number lacks the potential through unending augmentation to become an infinite number. Through this is shown that a continuous quantity lacks the potential [to become] infinite in parts. Consequently it is evident that it lacks the potential [to divide into] points that are infinite in number. We already explained this at length in our commentary on the *Physics*. Here we found it necessary to refute the position adopted by Ibn Rushd in his solution of this doubt, i.e., that a body possesses potentially and concurrently an infinite number of points into which it can divide. For if that were true then the doubts with respect to knowledge, and with respect to assuming the possible to exist, would retain their force. This is clear after a little speculation.

We have herein shown that there is nothing in the arguments brought by the philosophers that implies that God does not know these sublunar things in the manner that we have posited concerning His knowledge of them.

Chapter Five

One of the things that adds renown and completeness to what we have explained of God's knowledge of these things is that this position implies none of the absurdities that follow from Maimonides' position on God's knowledge, i.e., the five aforementioned characteristics that, according to that position, pertain to God's knowledge and which are inconceivable with respect to our knowledge.

The first of these characteristics – that a knowledge that is numerically one [nonetheless] corresponds and is equivalent to many objects that differ in species – is also a necessary characteristic of *our* knowledge, when our knowledge of these many things is from the aspect of their being unified.

This is when we intellectually cognize the intelligible orders that apply to them, and we apprehend some of them as the form and perfection of others. Now since we have already posited God's knowledge of these many things in this manner, i.e., that he knows the intelligible orders pertaining to them from the aspect in which they are ordered within Him, and He knows them from the aspect in which they are unified within Him, we are evidently not obliged from this aspect to posit the difference posited by Maimonides between God's knowledge and our knowledge. Rather, the difference between the two knowledges lies, in our opinion, in the way that the intellected things are one in God. For the difference between the unity that can be attained within our intellect and the unity within God's knowledge is so great that there is no ratio between the two unities. This is evident from what was mentioned previously in the first book of this work.

The second – i.e., that God's knowledge has as its object the nonexistent – is not implied by what we have posited concerning God's knowledge of these sublunar things. For we say that God's knowledge of these things from the aspect of their being ordered within Him refers to the intelligible order that pertains to them in His soul, which always exists, and not to the things that come about. For He does not acquire knowledge from them, rather they acquire their existence from the knowledge He possesses of them, i.e., their existence is caused by the intelligible order pertaining to them in the divine soul. Since this is so, it does not follow that God's knowledge has as its object the nonexistent, rather it has as its object what always exists as one unchanging thing.

The third – that God's knowledge encompasses what is infinite from the aspect of its being infinite – also does not follow from what we posited concerning God's knowledge. For we say that He knows them from the aspect in which they are a unity, and not from the aspect in which they are infinite and not unified, which is the aspect in which they are particular.

The fourth – that God's knowledge of things that come about in the future does not necessitate that the object known will be realized; rather its contradictory remains possible – is also a characteristic of our knowledge when we attain knowledge of such [future] things through dreams, divination, or prophecy. For we achieve knowledge of them from the aspect in which they are ordered, and they remain possible from the aspect of choice. Because of this latter aspect we receive the [predictive] information so that we may gauge the evil that is in store for us, and take counsel how to avoid it, as was fully explained in the previous book. We encounter the same idea when we examine the prophets' statements predicting some evil. For we find that they give counsel how to avoid that evil. You also find that when Joseph interpreted Pharaoh's dream he counseled him how to avoid the [evils of the] famine that lay in store for him in the manner predicted in his dream. You also find that when Daniel interpreted Nebuchadnezzar's dream about losing his mind and becoming an animal for seven years, he counseled him how to avoid that evil. Now since we have already posited that God knows these things from the aspect in which they are ordered, it is not odd that they remain possible from the aspect of choice. In this way we have removed the doubt that people have incessantly raised, namely, how can it be that God knows things that come about and yet they remain possible? This [can be] by virtue of their being two aspects and not one.[46]

The fifth – God's knowledge does not change when the things about which He had foreknowledge come about, even though the object of His knowledge has changed, for previously it was possible and afterwards actual – is a necessary characteristic of our knowledge as well, when the knowledge of these things is obtained from the aspect of their being ordered. For even if the opposite of what was known occurs, the knowledge remains the same from the aspect of these things being ordered, i.e. from this aspect the thing that was known would have occurred were it not for human choice, which is the cause of something not occurring that was ready to occur. Now since God's knowledge is from the aspect of the intelligible order of these things that is in His soul, and this order always exists in His soul as one thing, it is evident that His knowledge does not change when one of these things come about. For His knowledge does not have them as its object; but rather it has as its object the intelligible order in His soul.

One should not say that God's knowledge of things that are possible by virtue of choice changes when one of those things comes about. For we do not hold that God acquires knowledge from things that come about, nor that He knows them from the aspect of their being designated things, but from [the aspect of] what they possess generally and in common. From

---

[46] In other words, God knows a future possible event by virtue of its ordered aspect; whereas the event is possible by virtue of the aspect of human choice.

this aspect, their possibility, of which God has knowledge, is not removed [when they become actual]. This is very evident to one who examines this treatise.

Chapter Six

We should now explain that the view to which speculation has led us is also the view of our Torah. We say that the cornerstone of the Torah, and the axis on which it rotates, is [the view that] there are possible things in the sublunar world. For this reason the Torah commands us to perform certain acts and to refrain from performing other acts. It is a cornerstone of the prophetic statements in general that God will inform the prophets of possible things before they occur, as in the verse: "For God does nothing without revealing His secret to His servants the prophets" [Amos 3:7], and that it is not necessary for some evil predicted by prophets to occur, as in the statement: "For God is gracious . . . and reconsiders evil" [Joel 2:13]. One can maintain both these cornerstones only if it is assumed that (a) possible things are ordered in a certain respect, and this is the respect in which they are knowable, and (b) unordered in a certain respect, and this is the respect in which they are possible; and that God knows all these things from the aspect in which they are ordered, and He knows that they are possible. Now since this is the case, it is evident that the view of the Torah is what our speculation has led us to.

There is another verse explaining that our Torah's view is that God knows these things in a universal, rather than in a particular, way: "He who forms their hearts together; He who understands all their deeds" [Ps. 32:15], i.e., He formed together the hearts and opinions of men by having them ordered generally according to the patterns he bestowed upon the heavenly bodies. In this manner he understood all their deeds, i.e. "together," not that His knowledge terminates at each and every particular. Thus this verse clarifies that his "understanding of all their deeds" is in a universal way.

Moreover, the view of our Torah is that God's will does not change, as in the verse: "For I am God; I have not changed" [Mal. 3:6]. And Balaam, when he was a prophet, said: "[God] is not a man to be false or a mortal to reconsider" [Num. 23:19]. [Yet] we find in the prophetic statements that God does reconsider His acts, as it is said: "God reconsidered the evil He had planned to bring upon His people" [Ex. 32:14]; "For God is gracious . . . reconsidering punishment" [Joel 2:3]. Now this doubt cannot be resolved when we posit that God knows particular things from the aspect in which they are particular, but can easily be resolved when we posit that He knows these sublunar things in the manner that we posited. Hence it is evident that we should posit God's knowledge of these sublunar things in the manner that we have posited.

It is evident that what we have posited concerning God's knowledge of these things can easily resolve the doubt. For His knowledge does not judge that a certain accident will befall a certain man. Rather it judges [this] about any one possessing that pattern, from the aspect in which these accidents are ordered – together with God's knowledge that this may not occur from the aspect of human choice. However, when we posit that He knows the matter with respect to this particular individual insofar as He is particular, then this implies that God's will changes. In fact, nothing in the prophetic statements require that God's knowledge be other than what speculation has led us to posit. Since this is so, we should follow speculation on this subject. For when the Torah occasionally differs from what speculation has shown to be the case, according to what appears to be the simple meaning of some of its statements, we ought to explain them so as to correspond to speculation – provided that this does not destroy one of the Torah's cornerstone [beliefs]. This is what Maimonides did frequently in his noble treatise, *The Guide of the Perplexed*. How much more should we not disagree with speculation when we do not find the Torah disagreeing with it!

Now Maimonides relates in Chapter Two of Part Three of his noble treatise, *The Guide of the Perplexed*, that some of the people of speculation inclined to the view that knowledge has as its object the species, and extends, via the same notion, to its individuals. He said that this is the view to which every adherent of a religious Law[47] is necessarily led by speculation. It is thus shown that he holds that this view agrees with that of our Torah. It also appears that the sage Abraham Ibn Ezra (of blessed memory) is of this party, for he says in his commentary on the Torah that, "In truth, [God] knows every particular in a universal manner, and not in a particular manner."[48] Indeed, the agreement of the Torah's view concerning God's knowledge with the results of our speculation will be

---

[47] *Baʿal torah.*   [48] Commentary on Genesis 18:21.

even more apparent in the sequel to our discussion here, namely, the discussion on divine providence according to our Torah.

Herewith is completed the third treatise of this book. Praise be to the Lord (blessed be He) who aided us in its composition. And He will aid us, through His grace, to know Him, to love Him, to observe His Torah, and to ascertain the indubitable Truth.

7

Ḥasdai Crescas, from *The Light of the Lord* Treatise Two

On the cornerstones of the Torah, i.e., the foundations and pillars upon which the House of God is established. Through their existence, the existence of a Law ordered from God (may He be blessed) is conceivable; whereas if one of them is lacking, the entire Law falls, God forbid.

Upon investigation, we find there to be six cornerstones of the Torah: First, God's knowledge of existents; second, His providence for them; third, His ability; fourth prophecy; fifth, choice; sixth, the final end [of the Law].

There are six, for since the Law is a voluntary act from a commander, i.e., the agent, to one commanded, i.e., the patient, it follows of necessity that the agent is knowing, willing, and able, and that the patient is willing and choosing, not compelled or coerced. And since an act from the agent to the patient cannot fail to establish some relation between them, it follows that there will be a relation and certain conjunction between them, namely, prophecy. And since every act aims towards an end, whether that act be natural or artificial, or, certainly, voluntary and from an infinitely perfect agent, this perfect act cannot fail to be for an important end. For this reason we have seen fit to divide this treatise into six principles.

Cornerstone One: On God's knowledge of existing things
[Introduction]

This [principle] will explain this cornerstone and the manner of our knowing it. Now many of the philosophers have strayed from the true path, and have imagined that they could contradict the cornerstone as it is necessitated by authentic tradition. Even some of the sages among the men of speculation of our own nation "have imputed things that were not so" [based on II Kings 17:9]. Hence we have seen fit in this principle to explain this cornerstone according to the determination of the Torah and the contradictions which they imagined; to resolve the doubts; to respond to their opinions; and to comment upon our manner of knowing this cornerstone. Thus, we have seen fit to divide this principle into five parts . . .

Chapter One

On the explanation of this cornerstone, according to what the Torah requires.

As was mentioned above, it is evident that the Giver and Arranger of the Law, may He be blessed, must of necessity know what He commands and arranges. However, the manner of His knowledge has been a subject of great diversity of opinions among the commentators. Now there are three features that are required according to the root principles of the Torah, as we conceive them: first, that His knowledge encompasses the infinite; second, that He has knowledge of what does not [yet] exist; third, that He has knowledge of the disjuncts of the possible[1] without the nature of the possible being changed. Now, I shall explain why these are required by the root principles of the Torah.

As for the first feature, it is clear from the Torah that God apprehends particulars, from the stories, the particular commandments, the future divinely predicted events,[2] as well as from the Tradition,[3] where one finds many verses about this, e.g., "For God investigates all hearts and understands all thoughts" [I Chron. 28:9]. The psalmist in "You searched me O God, and knew my heart" [Psalm 139] greatly emphasizes His detailed knowledge; the entire psalm is based on this theme, i.e., His knowing and apprehending particulars, as in "You know when I sit down and when I rise up; You understand my thoughts from afar; You search out my path and my lying down, and are acquainted with all my ways" [v. 1–3]. The other verses that follow in that psalm indicate that His apprehension

---

[1] E.g., 'Socrates will go to the store' or 'Socrates will not go to the store.' Since Socrates' going to the store in the future is possible, these disjuncts are sometimes called below 'disjuncts' or 'parts' of the possible, or, in other words, future possibles.

[2] *Yiʿudim*, rewards and punishment for the performance or abrogation of the Torah.

[3] In this context, the books following the Torah in the Hebrew Scriptures.

is of particulars in their utmost detail. Once this is demonstrated, and it is clear from the particulars that they are infinite, it follows of necessity that His knowledge encompasses the infinite. That is the first thing [to be proved].

The second feature, namely, that He possesses knowledge of what does not [yet] exist, is clear from the divinely predicted events that appear in the Torah and the Prophets about things which did not then exist. Even though some verses indicate the coming–into–existence of [divine] knowledge, as in, "I will go down to see whether they have done altogether according to the outcry that has come to me, and if not, I will know it" [Gen. 18:21], the rabbis of blessed memory already explained in these and similar cases that "the Torah speaks in the language of men." Now this is certainly true in the case of things that already exist, for it is impossible that God was unaware of something and that his knowledge later came to pass. Rather, this occurred in a prophetic vision and was expressed in the language of men. However, the verse, "Now I know that you are a Godfearing man" (which was said in a waking–state at the binding of Isaac, as has come down to us according to the genuine tradition),[4] should, it seems to me, be taken in its plain sense. This is founded on a single premise that is demonstrated in political philosophy, namely, that actions form stable characters and qualities in the soul. They certainly reinforce those that are already acquired. With this premise accepted, it is no doubt that although Abraham was Godfearing before the binding, his fear was reinforced after his action, and was augmented to an additional degree. It is clear that this degree was not acquired by him before the action. This being so, and 'Godfearing' meaning "to a degree which is known by God," the sentence "Now I know that you are Godfearing" is indeed true. For before that action Abraham was not at the level intended by the phrase "that you are Godfearing." Consequently, it was impossible that God should know something different from what was. But He knew beforehand that Abraham would be Godfearing in the future, even though he had not yet reached that degree at the time. Consequently, His knowledge of what does not [yet] exist is entailed of necessity. That is the second feature.

As for the third feature, namely, that He has knowledge of the dis-juncts of the possible (i.e., knowledge that one of the disjuncts will occur

---

4 This appears to be an implicit criticism at previous Jewish philosophers (including Maimonides) who held that Abraham's prophecy was in a dream.

without the nature of the possible being changed), it is clear that the Torah requires this. For if His knowledge compelled one of the disjuncts, then [the act of] commanding would not apply to the commandments and prohibitions of the Torah. For there is no way to command someone unless he is assumed to be willing and not compelled or coerced. This is self-evident. Indeed, the aforementioned statement is self-contradictory because if His knowledge compelled one of the disjuncts, it would not be possible. For the possible is that which may or may not be. But if one of the disjuncts were compelled, then it would not be possible. But it was assumed possible! So it follows that His knowledge that one of the disjuncts occurs does not compel the nature of the possible. That is the third feature.

These three features are demonstrated completely in the aforementioned Psalm. For the first feature is demonstrated in the beginning of the Psalm, as was mentioned, and in its end: "My frame was not hidden from You, when I was made in secret, and skillfully wrought in the depths of the earth. Your eyes have seen my unformed limbs; and in Your book were all written. The days that were ordained for me, when there was *lo* one of them" [Psalms 139:15–16]. Now since the Masoretic text[5] has '*lo*' spelled with an *alef* [="not"], but we are to read '*lo*' with a *waw* [= "to him"], we must seek the meaning of both readings. The '*lo*' of the Masoretic text should be read 'was not hidden,' meaning that not one of the aforementioned details was hidden from him; whereas if *lo* is read as to him it should be taken to refer to God Himself, i.e., from His perspective, despite all his many cognitions, He is one through them. But from our perspective, the Psalm continues, "How weighty are your thoughts unto me" [v. 17]. So in explaining matters, a multiplicity of [divine] cognitions of precise particulars are brought in the Psalm. This is the first feature.

His knowledge of what does not [yet] exist is hinted at in the verse, "For there is no word on my tongue but that you, O Lord, know it well" [v. 4], i.e., the word that I will speak in the future is not yet on my tongue, which means that you will have known all of it before I mention it. This is the second feature.

---

5 The Masoretes were Jewish scholars (seventh to tenth century AD) whose job was to preserve the traditional Hebrew text of the Bible, and to indicate how it was to be read. On the whole they followed rabbinic Jewish traditions.

The third feature, i.e., that His knowledge does not compel the possible[6] is self-evident. For this verse appears to be founded on [King David's] defense for the days that he associated with bloodthirsty men, desperados, and debtors.[7] This is why he arranged praises of God with respect to His knowledge, as if to say that God knew the chambers of his heart and the secrets of his thoughts. And in a poetic fashion, he began with "You searched me O God, and knew my heart," as if God searched and investigated in order to examine his case, but He had already known him beforehand. This alludes to what is the truth itself, that God's knowledge is eternal and immutable. Then he went into great detail about it. The goal of all this was to justify himself, "O God, if you slay the wicked – away from me, you bloodthirsty" [v. 19], that is to say, If you had slain the wicked in my case, I would have said to the bloodthirsty, "Away with you!" Certainly I would not have associated with them, for all this is revealed unto you. Hence, he concluded the psalm, "Search me, O God, and know my heart, and guide me in the ways of the world" [v. 23], that his providence would be over him in the way of the world in which he walked, though what was visible did not seem proper. Hence it is evident that if His knowledge were compelling, there would be no need for such a defense. Thus, all three features have been shown in this psalm, which was the intention of this chapter.

Chapter Two: On the elaboration of the doubts that one may raise concerning this cornerstone, according to what has been assumed

Since some of the doubts are general and others particular, we shall mention first the general doubts which are raised concerning [all] the three features assumed in God's knowledge of existents.[8] There are five of them:

First, if God knows an existent other than Himself, then since knowledge perfects the knower, it follows that the superior is perfected by the inferior, which is absurd.

---

[6] Alternate version: the one disjunct.

[7] Following rabbinic tradition, Crescas identifies the Psalmist with King David.

[8] 1. God's knowledge encompasses the infinite; 2. God had knowledge of what does not [yet] exist; 3. God has knowledge of the disjuncts of the possible without the nature of the possible being changed.

Second, if God knows an existent other than Himself, then since the intellect becomes substantial by virtue of its knowledge, it follows that there is multiplicity in His essence. This is indeed His essence and what He knows, although it follows that the superior is perfected by the inferior. Now if the things known are many, then the multiplicity will be the same as the number of things known. And if they are infinite, then the multiplicity will be infinite, which is utterly absurd and disgraceful.

Third, because a particular thing is not apprehended except by means of a hylic faculty, like sense or imagination, and He has no hylic faculty, it follows that God does not apprehend a particular thing.

Fourth, since particular things are temporal, and time is an accident consequent upon body, then someone who is not described as in motion or at rest cannot apprehend temporal notions.

Now since it is evident that the three aforementioned features [in the previous chapter] establish knowledge of particulars, it is evident that these doubts, i.e., the third and the fourth, also cover the three features.

Fifth, the bad order found in the human species appears to imply that God does not apprehend these things. We shall not elaborate upon this doubt now, since it is more relevant to the second principle, the discussion of Providence.

As for the particular doubts, there are two concerning the first feature, that God's knowledge encompasses the infinite.

First, since knowledge is something that is inclusive and encompassing, and what is infinite is not subject to being included and encompassed, it seems to follow that "knowledge of the infinite" is a self-contradictory phrase.

Second, that if His knowledge encompasses the infinite, then what is impossible would be possible. It has been shown that a continuous quantity is always divisible into what is divisible. But God has knowledge of the infinite parts into which the quantity is divisible, it would be impossible for one of these part to be divisible qua quantity. For if it were divisible, then God's knowledge would not be true.

There are also two doubts concerning the second feature, that God has knowledge of what does not [yet] exist:

First, it seems that true knowledge must be of the existent. For things are true, when what is in the intellect is like what exists external to the intellect.

Second if the knowledge of what is not [yet] existent were true, then the content of His knowledge would be *It does not yet exist but it will exist in the future*. And when it does exist, the content would be *It exists now*. In that case, change in God's knowledge is inescapable. And since the intellect becomes substantial by virtue of what it knows, it follows that God's essence changes. This is utterly absurd.

There are also two doubts concerning the third feature, that He has knowledge of the disjuncts of the possible without the nature of the possible being changed. First, if His knowledge is of the occurrence of one of the disjuncts, with the contradictory disjunct remaining possible (and that seems to be the case) then when that disjunct occurs, that possibility is removed, and His knowledge has changed. Now since the intellect becomes substantial by virtue of what it knows, it follows that God's essence is in constant flux – but this is utterly absurd.

Second, let us assume that He has knowledge of the occurrence of one of the possible [disjuncts], with the contradictory disjunct remaining possible. Now it is evident that the possible is such that, when assumed to exist, no absurdity results. So when we posit [the contradictory disjunct] to exist, two absurdities result: first, His knowledge and essence changes; and second, his previous 'knowledge' was not knowledge but erroneous estimation.[9] All this is utterly absurd and disgraceful.

These are some of the doubts that caused some of the early authorities to disagree with this cornerstone as assumed here. They did so to such an extent that some of them ruled out God's knowledge of anything outside himself completely, while others ruled out God's knowledge of particulars that are generated and destroyed, but accepted it with respect to universals and eternal particulars.

Some of the sages of our nation were pressured by the Torah to accept God's knowledge of particulars. And since particulars are infinite, it seemed that such knowledge must encompass the infinite. And since the simple meaning of Scripture indicates that He knows particulars before

---

[9] Crescas here combines two of Gersonides' alternative readings of Maimonides into one objection. Gersonides had written (see pp. 164–5 above) that if God 'knows' that a possible event may occur, with its non-occurrence remaining possible, then that should be considered *opinion* rather than knowledge. On the other hand if God "knows" that a possible event *will* occur, and the event does not occur, then that should be considered *error*. Crescas combines these into the case of *erroneous estimation*, when God "knows" that a possible event will occur, but at t_1 the contradictory event occurs. Before t_1, God's knowledge is erroneous estimation. (The verbal form of the Hebrew term translated 'estimation' is used by Gersonides in the relevant passage.)

they come to pass, and that He makes them known to his prophets, as in "The Lord God does nothing without revealing its secret to his servants the prophets" [Amos 3.19], and this includes possible things involving choice, as in "For the king of Egypt will not let you go out unless by a greater power" [Exod. 3:19], they were forced to believe this cornerstone as assumed here. But when they were pressured by speculation (which, they imagined, rendered these things impossible), they thought "to confirm the vision, but they failed" [based on Dan. 11:14], by positing God's knowledge of particulars not insofar as they are particulars, but insofar as they are the parts of universals. And these universals [were said to be known] from the aspect in which some are the perfection of others, which is the aspect by virtue of which they are unified according to the universal order, the order which is in the essence of God in the utmost perfection, and in the soul of the active intellect, which is inferior to Him in perfection, and in the soul of the sphere, which is much inferior to them in perfection. They imagined that they accepted His knowledge of particulars, and accordingly that He knew them before they came to pass, and made them known to the prophets, not with respect to their being those particulars; rather His knowledge is from the aspect of the universal order which exists within Himself before these particulars are existent.

Whether speculation agrees with this view will be shown in the discussion below. But the doubts that imply the impossibility of God's knowing things external to himself can be easily resolved. The first doubt involved the notion that knowledge is a perfection for the knower, and that if God knew something other than Himself, the superior would be perfected by the inferior. The resolution of this is easy. For since the existence of what is other than God is acquired from His existence, and the intelligible of what is other than Him from His intelligible, it is not true that the superior is perfected by the inferior. For it has already been assumed that His knowledge of what is other than Himself is from the aspect of the intelligible order within His essence.

The second doubt rested on the notion that the intellect becomes substantial through what it knows, and that were He to know something other than Himself, that would imply multiplicity in His essence because of the multiplicity of things known. Its resolution is also easy, from what has been said. For His knowledge, which is His essence, bestows existence on what is other than Himself. Although the universal intelligible which is in Him includes many things known, there is an aspect in which some are the perfection for others, which is the aspect in virtue of which they are unified. For example, we say of *man* whose definition is *rational, sentient, nutritive*, that he is one through them, even though the definition includes many things, for one part is the perfection and completion of the other. Hence it is evident that God apprehends the things known from the aspect in which they are one, and therefore He does not apprehend multiplicity in His essence.

The third doubt rested on the notion that a particular thing cannot be apprehended except through a hylic faculty. Now it is evident from this notion that it does not imply that God does not know the intelligible order pertaining to things.

The fourth doubt rested on the notion that matters are temporal. Now it is evident that the intelligible order is not joined to time.

The fifth doubt rested on the apparent evil order that pertains to the human species. Now when it is shown that that [intelligible] order is of the utmost good and importance, then this doubt will be removed. This will be shown completely in the second principle of this treatise, God willing.

The first doubt regarding the first of the aforementioned three features rested on the notion that what is infinite is not subject to being included and encompassed, from which it seemed to follow that "knowledge [of the infinite particulars]" and "being encompassed by it" is a self-contradictory phrase. Now this doubt is easily resolved. For if these things were known from the aspect in which they are infinite, then there would be room for doubt. But according to what has been assumed, God knows them from the aspect in which they are finite, which is the aspect of the intelligible order.

The second doubt rested on [the infinite divisibility of] continuous quantity. Now it is clear that continuous quantity is not known from the aspect in which it is infinite, but from the aspect of its intelligible order, i.e., its potential to be divided infinitely.[10] Thus it is not required that God knows infinite parts from the aspect in which they are infinite.

The first doubt regarding the second of the aforementioned three features rested on the notion that true knowledge necessarily must be of what exists. Now when we say that God's knowledge of things is according to

---

[10] The Hebrew is awkward here; the idea is that continuous quantity's property of being infinitely divisible is part of the intelligible order and that is what is known.

the intelligible order within Himself, it is true that the object of knowledge exists, an existence which is of the utmost importance.

The second doubt rested on the change of knowledge that results from the change of things known. Its resolution is likewise easy. For if knowledge referred to particulars insofar as they are particular, there would be room for this doubt. But the knowledge, in the way it has been assumed, is joined to the intelligible order which is in Himself, and that is always one and unchanging.

The two doubts regarding the third of the aforementioned features rested on the nature of the possible. Now according to the position here,[11] there is no room for these doubts. For it is evident that possible matters are ordered in one respect and unordered in another. They are ordered from the aspect of the universal order, and they are unordered from the aspect of human choice. Now according to that position, knowledge concerning [possibles] is from the aspect of the universal order, which is the aspect in virtue of which they are determined and ordered. If so, then there will not be knowledge of them from the aspect in virtue of which they are undetermined and unordered. It thereby follows, according to this position, that there can only be knowledge of possible things insofar as they are possible, and not when one of the possible disjuncts occurs.

This is the import of their statements. And that was the intention of this chapter.

Chapter Three: On the elaboration of the even greater doubts that their position implies concerning this cornerstone

Despite what has been shown above, namely, that the roots of the Torah require that God has knowledge of particulars possessing the three afore-mentioned features – as can be seen from the stories, the [divine] promises, and the verses that signify this primarily and essentially – there will be those who wish to strangle themselves by "hanging on a great tree" and "uncovering sides of the Torah that run contrary to the law."[12] For scriptural pronouncements contain no arguments to compel the masters of

---

[11] I.e., the position of the Gersonideans, as understood by Crescas.

[12] Cf. *Pesaḥim* 112a and M. Avot 3, 11. The "great tree" here is probably Gersonides. Crescas' point seems to be that these Gersonideans cannot be convinced by citing the plain sense of Scripture since they know how to interpret verses to their advantage. The only method is to use reason to show why their arguments are defective.

figures[13] to give in, due to their stubbornness. Therefore, we have also seen fit to uncover the defects of their reasoning, whether according to the roots of the Torah, or according to speculation in their manner.

For they inferred necessarily two propositions; one, that God's knowledge is not of particulars insofar as they are particulars, but rather [of them] from the aspect of the universal order; and two, that His knowledge is not of possible things. Rather, He knows that they are possible, but He does not know which of the possible disjuncts will occur. A third proposition also follows for them, namely, that after the occurrence of the possible disjunct, He has no knowledge of it. This follows from each of the first two propositions: from the first, because knowledge of which possible disjunct occurs is knowledge of the particular insofar as it is particular, and this sort of knowledge had been ruled out; from the second, because since it is assumed that He has no knowledge of which disjunct occurs before it occurs, then were he to have knowledge after it occurs, there would be a change in His knowledge. Now this is what they tried to avoid because it was the greatest of the doubts that brought them to their position. Moreover, the claim that His knowledge comes to pass on account of some extramental reality implies that His knowledge has a cause other than Himself, and that He possesses "acquired intellect."[14] But this is utterly absurd and disgraceful, not to mention that one cannot conceive of something acquired if not by means of a hylic faculty. Hence it follows that this third proposition is required by them.

Now that this has been set down, let us explain the absurdities that result from this position, according to the Torah and according to speculation.

According to the Torah, their view leaves not one story true when understood literally. For from their inference that God's knowledge does not apply to designated particulars,[15] it follows that God did not know the Patriarchs, nor did He call them, nor did He promise them anything particular. Rather, the savants will say that God only knew the Patriarchs insofar as He knows the order of each one.[16] But Scripture cries out, "You said that you knew me by name" [Exod. 33:12] and "Whom God knew face

---

[13] *Baᶜalei zurot*. This is used by Maimonides and others to refer to makers of "talismans" that are used to bring down magical/astrological influences. Is this an oblique reference to thinkers in Spain who were influenced by Gersonides and by practical astrology, e.g. Shem Tov Ibn Shaprut (late fourteenth century)?

[14] On the acquired intellect, see above, p. 170.

[15] I.e., particulars that can be picked out or indicated through ostention.

[16] Lit.: 'He did not know anyone save one whose order was that order.'

to face" [Deut. 34:10], and several particulars that compel every believer to admit that God knows particulars.

Because of their inference that God does not know which disjunct will come to pass of a disjunction of possibles, they had to give the lie to the divinely predicted events that depend upon choice. So they explained that these are opinions and conjectures, and that such divinely predicted events were left to the heavenly configurations unless they were negated through choice. Thus, [Moses'] statement, "I know that after my death you will act wickedly" [Deut. 31:29] should be taken as "I suppose," etc. All this is devastation and denial of the roots of religion. Also, the statement of Samuel predicting to Saul that he would encounter a number of men on the way, who would tell him certain well-known things, etc. [cf. 1 Sam. 10:1–8], should also be understood as opinion and conjecture, although the prophet called them "signs." All this is madness and foolishness.

Because of their inference that God cannot know the disjunct after it occurs, the verse "Now I know that you are Godfearing" is meaningless. For 'knows' cannot mean *knowledge*, since they concluded that God does not have knowledge of things that come to pass. Nor can it be *opinion*, for the opinion that Abraham is Godfearing does not come to pass after his deed, not in such a way that would justify his saying, "Now I know." Thus it is evident that this view is against the Torah and the genuine tradition, several of whose verses testify that God's knowledge is of particulars in their utmost detail. It is superfluous to elaborate on this.

Yet I say that even according to rational speculation they did not emerge from most of the doubts they raised with their method. Indeed, they fell into much graver ones.

They did not emerge from those doubts, for it is evident that the knowledge they posited does not avoid a multiplicity of things known, perhaps an infinity of things known. This can be shown from several considerations. First, perfect knowledge of things is when they are known through their proximate and remote causes. Consequently, the knowledge of composite things from the aspect in which they are one will be perfect when the simples that make up the composites are known, for they are the elements and the causes of the composites. Hence we cannot avoid accepting that the things known are necessarily multiple when a composite is known.

Second, the notion that, as a rule, some existents perfect others, and on account of this they are unified, will be true of genera, for some are perfections for others, and genera are perfections of the species, as if you were to say that the vegetative is the perfection of the mineral, and the living of the vegetative, and the rational of the living. But it is not true of inferior species that some are perfections of others, for horses are not the perfection of asses, nor asses of sheep. Similarly, it is not true of individuals, which are primary substances, that one is the perfection of another. So when we posit knowledge of inferior species, we cannot avoid accepting that the things known are necessarily multiple.

Third, the heavenly bodies and the separate intelligences are eternal individuals that differ in species from each other. Now if it is assumed that knowledge of them is from the aspect of the intelligible order, it follows that they cannot be unified from the aspect in which they differ in species. If so, then knowledge of things that differ in species implies a multiplicity of things known.

Fourth, even if we concede that some separate intelligences are perfections of others, since some are the cause of others, and in this respect they can be unified, nonetheless the souls that survive are not the causes of each other. And if God knows them, then the multiplicity of things known is inescapable.

Fifth, if [God] knows particulars from the aspect of the order in the heavenly bodies, this order includes a numerical order, i.e., the number of rotations or the number of degrees. This is well known to any one who has a modicum of knowledge of judicial astrology, for it is from this aspect that the prophet can ascertain a definite time, as in the statement of Samuel to Saul. Well, if this is the case, then knowledge of a particular, e.g., 3 or 4, is inescapable. If it is countered that knowledge is not of this particular qua particular, e.g., this 3 or this 4, but rather any 3 and any 4, then if God's knowledge of some number is inescapable, who will inform me whether He knows all the rest of the numbers or not? And if He does know them, then since number can be infinitely augmented, His knowledge will be of infinite numbers. If he does not know all of the numbers, then of necessity there will be a limit, beyond which He does not know. Then the question will be: what accounts for His knowing the numbers until that limit and not knowing more? Did His knowledge become fatigued through exertion?! In any event, a multiplicity of infinite things known is inescapable.

Sixth, when [God] knows particulars with respect to the order in the heavenly bodies, the multiplicity of the things known is unavoidable. For this order is according to the position of the stars at the time of the nativity, the dominant planet, and the aspects, together with the other conditions that have not escaped the notice of the practitioners of this science. Now, the number of the positions of the stars in the spheres, by virtue of the ascendant, the dominant planet, and the aspects, is infinite, because the great circle that is on the sphere, on whose account the ascendant is [determined] in the [various] horizons, is a continuous quantity, which is always capable of [further] division.[17]

For all these reasons it is clear that they did not emerge from the doubts whose underlying principle is the multiplicity of things known.

That they fell in to much greater doubts will now be shown: In fleeing from attributing to God a multiplicity of cognitions, they attributed to Him the greatest of all defects, ignorance, in all three of their propositions,[18] and to the greatest extent possible.

Their first proposition – that God's knowledge is not of particulars insofar as they are particular – implies that God is ignorant of an infinite number of things, since particulars are infinite. And since what He knows is finite [according to them], the relation of what he knows to what he does not know is that of the finite to the infinite.

Their second proposition – that God does not know which of the possible disjuncts will occur – implies that He is ignorant of most things, since possible matters[19] are many, whereas necessary matters are comparatively few.[20]

The third inferred proposition – that God has no knowledge of a possible disjunct after it occurs – implies that He is ignorant of entire courses of events. For such things are complex because of their dependence on, and intermingling with, human choice. This is a perpetual feature of them, so that in a span of thousands of years many known possible disjuncts occur after other disjuncts, and this goes on for the entire period. For example, Jacob's descent to Egypt is a possible matter and dependent upon his

---

[17] Prof. Y. Tzvi Langermann explains this as follows: "Since the great circle on the orb (e.g. the celestial equator) will intersect a potentially infinite number of horizons (i.e. say a circle on the earth's circumference, also a circle infinitely divisible in principle), and since each interprinciple will produce a different horoscope (as the cardines are determined by the horizon), then, ergo, there is a potentially infinite number of horoscopes (nativities)" (Personal communication).

[18] I.e., the propositions mentioned at the outset of this chapter.

[19] Lit.: 'the matter of the possible . . . the matter of the necessary.'

[20] This is an odd assertion, since there are fewer events dependent upon human choice than there are natural events. Crescas doubtlessly intends the actions and events that are of interest to us humans.

choice. So when he chose to descend, God was ignorant and unaware of that choice. Now there is no way for Him to know all the consequences of that action, certainly not after the many choices of possible matters. This is their madness, heresy, and numbness of heart.

Marvel at them when they attribute to God ignorance of eternal things, as well as most existents, perhaps even an infinite amount. For the survival of souls after death results from the good choices men make when they are alive. Their survival, then, may or may not come about. And if it does come about, God cannot know about it. Now the increase in the number of surviving souls may result in a number much larger than that of the individual separate intellects and heavenly bodies. The nature of the number may even increase indefinitely, with the result that the amount of the eternal existents unknown to God will be much greater than that of the known. And this number will increase indefinitely. All this is utterly disgraceful.

I shall show further that it is impossible for God not to have knowledge of particulars insofar as they are particular. God is the agent of all existents, whether they are substances or accidents, and particulars insofar as they are particulars flow from His essence. Now it is evident that if He is ignorant of anything that flows from His essence, that His knowledge of His own essence is deficient, may He be exalted above that.

Moreover, it is evident from premises based on sense and tradition that prophets and diviners communicate particular things insofar as they are particulars to designated individuals. They must know these things from the one who has communicated them, and that is either God or an angel. Now if the communicant does not know [the communication in its particularity, including the designated individual], how can he communicate it? Would that I knew the answer!

Ibn Rushd was aroused by this doubt in [his commentary on] *On Sense and the Sensible*[21] but he didn't solve it in a satisfactory manner. For he said that just as the intellect gives the forms universally, and matter receives them in a particular manner, so too the intellect gives the universal order, and the imagination receives it in a particular manner. But this is the sort of thing that, although the mouth can utter it, the mind cannot conceive it. Rabbi Levi [Gersonides] (of blessed memory) made a similar point: particular existence flows from the universal order by means of material

---

[21] The *Parva Naturalia* of Aristotle.

nature, which possesses accidents by means of which each particular is individuated, and this by virtue of its zodiacal sign. But the imaginative faculty does not have individual accidents through which the communication becomes particular. And the communication pertains to these individual accidents. So how can this be?

Rabbi Levi himself attempted to resolve this doubt. He said that the communication does not pertain [to this individual] by virtue of it being *this* particular. Rather, what comes from the Agent Intellect is the knowledge of the order that pertains to this individual by virtue of the heavenly bodies – [not *qua* this designated individual but rather] *qua* any individual that happens to have been born at the time that the celestial bodies were in that position. [The prophet] happens to apprehend this individual because it happens that no other individual fitting this description is with him at this time.

But the mere fact that no other individual fitting this description occurs to the prophet at this time is clearly insufficient [to explain] the communication of something particular. Because the fact that this individual fits this description is not known to the prophet with respect to itself, and it is clear that the communicant should know that this description belongs to this individual, if it is necessary for the communication. But our senses show that [such information] is unnecessary for this communication from the diviners in our times, and even more so from the prophets, who used to communicate marvelous, time-delimited details, concerning the future or the past, as well as possible things.

I am greatly surprised at Rabbi Levi, for if we accept his resolution of [this doubt] concerning particular communications, his position on providence unavoidably implies particular knowledge, as we shall point out, God willing, in Chapter Three of Cornerstone 2.[22]

We can use another method to show that His knowledge must encompass an infinity of things known. Let us first make two assumptions. The first is demonstrated in *On Generation and Corruption*, and the second is self-evident. The first states that the form comes about in something composite by means of composition and mixture, such as the generation of oxymel from the mixture of vinegar and honey. The second is that when the proportion of the mixture changes the form changes, as when the proportion of the drug Theriac changes, the form of Theriac is replaced

[22] See *Light of the Lord* ii, 2, 3 (ed. S. Fisher [Jerusalem 1990], p. 162).

by another form. This is certainly the case when the simple [elements] of a composite change.

With these assumptions in place, I say that since the amounts of parts are always infinitely divisible, the difference in their mixtures are infinitely augmentable, and so there will be infinite forms of things differing in species. This implies, therefore that the Giver of Forms[23] apprehends infinite forms. And if this is so for it, then it is certainly so for His existence, may He be blessed.

This is sufficient for refuting what [the savants] imagined concerning this cornerstone, which is what we wished to do in this chapter.

Chapter Four: On the resolution of the doubts they posited concerning this cornerstone, according to the view of the Torah

Maimonides (of blessed memory) resolved these doubts in a different way, one which he frequently used to rebuke the philosophers. For the foundation of all these doubts is the analogy between His knowledge and our knowledge. And since it is evident from their statements that the term 'knowledge' is said of God and of us with complete homonymy; and it is well known that when two things are designated by equivocal terms, no demonstration should be brought from one to the other, it follows that there is no room for these doubts at all. For His knowledge is His essence, and just as His existence is elevated above ours, so too his knowledge is elevated above ours. So our efforts to know how He knows which possible disjunct will occur without compelling the possible would be as if we wished to know His essence. And in this way it is possible for him to know an infinite number of changing particulars before they come to be, without the nature of the possible changing, or His knowledge changing with the change of the things known, which is the view of the Torah according to the genuine tradition.[24]

But Gersonides (of blessed memory) raised several objections against him in his *Wars*, and imagined to tear down Maimonides' edifice with two premises: the first, that it is impossible for the homonymy between His knowledge and our knowledge to be complete. And the second, that it is impossible for what is confusion and error with respect to us, to be knowledge with respect to the true reality of God.[25]

---

[23] I.e. the Agent Intellect.   [24] See *Guide of the Perplexed* II, 20–1.   [25] See above, pp. 168–75.

Now the second premise is self-evident. But the first premise he explained as follows: 'knowledge' is said of us and of God by priority and posteriority. Since what is said by priority and posteriority is not said with complete homonymy, it follows that knowledge is not said of Him and of us with complete homonymy. The major premise is self-evident, since what is said with complete homonymy cannot be said by priority and posteriority, since the notions of which the term is said are unrelated. For example, the term *'ayin'* is not said by priority and posteriority of the water *'ayin* ('spring') and the sight *'ayin* ('eye'). The minor premise can also be easily shown. For one would think that when we affirm or negate of God something that we possess, we affirm or negate it according to our understanding, because we do not affirm or negate simply the name. Thus it appears that when we affirm knowledge of God, which is one of the things we possess, we affirm its meaning, which is 'lack of ignorance,' not that we affirm simply the name without its notion. Now since that notion is not said synonymously with respect to Him and to us, it follows that it is said by priority and posteriority. Thus the first premise, i.e., that it is impossible for the homonymy between His knowledge and ours to be complete.

After he had set down these premises, Gersonides imagined to destroy the wall of the edifice that Maimonides had constructed around the Torah's view. For since the term 'knowledge' is not said of Him and of us with complete homonymy, but rather by priority and posteriority, which is the first premise, it is proper that we reason analogously between His knowledge and our knowledge by priority and posteriority. The doubts raised from the multiplicity of things known and their changing will remain in full force.

Now since it is evident that what is confusion and error with respect to us cannot be knowledge with respect to the true reality of God, which is the second premise, then no matter how [God knows things], it is impossible that His knowledge of which possible disjunct will occur does not compel the possible. This is so because if it did not compel that disjunct, then its contradictory would remain possible. And the possible, when assumed to exist, does not imply an absurdity. If so, knowledge of that disjunct before it occurs will be error or confusion with respect to us. Nor can a change in knowledge after it occurs be avoided. But we already assumed that what is confusion and error with respect to us cannot be knowledge with respect to God.

This is the upshot of all his arguments and objections against Maimonides, even though he prattled on at length. We shall dispose of his doubts without difficulty in what follows, with God's help, but first we should show that the objection he made against Maimonides is not worthy of attention; indeed, the latter's remarks are correct and true, without a shred of difficulty or complexity.

Let us preface our remarks with the statement that it is necessary that the term 'knowledge' not be said of Him (God), and us, by priority and posteriority. For a term said of things by priority and posteriority requires that its notion be the same. For if the intended notions were different, then they could not have priority and posteriority. For they would have nothing in common save the name. This is self-evident. Let us take, for example, 'exists,' which is said of substance and of the other categories by priority and posteriority. The term 'exists' signifies in the various cases the same notion, for its intention is 'existence' and 'being,' which is understood as the same notion in all cases; the difference is only in the priority and posteriority. For existence and being belong to the other categories by virtue of their belonging to substance.

Now that this has been settled, [we say that] the term 'knowledge,' when applied to Him, refers to the notion of His essence, and His essence differs utterly from the intended notion of knowledge when said with respect of us. It follows thereby that the term does not apply to Him and to us by priority and posteriority. For homonymous names that are not said of things synonymously, nor by priority and posteriority, are said with complete homonymity. Indeed, Maimonides' statement that the term 'knowledge' is said of Him and of us with complete homonymity is on solid footing. For although[26] both share the [negative] signification of 'lack of ignorance' by priority and posteriority, nevertheless, since the term ['knowledge'] signifies affirmatively, and its affirmative signification is of things that are utterly different with respect to this notion, then it follows that this term is said of Him and of us with complete homonymy.

This is the proper understanding of Maimonides' remarks. For he reasoned analogously from knowledge to existence when he said that just as the rank of His existence is elevated above ours, so too the rank of His knowledge is elevated above ours. And he himself showed that His existence is His essence, and that others' existence is an accident accruing

---

[26] Reading *she-ᶜim* for *she-im*.

to them. Consequently it follows that the positive signification of the term 'existence' differs to the greatest extent [when referring to God and to others] like the difference between His essence and an accident that is attached to something apart from Himself. This is so even though the negative signification of the term 'existence,' i.e., the negation of privation, is the same for both [God and others.] However, since the primary signification of the term is positive, it is correct that the term 'existence' is said of Him and of us with complete homonymy. The same thing applies to the term 'knowledge'. Once this has been shown, we see that the foundation of the building that Maimonides set down is firm and permanent

The second premise, that it is impossible for what is confusion and error with respect to us to be knowledge with respect to the true reality of God, is true and self-evident. Nevertheless, the knowledge that He possesses of the occurrence of one of the disjuncts is true knowledge, clear and determinate. But His knowledge does not change the nature of the possible, for the nature of the possible pertains only to things that depend on choice, as will be shown in the fourth principle, God willing. Consequently, the nature of the possible does not change, and His knowledge is of the disjunct to which choice pertains.

One may object that once we assume that the nature of the possible does not change [when God knows the possible disjunct], then we can posit the existence of the contradictory [of what God foreknows], because according to the definition of the possible, no absurdity results from positing its existence.[27] To this we reply that no absurdity results on account of the nature of the possible, but an absurdity does result when we posit [the existence of the contradictory together with] His knowledge of the occurrence of the disjunct. It is clear that the absurdity is not on account of the nature of the possible, but rather because of God's knowledge of the choice. Still, *how* God knows the disjunct brought about by choice in matters that are assumed possible, can be understood only by one who understands His essence, because His knowledge and His essence are the same.

This seems to be Maimonides' method of resolving the doubts. It is a comprehensive method, first-rate, correct, and indubitable – whether the term 'knowledge' is said with complete equivocation, as in Maimonides'

---

[27] And then, God's knowledge would be opinion or confusion.

approach, or by priority and posteriority and signifying an attribute of His essence, as in ours, because knowledge belongs to His essence, as was stated in principle three of the first treatise.[28]

It remains for us to now offer a distinctive and satisfying resolution of these doubts, as we promised.

Let us preface this by saying that the distinguishing difference between God's knowledge and ours, as has been shown from speculation and genuine tradition and will be shown further in the third treatise, God willing, is that the things known have acquired their existence from His knowledge and the conception of His will – whereas our knowledge emanates and is acquired from the things known, through the instruments of sense and imagination, as has been shown in Aristotle's *On the Soul*.[29] This is the true and distinctive foundation through which most of the doubts will be resolved. For it resolves the four universal doubts that include the three features that distinguish God's knowledge.

The first doubt was taken from the notion that knowledge is a perfection of the knower, and this was thought to imply that if God knew something other than Himself, the superior would be perfected by the inferior. Now if His knowledge emanated from something other than Himself, there would be room for this doubt. But after it has been shown that His knowledge bestows existence on others, it is not true that the superior is perfected by the inferior. For His knowledge and His perfection are the same, and through knowing Himself, and the conception of His will, which is Himself, the existents other than Himself acquire their existence.

The second doubt was taken from the proposition that the intellect becomes substantial through what it knows, and that were He to know something other than Himself, this would seem to imply His becoming substantial through something else, and hence, His essence becomes multiple according to the number of the things known. Now if this commonly accepted proposition is true, [i.e., that the intellect becomes substantial through what it knows], then His knowledge of things known [still] does not imply multiplicity. For it is clear that His knowledge bestows existence and substance on other existents beside Himself, and it is certainly clear that He does not become substantial through something other than

---

[28] In the *Light* I, 3, Crescas argues against Maimonides that God possesses essential attributes.
[29] *On the Soul* III, 3.

Himself. If He were to become substantial through the things known, then that would indeed imply multiplicity in His essence. But once it has been shown that He bestows existence on others beside Himself, then He is the one simple source and the origin, through whose essential Eternal Will existence is bestowed on others, whether one or many. There is certainly no room for the [second] doubt if the proposition that was taken to be commonly accepted is untrue. That will be shown in the third treatise, God willing.

The third doubt, taken from the notion that a particular thing cannot be apprehended except through a hylic faculty, is peculiar to knowledge acquired from what exists. For a particular cannot be known or apprehended except through sense and imagination. But one need not know by means of sense and imagination with respect to knowledge that bestows existence on the sum total of existents – substance or accidents, species and particulars. Rather, the particular is that which acquires existence from the knowledge that is in Himself.

The fourth doubt was taken from the temporality of particulars, and from the claim that time is an accident consequent upon motion. There is no room for this doubt [even] if one accepts the premise, for His knowledge is that which bestows existence upon particulars and on time and motion – all the more so since the falsity of the premise was already shown in the first treatise, for time is not an accident consequent upon motion.

The fifth doubt was taken from the apparent evil order. Now when it is shown that the order is of the utmost good, then this doubt will be removed. This will be shown in the second principle, God willing.

Particular Doubts. The first particular doubt concerning the first feature was based on the [principles that] knowledge is something that is inclusive and encompassing, and that what is infinite is not subject to being included and encompassed. Now this is true of finite knowledge. But when we posit the knowledge to be infinite, when He knows an infinite number of things, then nothing absurd follows. For one infinite does not exceed the other.

The second particular doubt was based on [the knowability of] continuous quantity. Now when He knows the proportions of the parts into which [the quantity] is divisible, He already knows them infinitely, and he knows that there is no last part. There is nothing impossible about infinite knowledge becoming correlated with an infinite number of things known, as one infinite line can be correlated with another, since it does not exceed the other.

The first particular doubt concerning the second feature was based on the [principle that] true knowledge should be of the existent. Now this is true with respect to our knowledge, which is acquired from existing things. But it is sophistical with respect to His knowledge, which bestows existence on things. For His knowledge of things is of the most excellent type of existence that an existent may possess, namely, the existence which is in the Divine essence, may He be blessed, and which bestows existence on things and makes it flow into them. It is sufficient, in order for things to exist, that they be known to His eternal knowledge.

The second doubt was based on a change in His knowledge, and consequently a change in His essence, for the intellect becomes substantial through that which it knows. The resolution of this doubt is not difficult, based on what has been said, for this principle is incorrect. Even if we accept it, there will be no change in His essence when the time comes for the thing to exist, for it was already in his eternal will that the thing occur at the time that His wisdom determined.

The first doubt concerning the third feature was also based on a change in His knowledge when the possible disjunct occurs, for then the nature of the possible will be removed. Its resolution is like that of the previous doubt. For when we do not accept that the intellect becomes substantial by virtue of what it knows, there is no room for this doubt. Even if we accept it, there will be no change of knowledge. For since His eternal knowledge was that the nature of the possible would change at that time, then when the time comes, and the thing exists as was known, there is no change of knowledge.

The second doubt was based on the idea that if we posit the contradictory disjunct of what He knows to be possible, and indeed, to exist, then two absurdities result: first, His knowledge changes; and second, his previous 'knowledge' was not knowledge but erroneous estimation. Now it is evident that when we draw an analogy from our knowledge to His knowledge this [result] cannot be avoided, *unless* we hold that the disjunct which He knows is possible in a certain respect and necessary in another. From the aspect of its being necessary, no change in His knowledge and His essence comes about. From the aspect of its being possible, the [nature of] the possible in possible things is not nullified.

I can explain this [last point] as follows: When a thing is necessitated in a certain manner, this certainly does not imply that the thing is necessitated with respect to itself. This can be shown in the case of things that are possible with respect to themselves that exist now as sensibles. For knowledge that something exists absolutely necessitates that it exists, and its contradictory cannot possibly exist in any manner. But this necessitation does not change the nature of the possible, and does not imply the necessitation of the thing with respect to itself. So God's knowledge [of a thing] occasioned by choice does not imply the necessitation of the thing with respect to itself and does not change the nature of the possible at all. This will be shown at greater length in what follows, God willing, in principle four.[30] The indubitable truth of this will be explained there. Most men of speculation stumbled here, since they did not consider the [sort of] necessity that is compatible with Divine, religious justice.[31]

This is sufficient for our intentions in the present chapter.

Chapter Five: On the manner of knowing this cornerstone completely

I say that this cornerstone, as we have posited it, has been validated by tradition. But in addition to that, speculation has also confirmed it in two respects: First, it is enough to confirm this cornerstone by refuting the arguments and resolving the doubts that induced some men of speculation to reject [Divine] knowledge. For it is not fitting to attribute to Him the greatest of defects, ignorance. So when it has been shown completely that nothing claimed against this cornerstone can refute it, given what speculation has established concerning the nature of the possible, it is fitting and necessary that we confirm it according to our position. The second perspective is that we have shown above that it is impossible for God not to have knowledge of particulars insofar as they are particular, as was stated in Chapter Three of this treatise.

When we clarify fully the root principle of belief in creation below, this cornerstone will be revealed and clarified. For it will be shown there, without a doubt, that God is the agent and cause of the existence of all existing things through his simple will, and it is inconceivable that He is their agent without His knowing them. Now it will be shown easily

---

[30] Scholars have noted that the reference is more appropriate to II, 5, 3 and may be the vestige of an earlier version of the *Light of the Lord*, where the principle of choice was section four. It could, however, refer to II, 4, 2

[31] Lit.: 'that Divine religious justice tolerates.'

that once we have accepted the creation of all things through His will, including the natures of things, hence [these, too, are] consequent upon his will, i.e., fire burns because he wished to give it a burning nature; had he wished to give it a cool nature, although it is an extremely fine substance, or to give earth a hot nature, although it is extremely thick, they would have possessed such natures. It follows therefore that God stamped the nature of the possible, which is one of the existing things, according to His will. It is thus inconceivable that God willed not to know what He would have known had he not willed not to know it.[32] For if that were possible for Him, then it would be possible also that no absurdity would result from His wishing to stamp something with a nature over which He has no power, despite the fact that it is conceivable for something to have power over [this nature]. This thought is absolutely disgraceful and heretical. This principle will be explained fully in the third treatise, with the help of God.

Herewith is completed what we wished to explain with respect to this principle. Praise be to God alone, Who is exalted above all tribute and praise.

Cornerstone Five: Choice [Introduction]

We already stated above[33] that one of the foundations of the law is choice, and that power[34] has been granted to each individual. For the term 'commandment' does not apply to one who is compelled and coerced to perform a definite action. Rather, it must be left to one's simple will [to choose] any of the alternatives. In such a case, the injunction would be appropriate and relevant.

The foundation of choice is that the nature of the possible exists. The ancients struggled over this question. We have found in their statements that have reached us different views. Thus, we must investigate them according to the Torah and speculation. Since the views that we have found in regard to this issue are two contradictory disjuncts, we have divided this principle into three chapters. The first two chapters deal

---

[32] It is inconceivable that God willed to be ignorant of what was in principle knowable ("what He would have known had he not so willed"). The assumption, of course, is that future possibles are, in principle, knowable.

[33] See above, p. 192.   [34] *Reshut*, "power" or "authority".

with the two views and their arguments, as is implicit in their discussions. In the third [chapter], we shall report that which the Torah and reason necessitates [in respect to this issue], as it appears to us.

It is important that we are not indolent in this investigation, because this principle is an important foundation and pillar for [the belief in] God's knowledge of the existents, as we alluded to in the first principle, so that an error regarding this issue produces immense and enormous errors concerning God's knowledge of and providence over the existents. Therefore, we have added three chapters, as will be apparent from our discussion of this principle, with the help of God.

Chapter One: An explanation of the view of the one who maintains that the nature of the possible exists. This will be explained both according to speculation and the Torah.

According to speculation, [this view] is plausible for several reasons:

[First,] things, whether natural or artificial, can come to be only if they are preceded by four causes, namely the efficient, material, formal, and final cause, as is explained in the *Physics*.[35] And we see that some of the causes of certain things exist and some do not exist; thus, it is possible that all of the causes will come into existence or that some of them will not come into existence. Consequently, the possibility of its causes entails the possibility of the thing itself.

[Second,] we see that many things depend upon will. Indeed, it is evident that a person can will or not will certain things. But if this were compelled, there would be no will but compulsion and necessity. Consequently, it is evident that the nature of the possible exists.

[Third,] it has already been explained in the *Physics*[36] that certain things come about by chance, fortuitously, or by their own essence.[37] If all things were necessary, however, as would follow if the nature of the possible did not exist, everything would exists of necessity. Yet what exists of necessity can not be truthfully described as existing by chance. For it is not true of the sun's rising tomorrow that it does so by chance. Therefore, it is evident that not all things are necessary and that the nature of the possible exists.

---

[35] See *Physics* II, 1.   [36] *Physics* 195b–198a.   [37] I.e., not as a result of any external cause.

[Fourth,] if the nature of the possible did not exist, and human actions were compelled, effort and diligence would be futile. This would entail the futility of studying and teaching, the futility of all preparation and training, and the futility of applying oneself to obtain possessions and useful things, as well as the avoidance of harmful things. This is, however, contrary to what is well known and perceived by the senses.

[Fifth,] since a person's will is consequent upon his rational soul, which is separate from matter, it is not appropriate that things which are material, namely the corporeal spheres,[38] which act upon the bodies of the lower [world], act upon his rational soul. For, it is evident that the separate is designated to act, while matter is designated to be acted upon, as has been explained in the *Metaphysics*.[39] Therefore, it is not appropriate to suppose that the spheres, which are corporeal bodies, act upon and compel the human soul. Rather, will is devoid and negated of all necessity.

Thus, it is evident from all these arguments, that, according to speculation, the nature of the possible exists. Furthermore, according to the Torah, it is also evident for several reasons.

[First,] if all things were necessary and human actions were compelled, the commandments and prohibitions of the Torah would be futile, because they would be unprofitable, since human actions would be compelled and no one would have power or will over them.

[Second,] if human actions were compelled, God's reward and punishment for them would be unjust, God forbid! For it is self-evident that reward and punishment for actions apply only to volitional human action. Thus, it is not possible for there to be reward and punishment for compelled and coerced actions. Consequently, since reward and punishment are one of the root principles of the Torah, it is necessary that man possess a will that is free[40] of all coercion and compulsion.

From this, it is evident that the nature of the possible exists. This is the purpose of this chapter.

Chapter Two: An explanation of the view of the one who maintains that the nature of the possible does not exist

[This view] may also be demonstrated according to both speculation and the Torah. According to speculation, it is plausible for several reasons.

---

[38] I.e., the planets and stars. [39] *Metaphysics* 49b, 12–28. [40] Lit.: 'clean.'

[First,] it has been explained in physics that four causes must precede the existence of all generable and corruptible things. Furthermore, the existence of these causes necessarily brings about the existence of the effects. Therefore, the existence of the effects is necessary and not possible. When we inspect the existence of the causes, they must be preceded by other causes. These [preceding] causes necessitate the existence of the [subsequent] causes. Thus, the existence of the [preceding] causes is necessary and not possible. Moreover, when we search for [preceding] causes for these [antecedent] causes, the same will apply. This continues until one reaches the First Being, the Necessary Existent, blessed is His name. Thus, it has been explained that the nature of the possible does not exist.

[Second,] it is self-evident and commonly accepted that something which can or cannot exist requires a cause that preponderates its existence over its nonexistence. Otherwise, its nonexistence would be permanent. Therefore, when something possible comes into existence, a cause must have necessitated it and preponderated its existence over its nonexistence. Consequently, the being that was assumed as possible is [actually] necessary. Furthermore, when we inspect also the preceding cause, if one posits it as existing, the same thing will be true of it as was true of the first possible that was assumed as existing. This continues until one reaches the First Cause and Being, the Necessary Existent.

[Third,] it is self-evident and commonly accepted that anything which passes from potentiality to actuality requires an external cause that will actualize it. Therefore, when a will comes about in a man to do something, the will that was in potential and became actualized must have been actualized by something external. The cause of will is that which moved the appetitive faculty to join and agree with the imaginative faculty, as is explained in *On the Soul*.[41] Consequently, when this conjunction, which is the cause of will, exists, will is necessitated [to exist]. Likewise, the conjunction is necessitated when the mover exists.

One can claim that the mover of will is will itself, which is the contrary of necessity. However, from this claim follows one of two impossibilities: the thing will move itself and bring itself from potentiality to actuality, and this is contrary to the [aforementioned] accepted principle; alternatively,

---

[41] This point appears in Ibn Rushd's Epitome of Aristotle's *De Anima*, but Crescas probably is relying here on Abner of Burgos. See Walter Mettmann, *Ofrenda de Zelos (Minḥat Kena'ot)* (Opladen: Westdeutscher Verlag, 1990), pp. 29–30.

there is an antecedent will that moves will and brings it from actuality to potentiality, and [in turn] there exists another prior will [that actualizes] the former will. Consequently, one will would necessitate an infinite number of wills, which is absolutely ludicrous! Furthermore, each one [of the wills] would be necessitated by the antecedent one and therefore would not be possible.

[Fourth,] it is self-evident, as we have stated, that everything that is originated requires an originator that originates it. For a thing cannot originate itself. Therefore, let there be two people in identical situations, with identical temperaments, identical characteristics, and identical relation to a particular thing, and let them be indistinguishable. It is inconceivable and impossible that one chooses the existence of something and the other its non-existence. Rather, it is necessary that the one chooses and wills what the other chooses and wills. For, if their choice and will differed, then because the difference was originated it requires an originator. Would that I knew what is the cause of the difference, since they agree in all respects regarding temperament, nativity, and characteristics?! And even if it is true that the existence of such people is [empirically] impossible, the necessity does not result from its being impossible, but rather from its being possible. Thus, once it has been shown that their will must be identical, it is consequently necessary and compelled and not possible.

[Fifth,] it has already been explained in the first principle of this treatise that God's knowledge encompasses all particulars insofar as they are particulars, even if they are [presently] non-existent, not having come into existence. Consequently, it follows of necessity that once He knows which one of the possible disjuncts will come about, it is necessary that it will come about. Otherwise, He would not possess knowledge, but opinion or error. Therefore, what was assumed as possible is necessary and inescapable.

[Sixth,] if the nature of the possible exists, one would have necessarily to admit that the existence of a will toward one of two disjuncts without a necessitating cause is possible. Consequently, one would have to admit that His knowledge does not derive from His essence as is His knowledge of the existents which He has caused. Rather, His knowledge would be acquired and emanate from their existence. But it is absolutely absurd that His knowledge has an external origin.

[Seventh,] it is evident that divine providence of particulars, when it is not from the universal order, is impossible without a corporeal faculty – which God cannot possess. So since [by hypothesis] the existence of one of the sides [disjuncts] is without a necessitating cause, such an existence is not apprehended by the universal order.

From all this, then, it is plausible to conclude that according to speculation the nature of the possible does not exist. Moreover, this view can also be proven according to the Torah. For there is no doubt of its veracity from that which we mentioned regarding God's knowledge, namely that it encompasses all particulars, even if they do not [yet] exist. Furthermore, the prophets would presciently announce many of the particulars, even if they were not necessary with respect to itself, namely that they were dependent on choice, as in the case of Pharaoh. This is manifest proof that the nature of the possible does not exist. This is the purpose of this chapter.

Chapter Three: An explanation of the true view according to what Torah and speculation require

Since there are arguments that necessitate the existence of the possible and arguments that necessitate its non-existence, the only remaining alternative is that it exists in certain respects and does not exist in certain respects. Would that I knew what are these respects!

When we inspect the arguments which necessitate its existence, they only necessitate its existence in itself.

The first argument, based on the fact that the causes of certain things can exist without those things existing, begs the question. For the possibility of the causes is part of the question. Therefore, [this argument] does not provide the truth regarding this question.

The second argument, based on the [nature of] will, namely that it is evident that a person can will or not will things, also begs the question. For the advocate of the nonexistence of the nature of the possible claims that will possesses a mover that moves and necessitates its activity[42] towards one thing or its alternative, and that this mover is its cause. Thus, although the mover necessitates the activity of the will, the will remains will, neither necessary nor compelled. For in itself it has the capacity of willing one of the two alternatives equally, were it not that its mover necessitates it to will one of them without feeling any compulsion or coercion. Since in

---

[42] Lit.: 'occurrence of the will' (i.e., a volition).

itself it can equally will one of the two alternatives, it is considered will and not necessity.[43]

The third argument, based on the explanation of physics that some things occur by chance, implies only possibility in itself.[44] In this respect, it is true that they occur by chance. However, the existence of causes that necessitate their existence is not precluded.

As for the fourth argument, based on [the existence of] diligence and effort, it is evident that these only imply possibility in itself. That is to say, if it were true that a man was compelled to be wealthy by virtue of his essence,[45] it would then be futile for him to apply himself to obtain possessions. However, if it is assumed as possible in itself and necessary from the aspect of its cause, i.e., his diligence and effort, then his diligence and effort are not futile. Rather, they are the essential cause for his obtaining possessions and the obtaining of possessions are their effect. There is no way to claim that the cause is in vain for the effect unless the effect is necessary in itself, regardless of the existence of the cause or without it. It would in that case, however, not be an effect.

As for the fifth argument, it is evident that it does not provide the truth in all respects. For the rational soul is not separate [from matter] but is corporeal and is acted upon by the temperament of the ensouled person. Thus, it is possible that the bodies of the spheres, and certainly their movers, act upon the temperament of the ensouled person and move the appetitive faculty which, through conjunction with the imaginative faculty, becomes will, as is explained in *On the Soul*.[46] But whether the moving [of the appetitive faculty] is from the aspect of necessity, or whether possibility remains, is not demonstrated by this argument. Consequently, it is evident that none of the arguments from speculation implies the existence of the nature of the possible except with respect to the essence of existing things, and not with respect to their causes.

The arguments from the Torah also only imply the existence of possibility in itself.

---

43 The will is a capacity that (i) does not in itself necessitate outcomes and (ii) does not feel itself coerced or compelled. Hence, its activity can still be distinguished from natural necessity.

44 Possibility in itself (or, with respect to itself) is contrasted with possibility through another (or, with respect to another). According to Crescas, all created things are possible in themselves but necessitated through their causes.

45 That is, his essential nature necessitated that he would be rich and not just external causes necessitated this.

46 See note 41.

The first argument, based on the commandments and prohibitions of the Torah – that is, if things were necessary, then commandments and prohibitions would be futile, only implies the possibility of things from their own aspect. For, if things were necessary from their own aspect, then commandments and prohibitions would be futile. However, if things are possible from their own aspect and necessary with respect to their causes, then the commandments and prohibitions are not futile, but rather serve an important purpose. For they are causes that move things that are possible in themselves in the same way as other causes produce effects, such as diligence and application, which produce the obtaining of possessions and beneficial things, and our fleeing from harmful things. Thus, it is verified that there is nothing in this argument that implies the existence of possibility with respect to its cause.

The second, argument, based on reward and punishment – that is, if humans were compelled in their actions, God would be unjust in rewarding and punishing them – seems like a strong argument that invalidates any kind of necessity. However, when one inspects it, it is not difficult to resolve. For, if reward and punishment are necessitated from worship and transgression as effects are necessitated from causes, they are not considered unjust, just as it is not unjust for one who comes close to a fire to be burned, even if his approach was involuntary. This will be explained in the third treatise, with God's assistance.[47] Thus, it is evident that there is nothing in these arguments from the Torah or speculation that implies the existence of the nature of the possible with respect to the cause.

Likewise, when we inspect the arguments that imply the non–existence [of the nature of the possible], they only imply [necessity] with respect to its cause. For it is evident from the subject matter of the first, second, and third arguments, which are based upon the causes of things, and upon the movers that cause something potential to become actualized, as well as the fourth argument, that they only imply necessity with respect to the cause. Thus, they remain possible in themselves. The same can be said of prime matter; in itself it is able to receive all forms successively, yet with respect to its movers, the generation of verdigris from copper is necessary relative to its causes. Still, [matter] retains its possibility in itself. Thus, in generating verdigris, there is a temporal necessity with respect to its

---

[47] The third principle of the third treatise is devoted to explicating the issue of reward and punishment. There, Crescas does provide a naturalistic account of spiritual rewards. But the sharp deterministic formulation that appears here is not reproduced there.

cause, i.e., which is transitory, and an eternal possibility with respect to itself, which is permanent.

Similarly, it is evident that the arguments taken from God's knowledge of the future and from the fact that He informed the prophets of future events, even if they are dependent on choice, do not imply the annulment of possibility with respect to itself. But things are possible with respect to themselves and necessary with respect to their causes, and from the aspect of their being necessary, they are known prior to their becoming necessary. Hence clearly none of the arguments from speculation or the Torah imply the necessity of things in themselves.

Thus, the complete truth implied by the Torah and by speculation is that the nature of the possible exists in things with respect to themselves, but not with respect to their causes. However, publicizing this is dangerous to the masses. For, they will consider this an excuse to do evil, and they will not perceive that the punishment follows from the transgressions as an effect from a cause. Thus, Divine wisdom consigned them, i.e., the commandments and the prohibitions, to be intermediate movers and powerful causes to direct human beings towards human happiness. His beneficence and simple grace is responsible for this. And this is the divine equity that is alluded to in the verse: "God disciplines you just as a man disciplines his son" [Deut. 8:5]. It is well known that a father does not discipline his son with the intent to exact revenge, nor to render justice, but for the benefit of the son. So too when God disciplines human beings, His intention is not to exact revenge from them, nor to render political equity, which is only appropriate when human [actions] are completely volitional, without any compulsion or coercion. Rather, His intention is for the good of the entire nation, and this is what He intends by [the discipline]. Consequently, [the discipline] is appropriate even if [one] is necessitated with respect to his cause, because it is good for man.

It should be noted, however, that [punishing and rewarding] for these necessary [acts] is appropriate only when the agent does not feel coerced or compelled, which is the foundation of choice and will. But, when humans act under coercion and compulsion and not through their wills, the coerced and compelled actions are not acts of their souls, because they do not act with the accordance between their appetitive faculty and imaginative faculty. Thus, it is not appropriate that a punishment should follow. For commandments and prohibitions have no influence on coerced actions, so that they could motivate someone to do them or not do them.

Consequently, punishments for transgressions that human beings have no influence over would not be in accordance with divine equity, because no goodness would follow from it.

But the nature of will is such that it can will or not will without any external cause. This is the correct view.[48]

Now if we are preceding merely according to the Torah, we may posit the distinction [between absolute and hypothetical modalities] in the same manner as in the first principle of this treatise, i.e., a thing is possible with respect to itself and its cause, but necessary with respect to His knowledge.[49] When we posit a possible thing as existing and as known, it is possible with respect to itself, yet necessary with respect to its existing then, and its being known. If God's knowledge of things precedes their existence, then they are not possible with respect to His knowledge, because that which is necessitated prior to its existence is not possible; but they are possible with respect to themselves. And since God's knowledge is not temporal, His knowledge of the future is like our knowledge of existing things, which does not entail compulsion and necessity in the essence of the things.

When we object and say, "But is His knowledge then acquired from the existents?" as the last two doubts previously implied,[50] we shall reply and state that one does not know how He knows, because His knowledge is His essence. This is the way of Maimonides, according to our opinion.[51]

One could also reply that it is evident that things known are not known according to the nature of the things known but according to the nature of the knower. This can be seen clearly from sensory apprehension. For the sense of touch will apprehend its object when the person approaches and touches the object, and at the point of touching, senses whether it is hot or cold, hard or soft. [In contrast,] the sense of sight can apprehend colors from a distance; such is the case with the other [senses]. Therefore, since this knower is eternal and independent of time, it is proper

---

[48] Warren Zev Harvey has argued that the passages we have underlined here and in the subsequent paragraphs – passages that represent reservations about the correctness of determinism from the perspective of the Torah – were marginal comments that were incorporated in the body of the final version of the *Light of the Lord*. Whether they were made by Crescas or by others is impossible to say.

[49] See above, p. 211. The reference is obscure.

[50] See above, pp. 220–1 (the sixth and seventh doubts: if there are things that are possible with respect to themselves, then God's knowledge is acquired from existing things and not productive of them).

[51] See above, p. 208.

that He knows an object in a manner that accords with His rank and is independent of time, because of His essence. Thus, He apprehends in an eternal apprehension that which does not exist as if it were existing.

The principle that emerges from the above is that this possible material cannot escape being necessary with respect to its cause, and possible with respect to itself, as long as choice is not involved. When choice is involved, then if we maintain that the nature of will implies that it can either will it or not will it without an external mover, as is the correct view according to the Torah, then such things will be possible with respect to their causes *and* with respect to themselves, and necessary with respect to God's knowledge. And since they are possible with respect to themselves, diligence, commandments and prohibitions, and reward and punishment are fitting for them. For if one chose the contrary, God's knowledge would be of the contrary. Only the question how God knows the possible remains. And we already answered it, either according to the view of the Rabbi [Moses Maimonides], or according to our view. In general, since He emanates existence to the other existents, [His] knowledge of them is entailed [by this fact] and is fitting.

Whichever is true,[52] the principle point – "possibility from one aspect, necessity from another" – is inescapable.

The perfect man who entered and exited peacefully[53] already testified in regard to all these profundities in a brief statement: "Everything is observed and authority is granted. The world is judged according to goodness and all is in accord with the majority of actions."[54] By saying "everything is observed," he taught that everything is ordered and known. This is the great principle that is indubitably true, but over which some of our Sages stumbled. And this is what brought me to reveal this secret, because many of our nation have rebelled against it. By saying "authority is granted," he testifies about the secret of choice and will and that the authority with respect to itself is granted to each person, because the commandment cannot be administered to the compelled and coerced. By saying "the world is judged according to goodness," he testifies that the Divine equity in judgment, that is, in reward and punishment, is not for the purpose of revenge, nor is it for the intention of establishing political equity for the masses – this is so because of the necessitation with

---

[52] The reference is to Maimonides' or Crescas' explanations of why God's foreknowledge does not necessitate future possibles.

[53] I.e., Rabbi Akiva (cf. *Tosefta Ḥagigah* II, 2) [54] *Mishnah Avot* III, 15.

respect to its cause. But rather, it is for the sake of the good, as was stated previously – this is so not because of the necessitation with respect to its cause – but rather, it is for the sake of the good, as was stated previously. By saying "all is in accord with the majority of actions," he may be testifying to the necessity of proximate and remote causes, as is stated: "For a high one is protected by a higher one" [Eccles. 5:7]. Or, he is alluding to the well known principle of the tradition that the world is judged according to the majority.[55] Or he may be alluding to the great root principle that will be explained in Principle Six, God willing.[56]

Chapter Four

Whatever the [correct] view is concerning necessity, whether it is the necessity of something with respect to its cause, or with respect to God's knowledge,[57] it is alluded to in a number of places in Scripture, particularly in the Book of Ecclesiastes, and in the sayings of the sages. The sages stated: "No one bruises his finger below, unless it was so decreed against him above."[58] Moreover, regarding the verse: "If the one who is falling [*ha-nofel*] falls from there" [Deut. 22:8], they explained: "Already from the six days of creation the individual was suited to fall, for although he had not [yet] fallen Scripture refers to him as 'one who is falling.' But reward is brought about through a meritorious person and punishment through a guilty person."[59] Thus, despite the fact that many possibilities had occurred since then [i.e. the six days of creation], this individual was suited to fall since the six days of creation, and the proximate cause [of his falling] was the lack of a parapet. Although it is attributed to chance, and human beings are precluded from knowing it because their knowledge does not encompass particulars, since they are infinite, [knowledge of] it is necessary for someone who is infinite and whose knowledge is of the infinite.

Here is another statement of the sages that teaches this:

"David was not suited to do that deed, nor was Israel suited to do that deed. The point was to show us that if an individual sins he should be told, 'Seek the man who repented of his sin; so you should do repentance.'

---

55 *Qiddushin*, 40.   56 On the Final End of the Torah.

57 The rest of the chapter, which is largely based on Abner, only makes sense if things are causally necessitated. It appears that the first sentence of the chapter was altered to reflect later reservations concerning determinism.

58 *Hullin* 7b.   59 *Shabbat* 32a.

And if all the people sin then they should be told, 'Seek an entire people that repented; so you should do repentance.'"[60]

Despite their being unsuited for the deed, they were punished. And this [difficulty] can only be solved according to the approach that we have chosen.[61]

Here is another statement of the sages that teaches about 'necessity': "When God said to Israel: "Who might grant that they had such a heart always [to revere me and follow all My commandments" [Deut. 5:26], they should have said: "You grant." Moses only hinted this to Israel this after forty years . . . One can learn from here that a person understands completely the mind of his master only after forty years have transpired."[62]

The apparent meaning of many other [rabbinic] statements increase doubt and perplexity, but their literal meaning becomes intelligible according to this approach.

Here is a statement of the sages that teaches that effort is compatible with necessity: "If I am not for myself, who will be for me? And if I am for myself, what am I? And if not now, then when?"[63] There are many other similar statements that are not necessary to mention, e.g., the statement of the sages in *Sukkah* [29a]: "The sun eclipses on account of four things"; or the ruling that is cited in *Makkot* [2:6]: "If the High Priest died before the trial was concluded and another High Priest was appointed in his place and the trial was then concluded, the exiled slayer returns home only after the death of the second [High Priest]", to which the Talmud queries: "What should the [second] High Priest have done? He should have requested [divine] mercy that the trial should conclude with an acquittal

---

[60] *Avodah Zarah*, 4b–5a. The actions are David's illicit behavior with Bathsheba and Israel's worship of the golden calf.

[61] Although neither David nor Israel were responsible for their actions, they were punished by God. The example, which comes from Abner, shows that God does not reward and punish people according to the principle of retributive justice, but in order to produce good.

[62] *Avodah Zarah* 5a–b. Cf. Abner's explanation: "For by Moses saying that they should have said, 'You grant' he hinted that even the fear of God is within the power of God, and that He gives it to whom He considers good. Understand this utterance just like those who learned from it that a man does not truly fathom the mind of his master until after forty years, for Israel could not understand this opinion of Moses until he showed them and guided them in science forty years. Then he showed them it esoterically, so that only those who were worthy would discover it." Cf. Abner of Burgos, *Ofrenda de Zelos*, ed. Mettman, p. 71.

[63] *Avot* 1:14. According to Abner, the first sentence implies the need for endeavor; the second implies the need for Divine help (i.e., causal necessitation).

and he did not request" [11b].[64] All such statements can be confirmed only through our explanation that all things are arranged and known by God, whether they are natural or subject to choice. This is enough for our purpose. In the sixth principle, we will introduce things that agree and fit with this view, for truth is a witness to itself and is in agreement in all respects.[65]

Herein has been resolved the great doubt that we promised in the first principle to resolve. Many of the ancients stumbled over this, for they did not appreciate that necessity agrees with the divine equity of the Torah, even if it is incompatible with the political equity of the multitude. [Certainly according to the view of the Torah, which is the correct one, political equity agrees with [necessity].]

Praise be to God alone, Who is exalted above all tribute and praise.

Chapter Five

Further explanation of the view [two views], in which we resolve the immense dilemma about which the ancients were continually perplexed: How can divine equity regarding reward and punishment be in accord with the existence of necessity? And if they are in accord, what is the distinction between necessity with respect to causes *without* the feeling of compulsion and coercion, and between necessity *with* the feeling of compulsion and coercion?

It might be supposed that if actions that are commanded and prohibited are causes, and reward and punishment are their effects, and that actions are necessitated, then one should not differentiate between necessity without felt compulsion and between necessity with felt compulsion – such that reward and punishment is an effect of the former and not of the latter. For in either case, necessity is inevitable. But even if we accept the distinction (namely, that when there is felt coercion and compulsion, there is no place for reward and punishment, since in that case it would not be volitional at all, whereas when coercion is not felt, it is called 'volitional' even though there is compulsion, but it is not felt) how can there be reward and punishment for *opinions* about the fundamentals of the

---

[64] Since he did not request, he is now subject to the death wishes of the exiled killer's family. The point in both cases is that human endeavor effects the outcome, even though God knows and determines what is to happen.

[65] Treatise two, principle six, chapter two.

Torah? Would that I knew! For it is evident according to tradition that punishment for them is extraordinary, as it states: "But the apostates and heretics who deny the Torah and the resurrection of the dead [descend to Gehenna for eternity]."[66] Moreover, the Mishnah states: "The following have no portion in the world to come: [he who says the belief in the resurrection of the dead is not derived from the Torah, and that the Torah does not come from heaven.]"[67] But we see that will and choice have no influence[68] on opinions. This is for the following reasons:

First, if will were necessary for belief, then the degree of belief would not be determined by the force of truth.[69] For will has the capacity to will or not to will. And one could always believe contradictory disjuncts one after another, if one wanted to believe them. This is utterly absurd.

Second, if will were necessary for belief, then the reason that produces belief would be of dubious truth. For if the reason that produces belief is not of dubious truth, then there is no need for will. Now if the reason is of dubious truth, then the belief itself is of dubious truth.

Third, the following consideration shows that will has no influence on belief: belief is nothing but the affirmation that a thing exists extramentally as it exists in the soul. Now what exists extramentally is not dependent on the will of the believer that it is such. Therefore, belief is independent of will.

Having shown this I maintain that someone who believes a belief, certainly if the belief is demonstrative, must feel a necessity and a complete compulsion to affirm this belief. For the necessitation of the moving cause is strong and inescapable, since it is an absolute demonstration that causes [the resultant] belief to be a demonstrative one. Hence, the necessity and compulsion is evident and felt by him, so that he is internally prevented from believing the contradictory belief. So if reward and punishment were inappropriate for this sort of compulsion, I mean, felt compulsion, as was assumed, then I do not know how there can be reward and punishment for beliefs.

Here is the appropriate response in order to resolve these questions:

First, since divine equity is always directed to the good and the perfect, and the good and the perfect [includes] producing causes that motivate

---

[66] *Rosh ha-Shanah* 17a.   [67] *Sanhedrin* 10:1.   [68] *Mavo*, lit.: 'entry.'
[69] I.e., the degree of belief would be a function of the will and not of compelling reasons.

[people] towards good actions, the nature of divine equity necessitates the promulgation of commandments, and the associated reward and punishment, because these are causes that motivate [people] towards good actions. [The commandments] are motivating causes, since reward and punishment follow from [their observance], as the effect follows from the cause. So they move will and choice towards what is appropriate for them to approach, and away from what they should avoid. Hence we now grasp that it is appropriate for divine equity to be in accord with necessity.

Still, I maintain that it is appropriate to differentiate between necessity without felt coercion and compulsion, and necessity with felt coercion and compulsion. For it will be shown in the sixth principle [of this treatise], God willing, that the coveted purpose of acts of worship and good deeds is the desire and joy therein. This conforms both with the Torah and speculation, and it agrees with numerous rabbinic statements. Furthermore, this [i.e. the desire and the joy] is nothing other than the pleasure of will in doing good. This is so because God is love and pleasure to the utmost degree so that He emanates and brings about the good, and therefore the connection and conjunction [with God] is to follow in His path as much as possible. So when this desire and pleasure exists in the soul, it is a psychic action through which the conjunction and separation occurs. Consequently, it is appropriate that reward and punishment follows from it, as the effect follows from the cause. And when this desire is absent from the soul, as when one feels coerced and compelled in his or her actions, this action will not activate the soul, and conjunction and separation will not be entailed. For [in that case] the action is devoid of psychic volition, and hence reward and punishment are entirely inappropriate. We now grasp this distinction.

Still, even though we grasp this distinction, how do we grasp rewarding and punishing beliefs? For promises of reward and punishment cannot draw will and choice towards beliefs, nor can they be motivating causes for them. For it has been established that beliefs are not subject to human choice, and will has no influence on them.

Some of our sages have been seduced [into believing], as is implicit in their remarks, that justice and injustice are not relevant to reward for beliefs. For reward is natural and follows necessarily from the intelligible. In other words, once the soul of man realizes the truths of the beliefs, and they form intelligibles in him that are just as extramental [reality], then the soul has already become substantiated from them and will survive eternally. That is the ultimate reward for human beings.[70]

It is evident that this view has no place in the laws of the Torah, as will be explained further below, God willing.[71] Furthermore, if this were the case, then the few beliefs that appear in the Torah would have been sufficient for our guidance, and there would be no need for the great number of commandments, their branches, and their off-shoots, unless, by God, such commandments were derived from philosophy. Yet the number of [philosophical commandments] that appear in the Torah is quite small.

Now if souls were to become substantiated from the intelligible truths, then because there are very many intelligibles in [Euclid's] *Elements* and in [Appolonius'] *Conic Principle*, the geometer's soul would include many more truths than the Torah scholar's soul! But it is evident that this view is false according to the Torah, not to mention that the view that the ultimate reward is the survival of the intelligibles is itself far-fetched, as we shall explain, God willing.

Would that I knew whether the soul that cognized the intelligible that is demonstrated in the *Elements*, 'The angles of a triangle equal two right angles,' and no other, will become substantiated through this intelligible and survive eternally! And if it does survive, will it be like the soul that becomes substantiated through the intelligible, 'The square of a square's diameter is equal to the squares of two adjacent sides' and no other? If these souls differ, in what respect do they differ? No, all this is nonsense and false imagining. The Philosopher, unenlightened as he was by the Torah, yet pressured by strong indications of the immortality of the human soul, fabricated arguments and reasonings to confirm these indications, even though they are completely remote from the intellect and even more so from the Torah. Let us therefore abandon this method.

Now that we have shown that will has no influence on beliefs, but rather that the believer feels compelled in his beliefs, it is evident that we must relate will and choice to something that is attached and conjoined with beliefs, something that is adjacent to them. And this is the pleasure and

---

[70] This is the view of the Jewish Aristotelians, although it is not the case that they felt that justice is not relevant to reward for beliefs. This may be why Crescas says that this view is implicit in their remarks.

[71] Treatise two, principle six. For the relevant passage, see Daniel H. Frank, Oliver Leaman, and Charles H. Manekin (eds.), *The Jewish Philosophy Reader* (London and New York, 2000), pp. 265–70.

joy that we experience when God grants us His belief, and the diligence to apprehend its truth. This is undoubtedly subject to will and choice. For a true belief can be conceived without the believer apprehending a stirring of joy in his believing it. Therefore, it is evident that the stirring of joy, and the effort in comprehending [the belief's] truth, are matters that are consequent upon will and choice. This enables us to grasp the issue of reward and punishment [for beliefs], as we will demonstrate further in the sequel, God willing.

Moreover, it is also true, when one examines actions closely, that the reward is not primarily for [performance] of the actions themselves, but for the choice made by the agent to perform the act. For the man who performs a certain act has realized one of the contrary disjuncts that he had the power to choose equally. And since it is evident that the actual, insofar as it is actual, is neither potential nor possible for him, it must be necessary and compelled for him. It follows therefore that the reward and punishment resulting from choice and will is not for the act performed, but rather for his choice of the act to be performed.

How fitting is the statement of the Rabbis regarding this: "Thoughts of transgression are more severe than transgression" (*Yoma*, 29a). For the transgression is composed of two elements: the act itself, and its being chosen and willed. And the punishment that is received for it is only a result of the will and choice that are called in this statement "thought." Therefore, it is evident that the more severe of the two is the will, i.e., the "thought." This is also verified when we conceive them apart: the act without thought or will – what may be called a coerced act – or will without the act. For an agent will receive punishment for thought or will [without the act], as we learn from the genuine tradition: "The sin offering atones for thoughts of the heart."[72] He will not receive punishment for an action [alone], as our principle states: "In the case of coercion, the divine law exempts him."[73] However, it states "more severe" because the punishment for will when it is joined with an action is indubitably greater than the punishment for the will alone, when the act is not joined with it. This indicates that the punishment also results from the act, but the more severe [punishment] results from the will, especially when it is joined to the act. This is true without doubt!

---

[72] *Lev. Rabbah* 7:40.   [73] *Nedarim* 27a.

Thus, this great doubt has been solved, and it is now understood that reward and punishment of beliefs result from the desire and joy that one has from them and the diligence and effort in acquiring them. This is what we wished to explain.

Chapter Six: Explaining that what has been demonstrated through speculation agrees with the opinions of the sages

This is so because two notions have been demonstrated: first, that belief regarding opinions is not acquired through the will; second, that reward and punishment is for the will, because reward is for the desire, effort, and joy in being a party to the belief, and punishment is for the contrary.

These two matters are alluded to in a passage in the "Rabbi Akiva" chapter [of the Talmudic tractate *Shabbat*]:

"'They stood at the bottom of the mountain' [Exod. 19:17]. This teaches that [God] turned the mountain on top of them like a casket. [He said to them]: 'It is good if you accept it and, if you do not, you will be buried there.' Rava said: 'This supplies a strong disclaimer regarding [the acceptance of] the Torah.' He said to him: 'They reaccepted it in the days of Ahasuerus, for it is written: "They confirmed what they had accepted long before" [Esther 9:27].'"[74]

The explanation of this passage is as follows: Since it has been demonstrated that belief is acquired by means of rational principles, and certainly by means of the prophecy that was transpired at that noble gathering [at Mount Sinai], the will does not influence it at all. Consequently, they had to believe what they believed, whether they wanted to or not. Thus, they were compelled regarding the belief and this compulsion is likened to His "turning the mountain on top of them like a casket," so that they would accept it against their will, and if not, they would die there. This is recognizable coercion and compulsion, which is true of most of the great miracles. At the conclusion of that gathering, they necessarily believed in the Torah and that if they turned away from it, they would be turning away from the correct way, the way of life. This is designated as "death" and "burial." Thus, that sage said: "This supplies a strong disclaimer regarding [the acceptance of] the Torah." For the Torah is without doubt true;

---

[74] Crescas may be citing from memory; in the printed editions and the principal manuscripts of *Shabbat* 88a, the discutants differ (e.g., it is Rava who says, "They reaccepted it in the days of Ahashverosh", etc.)

nevertheless, because belief in it was coerced, the will had no influence over it. Perhaps they did not accept [the belief] of their own voluntary will,[75] which binds us to follow [the belief]. For although this belief is indubitably true, it is clear that if we did not accept it, then there is no way to the great punishment. Thus, they responded: "They accepted it again in the days of Ahasuerus, for it is written: 'They confirmed what they had accepted long before.'" That is to say, by means of the joy over the miracles and the deliverance that was performed for them in those days, "They confirmed what they had accepted long before," and the disclaimer dissipated. For the pleasure and joy on which the rewards of beliefs depends became perfected in the days of Ahasuerus.

All this is all a parable for what we have demonstrated: that beliefs in opinions are acquired without the will, and that reward is for the will and the joy in being an adherent of this belief.

Since this joy is a great pleasure and benefit for the adherent of this belief, and since our principle is, "It is forbidden for a man to benefit from this world without [reciting] a blessing,"[76] [the sages] instituted a formula for this blessing: "Blessed [is God] who has not made me a gentile, woman or slave." We shall explain this further in the sixth principle, God willing.[77] This is sufficient for now for our purpose. Praise be to God alone, Who is exalted above all tribute and praise.

---

[75] *Mi-reẓonam ha-beḥiri*, 'from their choosing will.'   [76] *Berakhot*, 35a.
[77] Treatise two, principle six, chapter one.

8

Joseph Albo, from *The Book of Principles*

Treatise One

Wherein is treated the number of laws,[1] and wherein it is shown that they are three: natural, conventional, and divine. The differences between them are given, and the principles of every one of them investigated, so that the principles of the divine law are made clear. Then is explained the test whereby the divine law is distinguished from the spurious law that pretends to be divine, and whether there can be more than one divine law at a time.

[Chapters One through Three are omitted] Chapter Four

I consider the proper way to enumerate the principles that are the roots and fundamentals of the divine Torah to be as follows:

The necessary and inclusive principles of the divine law are three: the existence of God, providence[2] in reward and punishment, and Torah from heaven. These three are the primary categories of the various divine laws, such as the Torah of Adam, the Torah of Noah, the Torah of Abraham, the Torah of Moses, and any other divine Torahs, if there be such, at the

---

[1] *Datot*. The Hebrew term '*dat*' signifies for Albo 'every guidance or regimen that embraces a large group of people, whether it consists of many commands . . . or one command.' (See below, p. 242.) Thus, *dat* should be understood as 'the law,' e.g., 'the law of the Medes.' Albo also uses the Hebrew term 'Torah' in this sense, but 'Torah' connotes a *divinely revealed* law, where *dat* is more inclusive. In our translation 'Torah' is left untranslated as a technical term, whereas *dat* is translated as 'law.'

[2] *Hashgaḥah*, lit.: 'supervision,' 'watching over.' The point is not so much that God provides for the world, as that He watches over it. Still, I have generally kept the traditional English translation 'providence.'

same time or in succession. There are subordinate and derivative principles included in every one of these three Torahs, which issue from the principle as a branch issues from a tree. Thus, God's eternity, perpetuity, and so on are subsumed under the existence of God. God's knowledge, prophecy, and so on are included within Torah from heaven. Reward and punishment in this world, and spiritual in the next are included within providence.

From these three general principles issue branches that are specific to the various divine Torahs, genuine or spurious, as follows: Subsumed under the principle of the existence of God is His incorporeality, which is a special principle of the Torah of Moses, and likewise His unity. Subsumed under the Torah from heaven is the root of the prophecy and mission of Moses. Subsumed under providence, and reward and punishment, is the coming of the Messiah, which is a special principle of the Torah of Moses according to the view of Maimonides. But according to our view the coming of the Messiah is not a principle. And if it is, it is not special to the Torah of Moses, for the Christians too regard it as a principle, and that too in order to abrogate the Torah of Moses. It is indeed a special principle for them, without which their law cannot be conceived. All these, and others like them that pertain specifically to particular laws, are included within the aforementioned three principles. The question whether there can be more than one divine Torah at the same time or at different times, will be discussed later with the help of God.[3]

That these three principles are the root and fundamental of the faith by which man attains true happiness is proved by the fact that the men of the Great Assembly[4] composed three blessings which they incorporated in the Additional Service for the New Year, going by the name of "Kingdoms," "Memorials," and "Trumpets." These three blessings correspond to the three principles and are intended to call our attention to the fact that by properly believing in these principles together with their branches, we shall win a favorable verdict in the divine judgment . . .

It may be that Maimonides had the same idea as the one we have just indicated concerning the number of principles, and that his list [of thirteen] consists of the three aforementioned primary categories, plus the branches issuing from them, as that they are all called by him

---

[3] I:25; III:13. The answer is that there can be more than one Torah addressed to different people.

[4] According to rabbinic Judaism, the Great Assembly (c. fifth century BCE) instituted many legal reforms and enactments.

"principles." Thus he lays down the existence of God, a primary category, as the first principle. Then he numbers four other roots that branch out from it, viz., the unity, incorporeality, eternity, and exclusive worship, as principles. Then he numbers the Torah from heaven a primary category, with three other branches as principles, since they issue from it: prophecy, Mosaic prophecy, and the immutability of the law. Then he lists divine omniscience and providence in reward and punishment as the third category, together with three other principles contained within, or issuing from, it: spiritual recompense, Messiah, and resurrection.

According to this explanation it is clear why he did not include the doctrine of creation, for it does not come under any of the three which we mentioned. He did not include choice and purpose because, though they are essential to divine law, they are not essential to it insofar as it is divine, as will be explained later.[5] The question still remains, however, why he did not enumerate under the principle of God's existence, "life" and "power" and other attributes, seeing that he included eternity and other attributes. The same criticism applies to the dogmas he derives from other principles.

All this will be made clear as we go on, with God's help. We must now return to analyze the principles according to our method, i.e., the three primary categories. We shall first explain the principles of nomic laws, and then we will treat of the principles of divine law, with the help of God (blessed be He).

Chapter Five

All animals live and thrive through three methods. Some cannot live and thrive together, such as beasts of prey. Living together would harm them, for if many of them gathered into one place, they would kill and feed on each other. Some are the complete opposite of the former; they can live only in associations and groups. Their society is necessary for their preservation, like the human species. By reason of his subtle [composition] and even temperament, man is affected by cold and heat and other contraries. He needs therefore clothing to protect him from heat and cold and properly prepared food suitable for his temperament. These things cannot be accomplished except by the aggregation and association of many

---

[5] Chapter 9.

individuals who assist one another. One sews, one weaves, one makes the needle, and so with the other arts, to the extent that every individual obtains the food and clothing that he needs for sustenance and support. Some other animals occupy an intermediate place between the two extremes. Aggregation and association are not injurious to their existence as it is to wild beasts and birds of prey, nor is it necessary as it is for the human species. But aggregation and association is better for them, like many species of grazing animals and gentle birds that move in flocks for the sake of company and convenience and for no other reason, seeing that it is not necessary for them as it is to the human species.

It is because aggregation and association are necessary for the life and support of the human species that the sages have said that man is political by nature.[6] They mean by this that it is almost necessary for man by his nature to live in a city with a large group of men, so that he may be able to obtain what he needs for his life and support. It is evident, therefore, that every human association in a city, district, or a clime, or all the human beings in the world, should have some order which they follow in their conduct, maintaining justice in general and suppressing wrong, so as to keep men from quarrelling in their transactions and business relations with one another. Such order would include protection against murder, theft, robbery and the like, and in general all those measures which are calculated to maintain the political group and enable the people to live in a suitable manner. The sages have called this order 'natural law,' meaning that it is necessary for man by virtue of his nature, whether the order emanates from a wise man or a prophet.

Such a law, however, is not yet sufficient to meet the needs of men and their social life, unless there is added to this a certain order or convention that embraces all the social and commercial relations and transactions of the people, like the laws of the Roman emperors, and the regimens of cities, and the statutes enacted by the people of a district or a kingdom to maintain conventional justice. Such an order as this is called a nomos or nomic law. This order or nomos cannot exist unless there is a governor, or a judge, or a ruler placed at the head of the association or city, who compels the people to remove injustice and to observe the nomos so as to perfect the welfare of the group. It follows therefore that the establishment of a

---

[6] Aristotle, *Politics* 1253a, 2.

king or a ruler or a judge is almost necessary for the maintenance of the human species, seeing that man is political by nature, as we have shown.

Chapter Six

If we reflect upon the formation of animals, and the perfection of their organs, we find that the Creator has supervised in a marvelous fashion their welfare and has provided for their every need, not merely those things which are necessary for the maintenance of the species or the individual, but also those things which are not necessary, yet which make their state a better one, for example, the duplication of the sense organs in animals to enable them to order their affairs in a more satisfactory and complete manner, though it is not necessary for the maintenance of their existence.

If we find such providence in inferior animals, certainly it befits Him to supervise the noblest species, and to order its affairs in accord with the species' perfection so as to enable it to achieve its perfection. If we reflect carefully upon the matter we shall find that the divine overflow that orders those things needed by the human species for the attainment of its perfection and end, is more necessary than [that which provides for] the many things which we see in the formation of the lower animals – I mean those things that have a tendency to improve their condition, but are not indispensable for their existence. This divine overflow may exist in a particular person only, yet this individual stands in the relation of perfection to the entire species.

Now this is so even though the various species coming under the genera do not form a hierarchy of graded perfection. I mean to say that although one particular species is more perfect than all the rest, yet this particular species alone is not the end of the whole genus, nor does it guide the genus to the perfection for which it is destined; for every species by itself contains in itself its own particular purpose and realizes its own perfection without reference to any other species. Now within each species there are similarly a number of groups of differing importance, e.g., the class of rulers has a greater measure of human perfection than the class of farmers; and the class of the sages is more perfect than that of the rulers. Similarly, within every class, some individual or individuals is or are more perfect than the other individuals of that class, and the celestial individual or individuals or class is or are not the purpose for which the species as a whole exists. Nevertheless [unlike the case between species] the celestial individual or individuals or class [within a species] is or are the cause of the attainment by the species of the purpose for which it is intended, because they stand in the relation of perfection to the species as a whole. I mean that they are like an instrument by means of which the species is enabled to attain its normal end and perfection, though the parts of the species are unequal in degree.

For example: every individual has many different organs, all of them necessary for an animal to exist, though one is more perfect than the other, and a third is still more perfect, and so on until we reach the most important organ which is the basis of an animal's existence. This organ stands in the relation of perfection to the animal, that is, it is an instrument by which perfect life flows to the animal as a whole. Thus, the heart is the basis of an animal's existence, and it is an instrument by which life flows to all the organs, and in particular the brain, which in turn transmits sensation and motion to all the other organs. Thus an animal's existence is perfected by the instrumentality, direct or indirect, of the heart. The same applies to men. All are equally human, yet human perfection reaches some individuals through the instrumentality of others. Just as all organs are necessary for the existence of the individual, and yet some stand higher in the scale than the others, and some receive their vital force through the instrumentality of others, so the class of wise men has a higher rank than the others, and it is from the wise man that emanates the order which arranges the affairs of men so as to enable them to attain human perfection. This order is called 'nomos.'

Now since, as we have said, it stands to reason that divine providence should take care that men receive this benefit, even as we find that it takes care of things of less importance in the lower animals, it follows that a divine overflow will accrue to some individual of the human race who is most ready for it, so that he may be an instrument by which men attain the perfection for which they are destined. This instrument may either be direct during life, or indirect after death, by inspiring the wise men who come after him to instruct men everywhere and always, according to the teaching such wise men receive from him, or to what they understand from the discourses in his writings. For the divine power is surely not unable to estimate this benefit so necessary to the human species, and to perfect it continually and everywhere, any more than it is unable to award the benefit that is necessary to the lower animals. This guidance that men receive from this individual is called divine Torah. Its relation to other laws and customs is the same as that of the architectonic art to the other arts which are subordinate to it.[7]

Chapter Seven

The term 'law' applies to every guidance or regimen that embraces a large group of people, whether it consists of many commands, such as "all that knew law and judgment" [Esther 1:13], or one command, such as "And a law was given out in Shushan" [ibid. 9:14]; or whether the law is divine, as in "At His right hand was a fiery law unto them" [Deut. 33:2] or nomic, as "the laws of the Medes and the Persians" [Dan. 6:9].

There are three kinds of law, natural, nomic, and divine. Natural law is the same among all peoples, at all times, and in all places. Nomic law is a law ordered by a wise man or men to suit the place and time, and the nature of the persons who are to be controlled by it, like the laws and statutes enacted in certain cities among the ancient idolworshippers, or those who worship God as human reason dictates without any divine revelation. Divine law is one that is ordered by God through a prophet, such as Adam or Noah, or like the regimen or law which Abraham taught men when he instructed them to worship God and when he circumcised them by the command of God, or one that is ordered by God through a messenger whom He sends and through whom He gives a law, like the Torah of Moses.

The intention of natural law is to suppress injustice and to promote justice, in order that men may keep away from theft, robbery, and murder, and that society may have a stable existence among men and every one may be safe from the wrongdoer and oppressor. The intention of nomic law is to repel the despicable and attract the fair, so that men may keep away from the despicable according to the commonly accepted view. Herein lies its advantage over natural law, for nomic law also improves men's conduct and arranges their affairs with a view to the improvement of political association, even as natural law. The intention of divine law is to guide men to obtain true happiness, which is spiritual happiness and immortality. It shows them the way they must follow to obtain it, teaches them the true good that they may take pains to secure it, shows them also real evil that they may guard against it, and trains them to abandon

---

[7] See *Metaphysics* 1013a, 14; *Ethics* 1094a, 14, 27.

imaginary happiness so that they may not desire it and not feel its loss. And in addition it also lays down the rules of justice so that the political association may be ordered in a proper manner, and the bad order of their association may not prevent them from attaining true happiness, which is the ultimate end of the human species to which the divine law aims. Divine law is in this way superior to nomic law.

Chapter Eight

Nomic law is inferior to divine law in many ways. The first is the one we mentioned, namely that nomic law improves human activity such that political association is improved. But it is not adequate to impart perfect doctrines, as we shall show in the sequel, so as to give immortality to the soul and enable it to return to the land of life from which it was taken, because nomic law deals only with the fair and the despicable. Divine law is adequate for this purpose, because it includes both parts upon which human perfection is based, viz., moral qualities and doctrines. Divine law encompasses the fair and the despicable, and distinguishes between the true and the false, i.e., the doctrines. That is why David describes it as perfect, when he says, "The law of the Lord is perfect, restoring the soul" [Ps. 19:18]. This means that the nomic law is not perfect because it does not encompass true doctrines, but divine law is perfect because it embraces perfection in moral qualities and doctrines, which are the two parts upon which the perfection of the soul depends. Therefore it "restores" the soul to God who gave it, and to the place which was its original home.

Another feature by which nomic law is inferior to divine law is that the former cannot distinguish between the fair and the despicable in all cases. For a thing may seem fair or despicable to us without being so in itself. For just as it is impossible that one should be born perfect in all the practical arts, though possessing a natural aptitude for some, so it is impossible that one should be born perfect in virtues and free from all defects, though possessing a greater tendency to certain perfections than to others. But it is impossible for someone to have all the virtues.

It becomes clear now that it is impossible for any author of a human nomos not to show a natural deficiency in some direction, and to regard the fair as despicable and the despicable as fair. His testimony concerning the fair and the despicable will therefore not be true. Thus Plato made a grievous mistake, advocating the despicable as though it were fair. For his idea is that all the women of a given class should be held in common by the men of that class. Thus, the wives of the rulers should be common to all the rulers, the wives of the merchants common to all the merchants, and similarly the wives of the men of a given trade or occupation should be common to the men of that trade or occupation. This is a matter which the Torah forbids; even the Torah of the Noahides prohibits it, for Abimelech was told, "Behold, thou shalt die, because of the woman whom thou hast taken; for she is a man's wife" [Gen. 20:3], and his excuse was that he did not know she had a husband. Aristotle, as is known, criticized Plato's idea in this matter.

This shows that no man's intellect is adequate to differentiate correctly between the fair and the despicable, and his views on this matter cannot therefore be relied upon. That is certainly true in the case of [theoretical] views, where it is clear that we cannot rely on a human view concerning profound problems, such as the creation or eternity of the world, for the human intellect is not adequate to know this with certainty. But "The testimony of the Lord is sure, making wise the simple" [Ps. 19:8], for it gives certain testimony on the problem of the world's origin, and on other important problems, and on the fair and despicable.

Another feature by which nomic law is inferior to divine law is that it cannot give full satisfaction to those who follow its requirements. The reason is that when a person is in doubt whether the thing he does is sufficient to lead him to the end intended, he cannot rejoice with his actions. But a person who follows the nomic law is precisely in this position. He does not know whether that which the law defines as just is really just or only apparently so. Hence he cannot rejoice with his actions. He, however, who lives by the divine law knows that what is defined therein as just is really just. Hence he rejoices in his actions. This is why "The precepts of the Lord are right, rejoicing the heart" [Psalms 19:9].

Another feature by which nomic law is inferior to divine law is this: Nomic law cannot define the specific acts which are proper in the several virtues. It can only make general statements, in the same way as a definition can be given of the general only, while the particular cannot be defined. Similarly nomic law cannot define particular acts. Thus Aristotle in his *Ethics* says repeatedly, in connection with the different virtues, that a virtuous act consists in doing the proper thing at the proper time and in the proper place, but he does not explain what is the proper time and the proper place. It is clearly a matter which not every one is capable of determining. Aristotle also says in various places in the *Ethics* that the proper measure must be maintained in every act, but he does not tell us what the proper measure is. It would seem therefore that his view was that the determination of this matter must be sought elsewhere.

Now there is no doubt that if it were within the true essence of a man *qua* man to know this determination, Aristotle would undoubtedly have discussed it. The reason he leaves this matter to another agency, i.e., divine determination, is because human nature is not capable of assessing it. For this reason Aristotle speaks of the virtues in a general way only, defining temperance as a mean quality between excessive indulgence in eating, drinking, sexual, and other pleasures on the one hand, and excessive abstinence on the other.[8]

In the matter of sexual intercourse in particular, the authors of human nomoi say that one may have sexual union in the proper manner, with the proper person and at the proper time, but they cannot tell what is proper in a given case. Divine law specifies that the proper manner is such as will lead to procreation and the perpetuation of the species; the proper person is the particular person who is the man's wife, forbidding marriage with certain women as being incestuous; the proper time is when the woman is clean, forbidding intercourse during or near the menstrual period.

Similarly divine law prohibits certain foods and permits others. It prohibits the drinking of wine when one is about to perform divine service or say his prayers. It explains that excessive abstinence is improper, as is clear from the interpretation which the Rabbis put upon the expression, "And make atonement for him, for that he sinned by reason of the soul" [Num. 6:11]. "By reason of what soul has he sinned?" ask the Rabbis, and they answer, "He sinned because he abstained from wine."[9]

In the same way the authors of human nomoi praise courage, and say that a person must not risk danger except when death would be preferable to life, but they cannot determine when that is the case! Divine law, however, declares that the proper time to risk one's life is when the name of God will be sanctified thereby, as in the case of Hananiah, Mishael, and Azariah, or in order to fight with idolaters so as to destroy them and eradicate their name from under heaven.

---

[8] *Ethics* 1117b, 23 ff. Cf. *Averroes' Middle Commentary on Aristotle's Nichomachean Ethics in the Hebrew Version of Samuel ben Judah*, ed. Lawrence V. Berman (Jerusalem: Israel Academy of Sciences and Humanities, 1999), pp. 137–8.

[9] *Nazir* 19a.

Similarly in relation to mercy and cruelty, the human nomos cannot determine the proper measure of each to indicate when each is proper and when not. The divine law makes clear that cruelty is proper in one's dealings with unbelievers, sectarians, and those who violate the law, who should be punished with stripes or death according to the magnitude of the offence, as the Torah determines; and that mercy is the proper quality to show to believers, and those who are poor and unfortunate, though it should be exercised differently according to circumstances. Thus in some cases it is proper to give by way of gift, in others by way of loan. This variety of method is indicated by the psalmist's expression, "All goes well with the man who bequeaths and lends, who conducts his affairs with equity" [Ps. 112:5].

"Bequeaths" refers to the charity given to a poor man without expectation of return; "lends" refers only to one who borrows a loan. And the one who does these two things is characterized as one who "conducts his affairs with equity," and one who "never will be shaken; the beneficent man will be remembered forever" [Ps. 112:6] because he confers benefits upon all men, by gift or by loan. The human nomos cannot determine properly in particular cases. Hence he who follows its sole guidance walks in darkness and does not know what specific acts he should do, or what way he should follow. But "the commandment of the Lord is pure like the sun, enlightening the eyes" [Ps. 19:9], and showing those who follow it the way they should go and the thing they should do.

Again, the author of nomic law is a human being, and therefore cannot determine the fair and the despicable at all times. For those things that pertain to the commonly accepted view may change, and that which is now regarded as fair may be regarded later as despicable and vice-versa. Thus we find that in the days of Cain and Abel and the ancient times generally, marrying one's sister was not thought despicable. The same thing was true in the time of Abraham. For Abraham in excusing himself to Abimelech said, "And moreover she is indeed my sister, the daughter of my father, but not the daughter of my mother" [Gen. 20:12]. Later the marrying one's sister came to be regarded as despicable. For this reason the aversion from the despicable which is acquired through the nomic law cannot last forever, because it changes with the times. But the divine law, by reason of the fact that it is determined by divine wisdom, declares the fair and the despicable for all time. And therefore the aversion from the despicable that is acquired through the divine law is not liable to change or destruction, for it is free from all error and impurity, and can therefore exist forever like silver which is free from all dross, as the Psalmist says, "The words of the Lord are pure words, as silver tried in a crucible on the earth, refined seven times" [Ps. 12:7].

The meaning of the verse is this: Impure silver made alchemically may stand one melting without betraying its impurity, but not two. In some cases it may stand two meltings, or sometimes three and four and five, but finally the impurity is discovered. In some cases the impurity is not discovered by melting it in a furnace, it requires melting "in thick earth" [1 Kings 7:46]. But silver which is purified "in thick earth" and refined many times is free from all impurity, dross and alloy, and can never change afterwards though it be melted many times. This is why the Psalmist compares the purity of the words of the Lord to pure silver which is refined in a crucible on the ground, that is to say in an open place in thick earth, refined seven times, in which there is not the slightest trace of impurity. Similarly the aversion to the despicable which is acquired from the Torah, is "clean, enduring forever" [Ps. 19:10], because it is not liable to the change and destruction to which nomic law is liable.

Again, the nomic law cannot recompense every man in accordance with his conduct or mete out punishment properly, so that one receives stripes, another be stoned, another strangled, another pays double damages, and another pays four- and five-fold, to make the punishment fit the crime. But the divine law gives every one recompense according to the wrongdoing, no more and no less. And though we see apparently the righteous man perishing in his righteousness, and the wicked man living a long life despite his wickedness, this appears so only if we test punishment by the standard of the goods of this world alone. But if we combine the goods of this world which the bad man gets with the evils and punishment which he gets in the next world, and similarly the evils befalling the righteous in this world with the good things he will get in the next world, we shall find that the sum of the two gives a just recompense though either alone is not just. This is the meaning of the Psalmist when he says, "The ordinances of the Lord are true, they are righteous altogether" [Ps. 19:10]. "True" refers to the measure of punishment, "righteous altogether" refers to the sum of punishment in this world plus the goods in the next, and vice versa.

I have seen a commentator explain this verse differently. We find instances in the Torah where the same thing is forbidden and permitted. For example, one may not marry his brother's widow, yet if the brother died without issue, he may; the fat of cattle is prohibited, but the fat of certain wild animals is permitted; the combination of meat and milk is prohibited, yet the udder is permitted, and so on. And one would think that two disjuncts of a contradiction cannot both be correct. Hence, the statement that "the ordinances of the Lord are true, they are righteous altogether," i.e., the permission as well as the prohibition. But the expression "true" is not a fitting one according to this interpretation. For "true" does not apply to the laying down of a law, but rather the term 'fitting,' or 'proper,' or 'right.'[10] The word true does apply to recompense, as we find, "Execute true judgment" [Zech. 7:9], judgment indicating recompense, as in the expression, "The Lord has made Himself known, He has executed judgment, the wicked is snared in the work of his own hands" [Ps. 9:17], or the expression, "only to do justly" [Micah 6:8]. The word 'altogether' is also unsatisfactory according to this explanation.

These are the defects of the nomic law, and a great many more might be mentioned. For example, human nomos can punish only a visible act, but not one that is secret, for man sees only what is visible to the eye, but the divine law lays down punishment for secret acts also, for God sees into the heart. The expression, "The ordinances of the Lord are true, they are righteous altogether," may also be explained as referring to visible and secret acts. There is no need to elaborate. I merely desired to enumerate those six points which are named by the Psalmist in the nineteenth Psalm, and which are contained in the expressions, "The law of the Lord is perfect," "The testimony of the Lord is sure," "The precepts of the Lord are right, rejoicing the heart," "The commandment of the Lord is pure, enlightening the eyes," "The fear of the Lord is clean, enduring forever," "The ordinances of the Lord are true, they are righteous altogether."

Having explained the six ways in which the divine law is superior to nomic law, the Psalmist shows that the divine law not only gives perfection in theoretical opinions, i.e., the true and the false, and in moral qualities, i.e., the fair and the despicable, as we have said, but it also gives perfection wherever perfection is imagined to exist, namely, also in the categories of the useful and the pleasurable. Hence the Psalmist continues and says by way of poetical figure that in the words of the Torah are also found the useful and the agreeable, "More to be desired are they than gold, yea, than

---

[10] Cf. Crescas, *Light* III, 4, 4, where a similar point is made.

much fine gold" [19:11], referring to the useful, and "Sweeter also than honey and the honeycomb," referring to the agreeable. The meaning is that the reward that is earned through the commandments is great, and is more beneficial than gold and much fine gold, and more agreeable than the honeycomb. This is so, provided one is careful to observe them. Hence he concludes, "Moreover by them is Thy servant warned; in keeping of them there is great reward" [19:12].

Chapter Nine

The first principles and roots of nomic law are choice and purpose. This is clear and evident, because why should someone who lays down a nomos fix a punishment for those who violate the rules of the code if the violator is not his own master to do what he likes? Similarly how can a king or ruler of a country compel people to do good if they are not their own masters to do good or evil? Even those who deny spiritual reward and punishment admit that man has absolute choice which is not interfered with, and through which he can choose what he desires and can direct his activities to a given purpose. That is why it is said that a nomos must be drawn up by a wise man or men, to define what is fair and what is despicable, what is wrong and what is right in the relations of the people of the city. And a governor, magistrate, and officer must be placed over the people to compel them to maintain justice among men and to suppress wrong, so as to realize the welfare of political association.

Hence it is clear that the writer who regarded choice and purpose as principles of the divine law missed the mark. For though the latter necessarily presupposes choice, choice is not a principle of divine law insofar as it is divine; it is a principle of divine law by virtue of being a principle of all acts and human conventions and of nomic regimens by which a political community is kept in order and without which it cannot exist. We do not say that the primary intelligibles are principles of divine law, though the latter presupposes them, as does any branch of learning and knowledge. In the same way, although choice is a root of divine law, it is not a principle thereof insofar as it is divine. For this reason Maimonides does not enumerate it among the principles, though he believes that it is necessary for divine law, as we said in Chapter Three. For only those principles which are the principles to divine law are enumerated.

Similarly *purpose*, without further qualification, is not a principle of divine law as such, but of all voluntary human acts, and in this respect it is a principle of nomic law. For as every one who does anything deliberately and voluntarily does it because he intends a certain purpose (whether the purpose be really good or one that seems to the agent good), so one who lays down a nomos intends in his commands and prohibitions that the people should attain a certain object in their acts, namely, the guidance of people, and their well-being through which political association is perfected. It is clear therefore that purpose is a principle of nomic law as well, and not of divine law insofar as it is divine. Nevertheless inasmuch as the purpose which results from the Torah, namely the future life, is different from the purpose resulting from nomic law and all the other purposes, Maimonides includes purpose among the principles, though he does not include choice.

Perhaps you will object that since choice and purpose are not principles of divine law as such, why does the Torah say, "See I have set before thee this day life . . . therefore choose life" [Deut. 30:15–19], an allusion to choice and purpose which is eternal life? We say again, as we said before, that though choice and purpose are not principles of the divine law as such, the latter necessarily presupposes them, as it presupposes the primary intelligibles, though they are not principles of divine law as such. Now no one denies that humans possess primary intelligibles, but there are those who deny that humans possess choice, like some astrologers, and there are also those who deny purpose in all acts, like the Epicureans, who believe that the world came by accident, and that no act has any purpose, but that everything happens by chance. Then there are those who admit purpose in human acts, but not so noble a purpose as the survival of the soul in eternal life. For this reason it was necessary that the Torah state this in order to abolish the views mentioned, which are self-refuting, because they nullify all human acts and human purpose, not to speak of undermining all laws.

Chapter Ten

The principles of divine law in general are three: the existence of God, Torah from heaven, and reward and punishment. There is no doubt that these three are necessary principles of divine law as such. For if we conceive the removal of one of them, the law will fall entirely. This is obvious from their meaning. Thus if we do not believe in the existence of God who commands the law, there is no divine law. And if we do believe in the existence of God, but there is no Torah from heaven, there is no divine law. And if there is no reward and punishment – corporeal in this world and spiritual in the next – what is the point of a divine law? If it is in order to maintain a proper order in human affairs and relations so as to perfect political society, nomic law is sufficient for this purpose. It is clear, therefore, that if there is a divine law, it is for the purpose of leading men to such perfection as a human nomos cannot attain to, viz., human perfection which depends upon perfection of the soul, as will appear later. It is clear therefore that the reward and punishment of the soul is a root and principle of divine law without doubt. And the corporeal reward which the righteous man obtains from God in this world for his observance of the commandments is a proof of the future spiritual reward. It follows, then, that reward and punishment in general is a necessary principle of divine law.

Since these three are general principles of divine law, our Rabbis (of blessed memory) enumerated them in the Mishnah in Chapter Ḥelek,[11] saying that one who denies any one of them is not to he reckoned among the adherents of the law, and therefore has no share in the world to come. Their words are as follows: "All Israel have a share in the world to come, as is said, 'Thy people also shall be all righteous, they shall inherit the land forever' [Isa. 60: 21]. But the following have no share in the world to come: He who says there is no resurrection of the dead in the Torah," i.e., a person who denies the divine recompense alluded to in the resurrection of the dead, which is a divine act in relation to body and soul that includes all kinds of recompense. For some of the rabbinical statements indicate that the expression "resurrection of the dead" should be taken in a particular sense as referring to the resurrection, and others indicate that it is said in a general sense, as referring to the world of the souls, the world-to-come, and the judgment day. They also explained the idea of the Messiah, which is a physical reward, in such a way as to allude to all kinds of reward.

Afterwards they list [as someone who does not receive a portion of the world to come] one who says there is no divine Torah, which is a second principle. Then they list the "Epicurean." According to the testimony of the ancients, Epicurus was a person who believed that the world came into

---

[11] The last chapter of *Mishnah: Sanhedrin.*

being by accident and denied the existence of God as the agent. Those who followed his teaching were called Epicureans. We see therefore that they list these three principles and say that he who denies any one of them has no share in the world to come because he is excluded from the community of adherents of the law.

It is true that, in Chapter Helek, "Epicurean" is interpreted as one who holds the sages in contempt, but the reason they say so is because not every man can know the existence of God by his own ratiocination. He gets this knowledge either by tradition or by demonstration from the sages. But he who holds in contempt the wise men who declare the existence of God to all, leaves himself no way by which he can know God, and hence is like one who denies the existence of God, and is therefore called an Epicurean. From the fact that, in the Mishnah of Chapter Helek, these are the only people who are denied a share in the world to come, it is clear that these three [categories] are the universal principles common to all divine law, which every adherent of divine law is obliged to believe. It is true that in the Gemara they name others who have no share in the world to come. But they are enumerated as being derived from the three principles, not as being principles themselves.

Index

Index

CAMBRIDGE TEXTS IN THE HISTORY OF PHILOSOPHY

Titles published in the series thus far

Aquinas *Disputed Questions on the Virtues* (edited by E. M. Atkins and Thomas Williams)

Aquinas *Summa Theologiae, Questions on God* (edited by Brian Davies and Brian Leftow)

Aristotle *Nicomachean Ethics* (edited by Roger Crisp)

Arnauld and Nicole *Logic or the Art of Thinking* (edited by Jill Vance Buroker)

Augustine *On the Trinity* (edited by Gareth Matthews)

Bacon *The New Organon* (edited by Lisa Jardine and Michael Silverthorne)

Boyle *A Free Enquiry into the Vulgarly Received Notion of Nature* (edited by Edward B. Davis and Michael Hunter)

Bruno *Cause, Principle and Unity and Essays on Magic* (edited by Richard Blackwell and Robert de Lucca with an introduction by Alfonso Ingegno)

Cavendish *Observations upon Experimental Philosophy* (edited by Eileen O'Neill)

Cicero *On Moral Ends* (edited by Julia Annas, translated by Raphael Woolf)

Clarke *A Demonstration of the Being and Attributes of God and Other Writings* (edited by Ezio Vailati)

Classic and Romantic German Aesthetics (edited by J. M. Bernstein)

Condillac *Essay on the Origin of Human Knowledge* (edited by Hans Aarsleff)

Conway *The Principles of the Most Ancient and Modern Philosophy* (edited by Allison P. Coudert and Taylor Corse)

Cudworth *A Treatise Concerning Eternal and Immutable Morality* with *A Treatise of Freewill* (edited by Sarah Hutton)

Descartes *Meditations on First Philosophy*, with selections from the *Objections and Replies* (edited by John Cottingham)

Descartes *The World and Other Writings* (edited by Stephen Gaukroger)

Fichte *Foundations of Natural Right* (edited by Frederick Neuhouser, translated by Michael Baur)

Fichte *The System of Ethics* (edited by Daniel Breazeale and Günter Zöller)

Hamann *Philosophical Writings* (edited by Kenneth Haynes)

Heine *On the History of Religion and Philosophy in Germany and Other Writings* (edited by Terry Pinkard, translated by Howard Pollack-Milgate)

Herder *Philosophical Writings* (edited by Michael Forster)

Hobbes and Bramhall on Liberty and Necessity (edited by Vere Chappell)

Humboldt *On Language* (edited by Michael Losonsky, translated by Peter Heath)

Hume *Dialogues Concerning Natural Religion and Other Writings* (edited by Dorothy Coleman)

Hume *An Enquiry Concerning Human Understanding* (edited by Stephen Buckle)

Kant *Anthropology from a Pragmatic Point of View* (edited by Robert B. Louden with an introduction by Manfred Kuehn)

Kant *Critique of Practical Reason* (edited by Mary Gregor with an introduction by Andrews Reath)